PENGU

LOVE ON THE WING

Sara Thornton chose to incarnate as a woman, born in Capricorn 1955. Her early years were spent in the Pacific, where she was joined by a soul sister, Billi. Today, having spent five years, five months and five days in prison, she has been reunited with her daughter Luise. When all legal proceedings have been exhausted, they visualize living in Cornwall. Whilst in prison, Sara dedicated her life to the goddess Isis. She harbours a vision of prisons as places of healing, and hopes to help bring this cherished dream to fruition.

George Delf was born in 1933 and spent his early childhood in India. He received his MA from Cambridge University and then lived, travelled and worked in East Africa, North America and Europe. A journalist, author and educator, his publications include a biography of Jomo Kenyatta, *Asians in East Africa* and *Humanizing Hell: The Law versus Nuclear Weapons*. His long-term concerns include the cultural decay implicit in nuclear 'defence' and the injustice of wealth inequality, and his current aim is to be a more conscious and creative human being.

Love on the Wing

LETTERS OF HOPE FROM PRISON

Sara Thornton
and George Delf

PENGUIN BOOKS

PENGUIN BOOKS

Published by the Penguin Group
Penguin Books Ltd, 27 Wrights Lane, London w8 5tz, England
Penguin Books USA Inc., 375 Hudson Street, New York, New York 10014, USA
Penguin Books Australia Ltd, Ringwood, Victoria, Australia
Penguin Books Canada Ltd, 10 Alcorn Avenue, Toronto, Ontario, Canada m4v 3b2
Penguin Books (NZ) Ltd, 182–190 Wairau Road, Auckland 10, New Zealand

Penguin Books Ltd, Registered Offices: Harmondsworth, Middlesex, England

First published by Penguin Books 1996
1 3 5 7 9 10 8 6 4 2

Copyright © Sara Thornton and George Delf 1996
All rights reserved

The moral right of the authors has been asserted

Filmset by Rowland Phototypesetting Ltd
Bury St Edmunds, Suffolk
Printed in England by Clays Ltd, St Ives plc
Set in 10/12 Monophoto Palatino

With Sara Thornton's agreement,
George Delf selected extracts from their letters for this book.
She plans to write a full account of her life story.

This book is dedicated to lovers everywhere,
especially those who live in a prison of their own.
Only love will free us all.

Contents

The Crime

Sara Thornton's crime, for which she was sentenced to life imprisonment at Birmingham Crown Court on 23 February 1990, is outlined in this Law Report:

'In 1988 Sara Thornton married the deceased, who drank heavily and on occasions was violent and assaulted her. In May 1989 he committed a serious assault on her, for which he was charged. She left home for several days and on her return the deceased tried to give up drink.

On the evening of 14 June 1989, after a weekend of rows, she found the deceased, who had started drinking, asleep on the couch and tried to persuade him to come to bed.

He refused, called her "a whore" and said he would kill her if she had been out with other men. She went to the kitchen to calm down and to look for a truncheon for protection. Not finding it, she took a long carving knife and sharpened it.

The deceased again refused to come to bed and said he would kill her when she was asleep. She held the knife over his stomach while he was still lying on the couch and brought it down slowly towards him, thinking he would ward it off. He did not do so and the knife entered his stomach and killed him.

She said that the death was accidental and she did not intend to kill the deceased but to frighten him. Psychiatric reports on her mental condition agreed that she suffered from a personality disorder which amounted to abnormality of the mind. Two reports for the defence stated that the abnormality impaired her mental responsibility for the acts she had done in killing the deceased, but the report for the prosecution did not think that her mental responsibility was impaired.

At her trial, her lawyers decided that her most effective defence would be that of diminished responsibility. The trial judge left the defence of provocation to the jury as an alternative.'

(Law Report on the Court of Criminal Appeal, *Independent*, 30 July 1991)

The Meeting

Widely separate paths led them around the world before converging in the grim setting of H-wing, Durham Prison, Britain's only maximum security unit for women. As her letters reveal, Sara's early childhood in the Pacific islands was a cocktail of terror, misery and flashes of joy in her tropical surroundings. By contrast, George grew up in India, enjoying much freedom and little schooling.

Sara returned to England and remained locked in a desperate struggle with inner and outer demons. A bird of rare vitality and wit, her wings were clipped. Only much later, in H-wing, with new-found courage and insight, new feathers grew.

Sara's letter in the *Independent* (8 August 1990) was their letter of introduction, a key moment in their lives:

Sir: In response to your leading article, 'Violence in the family' (1 August), I am a 35-year-old woman in my first year of a life sentence. I was found guilty of the murder of my husband by a jury at Birmingham Crown Court in February. I had no previous record.

My husband drank heavily and repeatedly attacked me. Although the police were summoned on many occasions he would only be verbally warned.

After a particularly vicious assault, which resulted in me being treated at hospital, I insisted that charges be pressed. My husband was arrested, charged and then released; he came home again.

A quiet two-week period then erupted in a weekend of violence. As a result I stabbed my husband once; he later died.

I have never denied inflicting the fatal wound. I had no intention of killing my husband. On the contrary, I summoned an ambulance straight away.

For the eight months preceding the trial I lived on bail with my 11-year-old daughter.

I am one of three women here, and many more in other prisons, who feel that if the police had taken our complaints seriously, our husbands would be alive and we would be free to live with our families today. Instead, we have lost our children, our husbands, our homes and our freedom.

Yours sincerely,

Sara E. Thornton

HM PRISON, DURHAM

2 August

For three and a half months after they met, George used a lightweight racing bicycle to reach Sara. The round trip from Stanhope, Weardale, up hill and down dale, was more than 40 miles. In December 1990 he rented rooms in Brancepeth Castle, 5 miles from Durham.

Sara:

Unlike Risley, I knew H-wing, Durham, was entirely inhabited by murderers – Britain's most dangerous women, qualifying for maximum security conditions.

I knew I wasn't dangerous. I knew I wasn't a murderer. How would I cope and survive in this environment with these monsters?

Arriving in Durham I was frightened. My first view of the prison deepened my fear. Thick high walls, tiny cell windows, hundreds of them. This looked like prison – a real prison.

It was lunch-time when I walked into H-wing. Women were sitting eating at tables lined up on 'the flat'. No strait-jackets, no ball and chain, no psychopaths, just a large group of ordinary-looking women. My surprise turned to delight. I was shown to my cell, someone made me a coffee. Another showed me around, and later in the day I was given a pickled onion. My mouth, which had been limited to the boring, bland fare of Risley, exploded into a culinary orgasm as I crunched.

It was not so bad after all. I could live here. I would survive.

George:

A rail traveller alighting at Durham's station in the sky has a dramatic view of the Norman Cathedral and Castle, perched on an island in the river Wear. Also in view, among the city's grey roofs, is a corner of H-wing where I first met Sara in August, 1990. In sight are a few

3

of the square, barred windows. As a cricket commentator put it, Durham can boast a castle, cathedral and prison, all in full view of its cricket ground. Power, prayer, punishment and play. All life is there.

My first visit to Sara was my first to a prison. I was alert, on edge as a female prison officer, expressionless, escorted me through seemingly endless locked doors. The jangling and clanging made a melancholy music.

At last, a short corridor and the visiting room, a tiny oasis of normality with its fitted carpet, curtains, easy chairs and coffee tables. Two prison officers chatted in a corner. A small, slim woman rose to greet me, in a peach outfit. Smart, neat, Sara's friendly smile reassured me. It was to be the first of many such brief commas in her life sentence. That room, for us, became home. The most secure home in Britain.

Letters

August 1990 – November 1990

August

Dear Sara Thornton,

I was interested to see your letter in yesterday's *Independent*. You may not need any more outside help but if there's anything useful I can do, I will gladly do it. The sooner you are free the better.

I am a journalist and author and have played a part in various pressure groups. I have a special interest in issues to do with justice and have some knowledge of the law (my last book was related to nuclear policies and the law, 1985).

I wonder if you come from this area? I live 20 miles or so from Durham. If you ever want a visitor I'd be glad to see you.

I know one of the Appeal Court judges! We were at school together many years ago and I haven't seen him since, but sent him a copy of the book I mentioned (it is heavily critical of lawyers and judges). He sent back quite a friendly letter saying it was 'interesting and provocative'!

If you think I may be able to help, please let me know.

With best wishes.

Sincerely, *George Delf*

Dear George Delf,

Your letter shouted at me across the dining table today. In most prisons inmates are restricted to four sides of paper, so one's writing becomes smaller.

After reading the article, 'Violence in the Family', I felt I must write something. I've been in prison five months (since Friday, 23 February), three months at Risley remand, the rest here. I have spoken to many women who like myself lived with violent men and, when denied assistance or support, cracked and committed murder, manslaughter, whatever you wish to call it. I never realized how widespread it is, how many children suffer the loss of both parents, how ignored we are.

7

Despite the tragedy of my marriage I loved my husband very much. Like all or many alcoholics he was a deeply sensitive man, who never hit me when sober. He never physically hurt my daughter. She is now in California with my sister Billi. It strikes me that we are breeding our next generation of wife-beaters, children who grow up to believe that violence is a normal way of life. In order to stop this (don't I sound arrogant?) I feel that society's view of women must change. At present it is fairly acceptable for a man to beat his wife. As long as they do it behind closed doors.

There is so much that I could write, like my experience with the social services, or police. I could fill pages and pages. Suffice to say, as much as I would love to be free again, there are other women just as deserving of your help and support. I should mention that my husband was an ex-policeman and knew the local police pretty well in his capacity as security manager of TNT.

I am not interested in me – I want to change the law. In Canada, I believe, if a couple are involved in a domestic situation where police are summoned, both must go for counselling. By law. Experts argue that counselling is ineffective unless voluntary. Personally, I disagree. But as long as men know that they can safely beat their wives, they will continue to do so.

Many women have asked me why I didn't skip the country. Bail was a mere £2,000 and I reported to the police station in Coventry once a week. Simply because I never believed I would be found guilty of murder. As you know, life is a mandatory sentence for murder. I do have grounds for an Appeal; would you believe, the Prosecution asked if I wore knickers! But I don't hold any hopes at all.

You ask if I come from Durham. I am in prison in Durham because it is the top security prison for thirty of Britain's 'most dangerous women'. Most lifers start here.

I was born in Nuneaton, Warwickshire. My mother was a marine biologist, my father a civil servant in Fiji. Daddy was for a time Governor, Mummy worked for the Hawaii Marine Laboratories. Returned aged fourteen, educated at Millfield, Somerset.

I guess you could say I am not your average British housewife, my eccentricities did me little good during my trial. I have a healthy disrespect for authority (that looks worse than it is) and I am at a loss as how to proceed from here. I have no outside help, apart from the friends I have left behind. My solicitor has just written to me and in legal language told me to shut up and quietly get on with my sentence. Every letter from my probation officer ends with, 'Sara, please behave. Be good.' All I have to go on is my faith in God and the overwhelming feeling that I just have to do something. That feeling is so strong that I am willing to stay in prison, sacrifice any chance of a successful Appeal, because I couldn't feel as if I've gone through so much pain without a reason. Do you understand?

Defence in a domestic murder is a very delicately balanced issue (I'm tired). If one puts the violence forward too strongly, then the jury feel that you had a good reason to murder. My Counsel decided it was a safer bet to plead guilty to manslaughter whilst balance of the mind was disturbed. Consequently, two eminent psychiatrists took the stand and made me sound as mad as a hatter. When the Prosecution Counsel, in cross examination, said that anything less than life would give me 'a licence to kill', I thought, 'Broadmoor, here I come.' We adjourned and asked for a re-trial. It was denied.

My husband's violence was very understated. I was made out to be a tart, and a greedy, cold-blooded murderer. I'm really not surprised the jury believed it. So now they just want to say, sorry and all that, you are in the system. I guess eventually, in about ten years' time, they'll let me out the other end, thoroughly cowed, demoralized, and no use to anyone.

I'd like it very much if you came to visit. I am allowed one visit a fortnight. I use a lot of my allowance to speak to my daughter once a month, but as I've been here nearly three months and haven't had a visit yet, my Visitor's Order balance must be in credit. I am sure you would have lots of questions to ask me. I'll answer them as best I can.

Believe me, a women's prison is a real eye-opener. I still find it fascinating. I'm starting a degree in psychology, come November (courtesy of Open University and the taxpayer). I will put a VO in with this letter. It is valid for a month. You phone the prison and say what day you are visiting and they will book you in. Apart from the security, it is pretty informal. Please bring a packet of cigarettes. I can roll my own but I'm not very good. Meanwhile I will reply to the other letters and see what the general response is. I hope you have some good ideas and you could go on from there.

I am receiving a lot of encouragement from the girls in here, though I can see many are bewildered by my actions and determination. It simply doesn't occur to them to question anything. They accept so meekly the condemnation of the establishment they profess to despise and distrust. It's frightening.

Sincerely, *Sara E. Thornton*

Dear Sara,

Many thanks for your interesting letter. I hope it's OK if I visit you this Friday morning (17th). I've phoned the prison and told them.

One question in particular: would it be possible for me, via your solicitor, to see your trial transcript at some point? Of course, you will probably want to meet me first to see what use I might be. Let's not make assumptions!

I'll try to remember the cigarettes – goes against my principles, but . . . !

In haste, I look forward to meeting you.

Best wishes, *George (Delf)*

Dear Sara,

I was very glad to meet you yesterday. Not having been inside a prison before I expected you to be in some sort of uniform, so it was a pleasant surprise to find you looking pretty and smart in your own clothes! The visiting area was quite a friendly space, too, considering.

I expect we were both quite tense at first, for many reasons, but I found you easy to talk to and began to understand more about you and your case. There are so many facts and events and comments, though, that I need a bit of time to sort them out. I want you to know that I am basically on your side – if you want me to do what I can to help, please tell me.

We must try to be honest about these visits. If you feel at any stage they are a waste of time (and there may be others you want to visit), just tell me. There is no need to be polite! I am interested in your case and the wider problems around it, but not sure yet whether anything I can do will be much use.

Because so much has to be crammed into a few minutes, I am not clear yet about the sequence of events and their timing. Would you like to write out a list of these, plus any comments you want to add? For example, I'd like to know your husband's record of violence against you, particularly in the weeks before his death.

There seem to be three areas of major concern for you.

1 The situation of women in violent homes and what can be done to help them.

2 Your own case and the possibility of getting your sentence reduced.

3 Your own personal situation.

I hope my visit did not disturb your routine life too much! For your own sake it's necessary to adjust to conditions around you, but it may be equally necessary to keep a lifeline to the outside world, however disturbing that may sometimes be. Don't become institutionalized. You have a whole new life starting (your old one is finished). Why not give yourself a *real* 'life' sentence? – to take part more fully in life than you have ever done? In that respect we are both novices! If we can learn from each other, so much the better. Take care.

With my best wishes, *George*

Dear George,

I woke this morning to the sound of Kiri Te Kanawa singing 'Ave Maria'. When I opened my eyes, I saw that my bed was covered in petals, the lilies had shed them in the night. Felt like a displaced corpse!

I enjoyed meeting you on Friday, I was so afraid that you would listen to me and say, 'Well, quite frankly I can understand why they gave you life!' Your warmth and understanding seemed to unlock something in me. I came upstairs and cried my eyes out! It was much later that I read your notes. I've carried them with me like a badge of triumph. Here is someone who understands, and is willing to help.

Saturday I received more 'fan mail'. I'll never be tired of it but it says something when one girl receives a red rose, another a mini book of love declarations, and I get a letter from a woman in Essex who tells me how her husband tortured her by holding her head under water till she lost consciousness! Well, you know what they say, 'One egg is *un oeuf*!'

I got a very interesting letter from someone called Shakila M., I take it female, who is researching a documentary on women and violence, and asks me to send a VO so that she may visit and interview me. She has also taken the precaution of asking the Governor's permission. I shall of course write and accept, do you have any particular advice you wish to give me before I see her? My instincts tell me that I could very easily blow everything through over-enthusiasm or naivety.

I agree with what you have to say about a mother sharing her identity with her children. It's a very important point. I have no knowledge of how the law stands on this. Nobody from the *four psychiatrists* to my Defence Counsel ever mentioned this. However, I shall write to Kathleen O'Donovan, the Professor of Law at Kent University, and ask her. I also think that it is important to have a favourable psychiatrist or psychologist to back this up. I still can't remember the name of the professor I saw at Leicester. He called me arrogant, because I asked for a cup of tea after a two-hour drive and a two-hour consultation, which was private, not NHS. So maybe not him. Someone new. If I wait long enough, and pray hard enough, one will contact me.

As to the other 'dangerous women' in here, a strange phenomenon has occurred. Overnight my room has become a 'get-it-off-your-chest' surgery. I have heard more stories of violence, betrayal and heartbreak, since a film company has shown interest, than I ever thought possible.

There is a fear that I will rock the boat. These women have cocooned themselves from the outside world and all the pain that goes with it. They are quite understandably reluctant to open the wounds again. But I'm getting there.

I don't want to quote a case and then get a nasty shock when someone lies. But if these women want to be included, then all I can do is give your address and ask them to contact you.

It strikes me that we don't put enough emphasis on the life and welfare of a child. Looking around me in here, there are cases of infanticide where no life sentence has been imposed or if it has, a low-tariff date. (Do you know about tariffs?) In fact, that's one of the problems in our judicial system, it's so bloody inconsistent.

I am writing to my solicitor informing him of your interest, my intentions and giving you permission to have any papers relating to my case. If he fires me, you'll have to find me another solicitor. I suspect you'll find him condescending, abrupt and very probably angry. Don't let him get to you. If you pay taxes, you are no doubt paying a very large proportion of his salary.

It's my daughter's birthday in September. I am speaking to her on the 2nd, two days beforehand. She will be twelve, and my sister tells me she's developing physically. It hurts very much that I can't be with her.

Later

My judge was called Judge Judge! I only had eleven jurors, one of whom, an 18-year-old, slept so much, that my sister complained to my Counsel. One was an Indian, who found it difficult, I think, to understand the forensic evidence on drugs and alcohol. As a matter of interest, I had a blood test which showed up negative for alcohol and a slight amount of Mogadon, which I took earlier that evening in order to calm down. As far as witnesses go, I called few, mainly psychiatrists, none attesting to Malcolm's violence. Martin, Malcolm's son, was a witness for the Prosecution, but he stated quite clearly in his evidence that Malcolm was in an ugly mood that night, and he felt it wise for us (him and me) to get out for a while. He said he was scared. Martin is 6' 2", twenty years old and fit.

Your visit prompted many memories which hitherto lay dormant. Malcolm, as I told you, was very friendly with the local police. They frequently came round whilst on duty to drink and talk 'cop shop'. Malcolm always kept a bottle of Grouse for them, which he bought on his expense account. Naturally, after his admission to the Nightingale Clinic in London, I put a stop to that ... Didn't go down well. I wonder if I am being unfair, perhaps the local police were reluctant to prosecute Malcolm for his violence because of their relationship rather than their policies? Suffice to say, I did bring that up in court, against the express wishes of my Counsel, who, very firmly quashed it. George, what are you going to do? Are we a team? What do you want me to do?

Sara E. Thornton

Dear Sara,

Neither the Advice on Appeal nor the Grounds for Appeal make *any mention* of M.'s violence towards you *except* in a brief description of the *prosecution* case. This seems very stupid and gives the impression in the Appeal that you simply stabbed a man lying on a sofa in order to 'frighten him'. My view at present is that the Appeal (like the defence case in court) is directed at secondary issues which obscure the main point, that you were driven to this act by repeated, unpredictable drunken violence. Is this not so? I found some interesting examples of behaviour in war under stress which parallel your so-called 'bizarre' behaviour. Not mad – *shocked*. A form of emotional concussion . . . We can discuss all this if you wish, and anything else.

Keep well, *George*

Dear Sara,

Many thanks for your letter – I'm glad you left the high heels behind! Don't risk your ankles, you need them. Sounds like you and the others could open a boutique in there, and a hairdressing salon, and then open them to the public. Just call it 'privatization' and I'm sure the Home Office would approve!

OK let's be a 'team' – both of us 'captains' so we're both in charge, with nobody to boss around! Maybe we can adopt the canary as our symbol, because it is the symbol of my favourite football team (Norwich City) – more important, the canary is, or was, used in coal mines to warn of poisoned air.

At this early stage, I feel it's best to stir ideas and needs around, to see what is most wanted. Then we can begin to define aims and means a bit more clearly.

Re: the film interview; the only thing I'd suggest is, ask for a full description of the programme *before* you see her. So you can take a good look at it. Otherwise you may well lose any power over the purpose and content of the thing. Behave like a co-producer, not a grateful 'extra'. Such is the power of TV today that almost everybody falls on their knees to worship it. I can remember a political candidate saying once that his constituents only took him seriously after he appeared on TV. More 'real' in glass than in the flesh! Crazy.

I liked your lily story – maybe waking up under petals symbolizes your death and rebirth? 'Life' can be *LIFE* ... Ophelia in reverse ...

There's one thing I hope you and I can do – make links between personal and social/political violence – and links between violent creative energies. My feeling, for example, is that the exceptionally low level of creativity (and I don't just mean art) in this country at present is related to its refusal to confront its own violence. Most children seem to grow up with a very low estimate of their own creative potential. If they don't believe in themselves, how can they believe in anything else? So life becomes a perpetual escape from inner dis-belief.

A lot of positive things beckon! *George*

Dear George,

Tomorrow is my anniversary. I'll have been in prison six months. It doesn't seem possible. The PO told me that I can expect a tariff of nine to sixteen years, so looking on the bright side, only eight and a half years to go. Time enough to do a Masters in Psychology, roll perfect fags, and figure out where the odd socks go when you do a load of washing! Think positive, that's the secret!

Dr F. – he worked as a family GP and a police surgeon. He is a brilliant man, totally eccentric. I really think he saved Malcolm's life, when he found Dr Max Glatt in London, and made it possible for me to take him to the Charter Nightingale Clinic.

I love your letters, even if you can't help me, which I don't think for one minute, just keep writing. Some letters are just letters, very pleasant and all that, some letters caress one's spirit, and can be read over and over again. Tracey says I glow when I read your letters.

How is Norwich? Last time I was there, I threw a chicken drumstick at Colin Chapman (head of Lotus Cars). I had a boyfriend who was working on the John Delorean gull-wing cars down there, stayed at a huge farm which produced eggs. Beautiful, but I thought of those hens locked up in little boxes all the time I was there, so I left early.

No, I haven't been in prison before! That's a major point in my favour, no criminal record, no record of violence.

I was forced to bed yesterday afternoon, just a sickness bug going round. So last night, I started on your book. Heavy going, but interesting. Your comments on lawyers and solicitors remind me of my solicitor. Kitty Hart's observations on concentration camp behaviour are very interesting. I see the same thing here, although more pronounced. If you are interested, though it isn't really relevant, we can talk about it. Understand?

I will, before your next visit, write out and post the sequence of events that led to Malcolm's death. It's painful, George, but I'll do it.

For your next visit, I'll dress normally. I've put my peach trousers back into property. We are allowed four sets of clothes out in one go. I'm afraid I like to wear my gym stuff most of the time.

I had a letter from my dear sister Billi today. Someone, not me, sent her a copy of my letter to the *Independent*. She's proud of me, says I've got balls, but can't help laughing. Will I ever give up? No! I hope you don't object, George, but I gave her your phone number in my reply. Billi came over for my trial and there might well be things she remembers that I don't. She's been very involved and very supportive. I don't want her to feel left out.

Regards, *Sara E.*

PS M. was *not* asleep, he had woken when I returned. That he was asleep, I vehemently deny now and did during the trial.

Whilst the judge was summing up, he pointed out the tears I shed during the telling of that part of the night, M. calling me a whore, and saying he would kill me.

Must go, its 12.30 a.m. Tracey, my friend, is being confirmed tomorrow, by the Bishop of Jarrow. I hope he's not pompous, it's like a red flag to a bull, as far as I'm concerned. Sometimes I can see that sort of visitor is scared of us. It's a great chance to wind them up. Once, when a member of the Board of Visitors was watching us pick the fur out of visible seams in a soft toy, I responded to his enquiry by telling him that sticking needles in rabbits was therapy for my sadistic tendencies. He ran!

Luise has been diagnosed as quite severely dyslexic. I got her into a special school for three mornings a week, but it was a hell of a fight.

One of the reasons I didn't want to leave my home and Atherstone, was because I knew I wouldn't find another school for dyslexics. I also fought and won a couple of battles for other children in a similar position.

I really do have to go now.

Sara

Dear George,

Shakila from Faction Films was supposed to visit me today, but it has been cancelled. Mr Hicks on two occasions told her that she must go through the Home Office. This is a precaution to protect us women, as much as the prison. Durham H-wing has a fearful reputation with the media. It's very important that I follow the rules, or the prison could make things very awkward for me. They could try and stop you too, though I would definitely class you as friend more than journalist. I've got to be so careful, and my gut instincts are to trust you, don't let me down.

Joyce is my sister's mother. My sister was adopted when she was six weeks old. So, now Joyce has come back into our lives. She has now returned the favour and 'adopted' me. We've never met.

Can you try and come Tuesday afternoon? It's not important, it would be nice.

Take care. *Sara* x

PS Martina says one kiss is all right!

Dear George,

Good to see you this afternoon. My full attention didn't come with me, no insult to you, George. I can't stop thinking about Luise and her birthday. I remember how tremendously excited she used to be in the days leading up to it, the endless questions and little hints from me as to what I had bought her. Icing her cake; the last one was a strawberry cheesecake, we stuck the candles in whole strawberries. Very popular choice. All this is remembered with ineffable sadness, it clouds everything, I feel bogged down, unable to formulate even the simplest plans. I've just lost my spirit. I shall probably sob my heart out on Sunday, after I speak with her, and feel better next week. It's only a temporary defeat. Write me some strong encouraging words, George – don't criticize me. I feel emotionally battered and vulnerable.

When I went to the hospital yesterday I seemed to see children everywhere. Brown, blond-haired, in T-shirts, lovely summer children. I could have scooped one up in my arms. I have a list of things I miss in prison, rain, olives; I never thought about it, but I haven't seen a child for six months.

The girls are very sensitive to each other's moods, they've noticed my sadness, and this evening dragged me off to watch some rubbishy horror film.

You are so organized and methodical. I make lists and then lose them. I can write far more candidly than I speak. Billi says she only knows the 'real' me through my letters. Sent off Luise's birthday card this afternoon, late, we are only allowed a set number of letters per week.

What you must have thought when you came this afternoon! Within five minutes you'd learned that I do crazy things with bodily samples, and am quite likely in the near future to have webbed feet (toe op).

You looked healthy, brown, you looked good. I like your face. I couldn't really remember it last time; Tracey saw you waiting to leave, she knew straightaway who you were. She was going to say something but you quickly left. I didn't come to the door, because we are not allowed out, it is so unnatural, to hear and see a door slamming behind you.

General consensus of opinion is that I should: a) fight for my own freedom, and b) change solicitors. Can I change Counsel too? When faced with the possibility of ten years in prison, you find that one suppresses all desire for the outside world. I've done that very well. When I went out yesterday, looking at the world through the windows of the bus, I didn't feel a part of it. It was like watching something on TV. If that's what six months can do, how do you think a person would be after a few years? Do you want to visit again? Let me know, I'll send you a VO. I hope you do.

We have our discussion group tomorrow. I have to think of a 'happy subject'. Last week we were disrupted by the rain. I can't think of a happy subject. Maybe I could get them all to tell their favourite jokes – I love jokes, best of all I love malapropisms. My best effort was, 'Looking at the world through rose coloured testicles'. Children are the best. During my horoscope period I heard Luise ask someone if they were Virgo or Catholic.

Mr Mogg (Governor) brought in the photos of the barbecue. Would you believe, someone nicked three?

If you write to Billi, ask her what she thought of the trial. I never really got to know, I think she was disappointed in the Counsel.

Take care. I'm going to read another chapter of your book. That'll put me to sleep.

Sara

Dear Sara,

I've just tried out my new (old) racing bike and my old (old) legs – to the far end of the dale and back (about 16 miles). I flew down the dale, chased by the wind, and crawled back uphill.

I wondered about showing you the photos, in case it made you miss the countryside, etc. I'm not squeamish – you can tell me what you think, feel, or be critical. Friendships are not based on pure love – we have to struggle for the truth sometimes. You should know that I'll stay with you in this experience, whatever happens, unless or until you don't want it. I like you – your mischievous spirit. You're no angel, but no devil either!

I like Plato's definition of a human being as 'a biped without feathers'! I think you have a rather manic-depressive temperament (true or false?) with steep highs and lows. Maybe this goes back to a childhood of natural vitality versus adult gloom? Maybe you're still trying to escape from oppressive adult pomposity? Have you thought about the rather interesting parallel between marrying an ex-police Security man and getting into a High-Security prison? Your natural lively spirit seems paradoxically chained to this Security factor. Don't fight your father – understand him and let him go. The awful truth is that young children often assume the burdens of adult/parental failures.

I hope you never owned Rottweilers, Alsatians, guard dogs, etc.! On Hampstead Heath on Wednesday I saw an ultra-fit, shaven-headed young man with *seven* Dobermans. He was shouting orders at one like an SS officer. One of them wandered off and he barked at it, 'Come back, Rommel!' God knows what the others were called.

Thanks for the Home Office approved kiss! You can have one back, and a long hug.

George x

September

Dear Sara,

Thanks for the photo – a cheerful handful! Is that a characteristic pose of yours? Eyes closed, chin forward – reminds me of someone's translation of 'Nil Desperandum' as 'Don't let the bastards get you down!' I bet you were a cheeky kid who drove your pompous father mad.

I hope the sadness of missing Luise's birthday will wear off soon. It must be awful.

It's amazing how often disasters of one kind or another wake people up to hidden energies. So-called normal life seems an anaesthetic, doesn't it? I've come across loads of men who remember 'the War' as the highpoint of their lives, the only time when people really cooperated, etc. Sad. I find ordinary life full of drama.

I'm 'organized' occasionally, and in chaos most of the time, so don't worry. Chaos is part of creativity, I tell myself. If it was Tracey up on the landing, then I saw her too – the whole set-up is smaller than I imagined.

If my book sends you to sleep you must be like most people in this country, cut off from such small realities as the survival of civilization and life on earth. It's supposed to wake you up! I'm just exchanging my sarcasm for yours!

I don't know who reads these letters, but I hope they realize how privileged they are!

Look forward to seeing you soon. *George* x

Dear George,

My world is once more a sunny place to be; funny, when these depressions hit me, nothing seems to go well. I find it hard to climb out of the 'deep pool of sadness', as you wrote of it. Sometimes just keeping afloat is hard enough. I stop eating too, which doesn't help.

Thank you for your letter on Saturday, especially the long hug. I grabbed it and took it to bed Saturday afternoon. Slept most of the day. Maybe, just maybe, I'll agree with you on the manic temperament bit. First I want to find out more about it. I think you are right about my father – and you come agonizingly close with my childhood. Things happened which I can't tell you about. My sister has been going to counselling sessions with Luise, and she wrote that she was starting to remember. Gives me goose-pimples just writing about it.

Had my phone call yesterday. I had to ask the officers to shut the door so I could hear, and two of them talked to each other whilst I was on the phone. Most disconcerting, is all I will say here. Luise got her first bra! And a gum boaster, whatever that is. Tomorrow at 6 p.m. I have to have a drink and wish her Happy Birthday – she will do exactly the same at 10 a.m. her time.

Tuesday night

Your point about creating drama should your life lack it, I clearly remember Helen Thomas saying on the stand, 'Well, things just happen to Sara!'

Music – I love everything; my father's mother was a concert pianist, and from her I have a talent for playing by ear. This wasn't realized until I was twelve and was bought a cheap mouth organ. I just sat and played every tune I knew. (I've just listened to *Spitfire Prelude and Fugue*, beautiful!) I can just about pick out any tune on a piano. One night I had the Atherstone football team near tears with my rendition of *Love Story* and the *Dr Zhivago* theme! Then I got over confident and started *Zorba the Greek*. When they tried to dance with pints on their heads, the piano was locked! If I play *Isa Lei*, which is the Fijian national anthem, I choke up.

I played in church a couple of Sundays ago–'Amazing Grace'. I didn't realize there were four verses, so stopped after three and put down the guitar. They gave me a funny look and carried on without me!

Luise doesn't keep in touch with her father, she wouldn't know him. She was eight months old when I left. I never wanted alimony, he never wanted Luise – end of story!

CD gadget comes Saturday, but first Security has to take it apart to look for Semtex, drugs, etc. So I probably won't get it till Monday.

Sara x

Dear Sara,

I had a long and interesting phone conversation with Kathleen O'D. She's coming up quite soon if you send her a VO. I think she could be useful, particularly in getting information about similar cases in the USA and Europe, etc. She also has a daughter, aged eleven.

I have a strong hunch you are totally miserable about Luise. I wish I could give you a long hug.

I have an owl for you, from India.

Here's a joke – true. When my younger son, Jason, was about four or five I went to say good night to him and he sneezed. I said 'God bless you' and then asked if he knew who God was. 'Yes' he said, 'when the robber steals something the God shoots him!' Being half American, he thought God was GUARD!

Hope your brave spirit revives soon – there's a lot to think about and discuss.

With love and hugs, *George*

Dear Sara,

Whatever you want me to 'divulge' about myself, my life, just ask. I'll try to tell at least part of the truth!

Really good father–daughter relations are as rare as gold dust. Why? I feel it's got something to do with the appalling collective shock of two world wars – the male ego is badly dented, which affects everything. It's a disaster! I've always wanted a daughter, but never been tested. Maybe just as well.

See you soon. V. told me to cuddle you, so be prepared!

With love, *G*.

Dear George,

The appointment in hospital. I think it is to see the plastic surgeon. I hope it isn't the actual op. as I still have a lot of questions to ask. We were talking today – general consensus is I should have my foot stitched to my mouth.

I got to give you a hug today! I'm not too comfortable with hugs, cuddles, and kisses, though I am getting better. The girls in here are very affectionate towards each other, only natural, I suppose. I remember one day when I had been here about a month I was waiting at the door, and another girl put her arms around my waist from behind. I stood it until I felt the sweat run down my back. When we are called to 'our rooms' for lock-in, there's a round of good-night kisses and cuddles, but I don't participate. They know my problems. However, the girls said I was 'really glowing' so I guess you must have done something right.

I couldn't have the owl – it was pointed out to me, quite correctly I am sure, that legal advisers do not bring gifts. I'll have to give it back to you next visit. You can look after him for me, don't think you are getting it back permanently! Also, don't expect a drink next time either – solicitors are not entitled to coffee!

Mr Hicks (Wing governor) put a plug on my CD adaptor, he was quite insulted when I whispered, 'Brown on the right, blue on the left, green at the top!' Rules are that the workmen should do these jobs. I said to Mr Hicks, 'Hang on, let me see if anyone has a screwdriver.' He replied, 'If they have, I want to know where they got it!'

I have been thinking over your suggestions about the book. My gut feeling is yes, talked to the girls, they think it would be marvellous. I suppose, I would have to tell you all those awful things about me, like how I used to pick my nose, turn my eyelids inside out to frighten the boys, and – my worst secret (piss in the bath so Billi would get out!). I can be so irreverent, George, the more something hurts or is dangerous, the more I joke. Hey, you looked snazzy today – I liked it. What is all this bullshit about adopting me as a daughter? If that's the way you think, then I'm incestuous (well the thoughts are). I also talk too much to cover a certain amount of emotional confusion.

I had a letter from my faith healer, Keith Lee. Did I tell you about him? He's a marvellous man – I met him through the Methodist Church. When M. came out of the clinic, he felt he had had a sort of religious awakening. I don't know whether he did or didn't. I do know that if you create a vacuum then you must fill it with something else. Why not God? Anyway, this experience didn't see him through, we togged up for church every Sunday, but the reality meant that M. actually went to the pub earlier. 'We're all dressed up, let's pop to the Such and Such,' quite often dropping Luise off at the swimming pool. I'm ashamed to say I usually agreed. To ask to go home meant a row.

Keith came to my birthday party, just before my trial, and healed all my friends – back problems, etc. I was jumping up and down saying, 'I *want* to be healed – heal me!' He just looked at me and said, '*you're fine*'! I was so disappointed. I mean, everyone was worrying about me and my trial and he ignored me.

Meanwhile, take care, keep writing, it's great to see an envelope with your big bold handwriting waiting for me!

Love, *Sara* x

Dear George,

I'm still a little tearful, but am coming out of it. Mopped the landing during breakfast, sobbed my way around the floor – must have looked a comical sight. Everybody is being so kind, it makes me cry more. Tomorrow I am going to try and crack a joke! I think even if it's a bad joke everyone will laugh, relieved I am back to normal.

Sunday evening

I had a chat with the No. 1 Governor, Mr Mogg, this morning. As my legal aid doesn't cover either solicitor or QC, I am preparing my own defence! In view of that, he is going to allow me one visit per week with legal advisers. Guess who is my top legal adviser? So don't use the VO I sent you, just phone and book. You might be my top legal adviser, but for God's sake don't dress like one, or you'll be fired! Stay as you are.

Love, *Sara*

Dear lovely Sara!

It was good to see you in the new official legal box. Sorry if I was 'brusque'! I don't feel in the least brusque about you – exactly the reverse. In fact I'm amazed and delighted at our friendship – exactly one month ago since I met you. I don't know what it means to you, but for me it's already a jewel of an experience. Life is a marvellous process of redemption, isn't it?

You remind me of a cartoon by Steinberg: two very ordinary birds are standing together looking up at the American heraldic eagle, with '*E Pluribus Unum*' on its chest and clutching arrows in its talons. One turns to the other and says, '*RARA AVIS*' (rare bird, if Millfield didn't teach you Latin!). You're a rare bird and I love you for it. If you want me to stay as a 'tramp' (cheeky woman!) you must stay as a *rara avis* . . . *Rara Sara.* You certainly have a rare spirit. Never let it go.

Re: the Appeal, the problem is how best to *add* to the Appeal argument various facts about the stress you were under, the police role, etc.

My love, *George*

Dear George,

The atmosphere is euphoric, no other word could describe it. I've cried, not often that someone gets released from here like this. It's normally the Appeal Courts or another prison. Sonia, bless her, is just bubbling over with happiness. I've done the card and notelets delivery with a great grin on my face. From your letter, not Sonia's news.

I am practising hugs – so next time you come I'll be better. I'm all choked up – I'll answer the points you've made later tonight, when I've more time. I just want to get this letter out – all I'll say is my feelings are a delicious secret. I just want to hug them to myself for a bit longer.

Love, *Sara* x

Dear Sara,

You must be addictive! I miss you. Thanks for the canary letter. I like the colour – but I think that bird is for the pot! *Please*, by all means use the paper for people who know you well, but don't send it to fans, TV people and other riff-raff till I've had a chance to discuss it with you. Anyway, be patient and let's discuss it.

I've got a good book on criminal procedure and have looked up a lot of stuff about Appeals, provocation, etc. Legal jargon – I'll discuss it with K.O'D. and then let you borrow it.

What are all those 'delicious secrets'? Or are they too secret? Father nostalgia may be off the menu but I'm sure I would have adored you as a little girl.

I feel your case is a huge challenge; interesting, heartening, mind-bending – a real test of each of us. I'm not optimistic but I'm certainly *hopeful*! See you soon.

A lot of hugs and love, *George* x

Dear Sara,

I was quite disappointed this morning not to get a letter from you – just a library card and an official looking OHMS envelope. Then I noticed the stamp on the letter was upside down, and opened it to find your letter and Faction stuff. Have a nice day . . . Thanks!

Billi phoned last night and we talked for half an hour – I hate to think what her phone bills are like. It was very good to talk to her – she sounds very American. (Next time I'll ask her what she feels about your tricks for getting her out of the bath! No I won't . . .) She said, incidentally, that when you were asked in court if you had been 'provoked', you said, 'No'. Is that correct? I thought she had a parrot on her shoulder squawking, but she said it was a two-and-a-half-year-old child! She says the trial was a farce, with all sorts of blunders.

A 'snazzy' tramp, hey? One day I'll hire a pin-stripe suit and white tie and shock you! Most lawyers are would-be actors – I know one in London who wears capes, bangles, God knows what.

I'll gladly drop the father–daughter role if you offer me something better! And if you discover a link between webbed feet and orgasm you'll be able to write a thesis on it for your Ph.D. Be nice to the captain and crew of HMS *Invincible* or they'll make you walk the plank for mutiny! Take care and a real live hug/kiss ready please.

My love, *George* x

Dear George,

Hello, how are you? I've had a wonderful day – as the rhyme goes, 'Visions of swans have danced in my head'. I got the CD out at lunchtime, and set myself up in the association room. I love music so much.

I had five letters this morning, one from Billi expressing great curiosity about you, so I wasn't too surprised to read in yours that she had telephoned. Did I say 'No' to provocation? I thought I was made out to be: 'I'm just a girl who can't say No!' (Stupid joke – but I'm in such a great mood!) I think on reflection I did – in fact, much of the time I answered questions with a monosyllable! I was so god-damn scared, George. I really felt like nobody in there was on *my* side. I have the Prosecution being downright nasty, the psychiatrists telling me, 'Don't worry, we are going to say some awful things about you, but don't worry.' And then Barker QC, he reminded me of my Father. I was terrified of that man. I only met him once before the trial. I had no empathy with him, he really came across like, 'You have been a naughty, silly girl, but do as I say and hopefully everything will turn out fine.' He gave me no due respect for my age, intelligence or ability. I felt crushed in his presence! On reflection, the whole thing was a big mistake. I didn't meet him till four weeks before the trial, it was all so rushed. Like Billi said – a fiasco. Let me tell you something, George, being on trial for murder is probably the most frightening thing that can happen to a woman. If they had accepted my guilty plea to man-slaughter, then it wouldn't have been half so bad. Many of the women here were not allowed on the stand by their defence counsel, because it's so bad. Also, I did not understand the full implications of the whole subject of provocation – I thought they meant, had he just hit me, to which the answer was of course no, but he did tell me he was going to kill me, and I believed him. If I get a retrial, we'll do it my way.

I'll come to Finland with you, if you: (a) let me bring my guitar; (b) keep me warm with whatever means are at your disposal; and (c) feed me salted olives on cocktail sticks.

Let me tell you a funny story – just to prove that even in the most tense, fraught situations there is humour.

On about the third or fourth day of my trial, Billi, V., K. and myself were sitting on a long seat outside the court. I was due to go on the stand – and I was very frightened. We were all praying, smoking, etc. Two rather dilapidated old men sat down opposite us. One turned to his friend, who was obviously deaf and said very loudly, ' 'Ere, let's go in this one, Bert, it's a real juicy murder.' 'Ye what?' replied Bert. 'Murder,' said his friend. 'Some lady knocked off her old man – bet he was 'aving a bit on the side.' They sat, and then looked at us. The friend said to K., ' 'Ere, are you part of this trial?' to which K. just nodded. 'What about you?' he asked, looking at Billi. 'Are you a friend or summat?' Billi nodded, saying, 'Yes, I'm a friend of the lady.' 'Ooh er, Bert, you 'ear that?' he asked, nudging Bert, who by this time was beginning to catch on to the fact that they had hit the big time. 'Bert, Bert, she said she's a friend of the lady!' Bert sat up higher as they both digested this information. By now I was having a hard time keeping a straight face and I could feel V. shaking silently next to me. She kept her head down, so the next question was directed at me. 'What about you then, you a friend an' all?' I waited a split second, lifted my chin higher and staring straight at him, replied, 'I am the lady!' It was wonderful, and I will always remember it as one of the highlights of my trial. Bert and friend were over the moon, though we refused to speak after that. There was a sequel though. A couple of days later we were again waiting, when Bert's friend came up, sat down next to me and put an arm around my shoulders. 'Don't you worry, love,' he comforted, 'I've seen a lot of these trials; mark my words, you'll get off – hefty fine and a suspended sentence.'

My Defence didn't take any statements. Most were composed by bloody psychiatrists. They obviously thought, oh, we'll do it with DR (diminished responsibility), before they even met me! Dr Henrietta Bullard was a great lady. She came to see me in Coventry one week before the trial. She was absolutely adamant that I shouldn't be charged with murder. I liked her, a strong, strong lady, she wanted to bring up all the problems of living with an alcoholic. For some reason she didn't. She'll probably do her best to convince you I'm nuts! Frankly I'm convinced of it myself at present! But I don't care, it's a wonderful feeling, you've given me something, George – Desire, a desire to be free! I'll write more tomorrow, sleep well.

Love, *Sara* x

Dear Sara,

A quick, *non*-brusque scrawl!

A red squirrel appeared outside this morning, collecting berries for the winter . . . I love them (squirrels, not berries). Hope to come Friday and do the owl exchange. And discuss K.O'D.'s visit and get a hug or more.

Much love, *George* x

Dear George,

It's Tuesday – where are you? Then I heard the weather forecast, and this morning I went outside, pouring with rain, so I understand.

So you don't like my bird. It's only a joke bird, George – not a big deal. I was thinking of sending you one with a tramp . . . I think I hear what you are saying – I shouldn't be so glib – I feel suitably chastened. I *hate* being told off, one of my very worst points.

There's been a lot of talk over the last few days about crime and culpability. I guess many of us, including myself, tend to blame others. It's only in the time that I've been in prison that I have understood how wrong I was; so many people felt that M. deserved to die, but *nobody*, George, deserves to die, at least not like that. I think one of the reasons I'm fairly happy in prison is because I can accept my guilt and punishment. I love being locked up alone for twelve hours. I'm so looking forward to my studies. Never before have I had such a chance to really get to know myself, and perhaps understand. But the main point I think I want to make is that I and the other women mustn't make life appear *cheap*. Of course, the whole aim is to stop the violence before anyone dies, but I don't think women should be just freed. Life is very precious, no matter how badly M. behaved, he was entitled to his life, and I took that away, however accidentally it was. Just as I feel if someone goes driving whilst drunk, then they are just as guilty of manslaughter should they knock someone over. Being in prison helps assuage my guilt.

Off to hospital tomorrow to see the plastic surgeon! I'm looking forward to seeing the world once more; there'll be few children – they are all at school!

Had a letter from Billi – just a short note to say that she had phoned you – and thought you were OK! At least she says you are OK to talk to, she called you 'strong' and quietly spoken! I'm glad she approves.

Lots of hugs and kisses prepared, *Sara*

Dear George,

Congratulations, you finally wrote me a letter that had no mention of 'old', 'father–daughter', etc. Has it finally sunk in? How many hints must I write? I can't be as forthright as you – circumstances, insecurities, but I'm certain I feel as you do, and probably have for a lot longer. I just didn't realize. Everyone close to me did, though, which makes it doubly infuriating. I expected to feel many varying emotions in prison, but not this. I'm walking round in a daze half of the time, with a lunatic grin on my face! But it's hard, I'm torn between elation and nagging doubt.

Foot expedition was satisfactory. The surgeon is not going to sew my toes together. Instead he will take a graft off the top of my foot. This damn thing has got so big and deep, he can't just leave a hole. He's booking me in, don't know when though. I won't be told till the day before either (security reasons) so it could be one week or one month.

Charlotte and I had another portion of stew, so I'm bloated and burbling. Darn thing gets hotter every time we reheat it! Come Friday, it'll be unbearable. Kiss me at your peril! But kiss me anyway!!!

I've just made an 'app.' to accept your owl in if you come Friday – 'permission to return owl and permission to receive owl'.

I'm glad you liked my story, being on bail whilst on a charge of murder was at times very funny and strange. The weekend after M. died, when the euphoria of being on bail and surrounded by caring friends had subsided, I felt totally bereft and wandered off one early Sunday morning. I eventually found myself in a church. The service was nearly over and as I waited to go in, a man of the cloth asked me if I was all right. I told him I had just murdered my husband (I was crying) – he backed away, looked at me for a minute then whispered harshly, 'Have you told anyone else?' I realized he was frightened and unable to help at all. I just left. I often wonder if he told anyone. I find that story sad, so typical of the Church today. I have asked if I can preach in our service here, but I don't think they will let me. I feel they guard their so-called access to God very jealously. Being a *Christian* in prison is very difficult. At times I feel spiritually lost.

I feel very close to God when I pray in my room, or out on exercise. I often take the Bible to the loo with me, but I cannot in all honesty say I find much comfort from the dogma of the Anglican Church. I love the hymns though, and always manage to get a good slurp of the communion wine!

I'm so looking forward to seeing K.O'D. tomorrow, it's a great help that she's seeing you first. I'll only have an hour and a half, you know well how quickly that seems to fly.

I have a funny feeling that we are going to be restricted on what we can enter on behalf of me as Appeal material. Hurry up with your 'sawdust', I want to read it please. I feel useless without having any reference books to read.

Reading your last letter again, may I point out Mr Delf, that if I should ever find myself in a forest in Finland sharing a sleeping bag with you, playing the guitar is not an occupation that springs to mind.

I am scheming to print you some headed notepaper. It's just ideas. Your comments hurt me terribly, I just want to hit back. I won't. However, I have one in mind . . .

Lots of love, *Sara* x

Dear Sara,

It was good to get your letter this a.m. – it and the one I got yesterday make a very good combination – all sides of you, happy, high-spirited, 'chastened' and thoughtful. Don't you realize yet that I love you – which means *all* my (mildly) critical comments exist in a context which is warm and supportive and loving. Where would you sleep here? Either with me or out with the owls. Take your choice.

I hope the 'chastening' has been and gone. I don't like being classed with bullying QCs and other flotsam. I'm glad you expressed those feelings about Malcolm. Exploring all that loss and sadness is all part of freeing yourself from your past – maybe you must free yourself before it's worth getting the prison to free you physically? Lots of people drift through all of life and *never* explore their own deepest feelings – you have given yourself no option.

Are the swans still dancing? How about this saying of Hildegarde of Bingen (around 1100)?

'I am that living and fiery essence of the divine substance that glows in the beauty of the fields. I shine in the water, I burn in the sun and the moon and the stars . . . I breathe in the grass and in the flowers, and when the waters flow like living things, it is I . . . I am wisdom. Mine is the blast of the thundered Word by which all things were made . . . I am Life.'

That's you.

There's a pub in Durham called the Swan and Three Cygnets, about 300 yards from your abode. It's my favourite – let's go ... See you soon.

Much love, *George* x

Dear, dear George,

I'm skipping lunch in order to write this. I took a brief look at what was on offer. Shepherd's Pie with the 'Shepherd' very much in evidence. No, thank you!

We've been given such an opportunity, George, don't let's blow it with preconceived notions of age or whatever. At the risk of making myself vulnerable, I love you too, and I think you are an incredibly sexy man! I spent most of today's visit gazing at your face. All I wanted to do was hug and hold you! Every time I took your hand you pulled away. But I don't feel hurt, a little amused at your bashfulness, and just thoroughly glad to see you and cement this wonderful feeling I have for you. Enough.

Chris just came to see me – 'How was your visit, etc.?' She says she wishes she had been in there with me, she'd have said, 'For God's sake, George, give her a big kiss and put us all out of her misery!'

It's cold – I'll spend this weekend in bed with a hot-water bottle, my pen and erotic thoughts of *you*. I feel really good, peaceful, but anxious to see you again.

Love, *Sara* x

George,

Have you ever had a flash of understanding that was so deep it took your breath away?

Lying here thinking about prisons, Daddy, Mummy, me. Your comment about loving me and any criticisms being in the context of love, etc. I don't know that sort of criticism. Then it hit me – of course I don't. As a child all criticism was demoralizing, degrading. Mostly from Mummy. Then I started thinking that my real prison is the past, the way I think of myself – why Daddy doesn't love me (us); why does he always call me a liar, etc. Well it hit me. Whenever Mummy had been hitting us, she always explained our crimes, punishment (whip, locked in room/cupboard, no supper, etc.) were because we had been naughty, lying, cheating, etc. I guess Daddy believed her – or wanted to. Poor Daddy, poor us. I feel like crying.

When I cut my throat, Billi found out several months later, and when she asked Daddy about it, his comment was, pity she didn't succeed! I'm not such a bad person that I deserve my own father to say that about me. God, that hurts even now. I don't want to store a catalogue of grievances – but I know now why I married Malcolm – Daddy approved, I finally belonged. I was accepted. Daddy even visited my house in Atherstone and thought Malcolm a 'super chap' (he'd just come out of the clinic). I lived five years in Coventry as a single parent – Daddy never even phoned me!

The only time Daddy was nice to me was when he was drunk – or had been drinking heavily – maybe just maybe that's why I tolerated Malcolm's drinking for so long!

I've just heard about a 32-year-old man who received a six-year jail sentence. His crime? He killed an old man – smashed his back in three places, broke all his ribs, then took his £75 and calmly walked to the pub. Admitted manslaughter through diminished responsibility – he was depressed at not being able to find a job. I am disgusted and hurt!

I want to make you something in pottery – but it requires a bit of research. I'm *not* artistic! The apple I made for Luise took two weeks – and it started out life as a hedgehog. However, I am going to try – that's all I can do, isn't it? Don't hold your breath, though.

I guess a woman in love must shine like a beacon. I do – it's embarrassing. I'm in an agony of suspense – I can't wait to see you tomorrow, I'll probably be tongue-tied.

I looked up Leo – do you think you are typical?

Love you, *Sara* x

Dear Sara,

The ride back took one hour longer than going in – a howling gale! One day, Ms Thornton, I'll get my own back for all this cycling – when we go to Finland. I'll insist that before you're allowed in *our* sleeping bag you'll have to cycle at least once around Finland!

I'll make only one last comment on the dreary subject of age – please, never make assumptions about *time* regarding us.

I love you in your glasses, just the secretary I want! I love hugging you even more.

Your description of the church encounter is *chilling*. You say, 'as a Christian', etc. Why not, 'as a human being'? Doesn't what you and I are trying to do and be add up to a spiritual quest? The challenge we face re: law, people, hostility, bureaucracy, prejudice, ignorance, etc., etc., is all of life rolled into a ball – power, psychology, feeling, fear, hope, love, everything?

One of the things I love about you is your great reserve of courage/ spirit/hope. It's a miracle it survived all that devastating emotional paralysis and cruelty.

If I really hurt you, I'll kiss your re-designed toe in penance! I *am* sorry. Keep complaining. You don't have to hit back. I think one emotion in me your aggro-bird aroused was a dislike of women acting like men, with wide shoulders – aggressive gestures. That's an excuse. I *am* sorry. How many kisses and hugs in payment?

Much love, G. x

Dear George,

I was the last on the landing to be locked in. Normally I am the first as I'm usually in bed writing. Being last gave me a chance to turn Sonia's lights off. You should have heard her holler! She has only one day left, there'll be tears tomorrow, not everyone is feeling euphoric about it.

Saw Mr Mogg today, he enquired about my campaign. One of the officers brought in some CDs to play – very nice. Tina Turner shriek-ing, 'I think you're the best!' I do as well.

Wrote to Faction Films today, in fact spent most of the afternoon on it. Very difficult to be truthful, without distorting the facts. Nowhere have I mentioned that Malcolm was a former policeman.

I wish you'd come and see me before I send it off.

Your last letter talked about jealousy, and lack of faith between couples. Jealousy is something I cannot understand. M. was very jeal-ous, perhaps his alcoholism made it worse. I think if a person feels truly secure in the love they have, there's no need to be jealous. But people do like to play silly games, don't they, and I've found that men only believe you love them if you get jealous.

Malcolm used to shove his ex-wife down my throat, with her sewing talents and big boobs, etc. I merely retaliated by nicknaming her 'wonder wife'. I stopped playing pool, after one incident when Malcolm left me in a pub. When he finally came home, he asked why I had to play with big hairy men – I replied, because I couldn't find any big hairy women. I was a pretty good pool player too. Yes, on reflection, I gave up a lot for Malcolm, but it wasn't love, it was weakness. However, I don't think I am an easy person, I think nothing of being the first on the dance floor at a 'do' – going to a pub on my own. Wearing shorts, going topless. I *never* wear a top in my garden. I think a lot of it had to do with being brought up to treat men as equals – not as prospective lovers/husbands etc. I generally get on better with men than women. (At least I did!)

I think freedom comes from within, it is dependent on what you want out of life, not what someone else does. 'Live your life the way you want as long as you don't hurt others.' I used to think that made a lot of sense, now I think it's a load of bullshit. I no longer want to feel responsible for what the world feels. Just for once I am going to think of myself, and that gives me freedom. I maintained a façade of 'happy, normal housewife' till M. died – not because I wanted it, but because society wanted it. I've lost nearly everything of any material value; it used to hurt, but not any more. Maybe I'll feel different when I'm out of prison, but I don't think so. Does any of this make sense or am I rambling?

I write lots of poetry, not heavy stuff though. I just like playing with words. I remember one I wrote for M. started, 'I wish my husband was a camel, and could go two weeks without a drink.' Disaster!

Found a letter I wrote to you yesterday, written in a mood you haven't yet seen, 'pissed off Sara'. Tore it up, but the last line I'll repeat. 'I wish I was with you, sipping a hot toddy, listening to music and being loved.' See you *soon*.

Love, *Sara* x

Dear Sara (this form of address is getting ridiculous!),

The awful truth is that I could write to you all day and then nothing would get done, and you'd get saturated. And the censors would go on strike!

Don't over-stress your sexy body, please. Will they plaster your toe? I suppose not. Go easy on the wooden horses, etc., they might throw you off. Will you be my gym mistress? (Feeble joke!)

You have looked better, weller, prettier each time I've seen you – which must prove something!

We've proved one thing, at least, that kisses and hugs are *far* better in real life than on paper . . . So let's remember the last and promise the next!

Love, *George* x

Dear George,

Quite late, well very late, (all right) Thursday morning. You're right, it is stupid.

Dear, wonderful George. That's better!

Had a portfolio of work from Luise, paintings, poems, etc. Spent the last day laughing and dare I say crying. Her first poem reads, 'My dog is company when I'm alone, but not great company when I have an ice-cream cone.'

Made me think of my mother – a memory. When I was about nine, ten years old, Billi, five or six, we made a swing on the branch of a flame tree in our garden (in Fiji). It was pretty poor, just a piece of green nylon washing line which I put up with a couple of slip knots. Mummy came out, and told us in no uncertain terms to take it off. Why, I don't know, it wasn't dangerous. I tried very hard, but the slip knots had become very tight with our weight. She came back about twenty minutes later, was furious that I hadn't done as she said. She wouldn't listen to me, took it off herself and whipped me with it. Whipped me, George, on my legs. I was wearing shorts. I remember her chasing me with it, as I leapt up and down trying to avoid it. As a mother now, I look back with disgust at her cruelty. As a child it seemed normal. Writing this down I feel as if I've spewed up bitter bile; it's almost a physical release to write it. The line was nylon coated – quite heavy!

I spoke to a trainee probation officer called Elizabeth. Took her on a tour of the centre and introduced her to a few people. Showed her my 'article' and explained a little about what I was hoping to achieve. To my horror, she sat at my desk and broke down in tears! Are they catching? Do I have this effect on people? I mentioned your name.

Some of the girls are getting a bit excited over an article that appeared in the *Independent* not long ago. It seems that MPs are debating the issue of conjugal visits. I gave Susie the article to read whilst we were waiting to go to work. She read it through, then looking at me asked in her gravelly cockney voice, 'What's conjugal visit mean, Sara?' A hush as the girls awaited my reply. 'It means you fuck and fuck and fuck all weekend, love!' Uproar!! ('I want a conjugal visit, George' – Susie)

You are right about my balance and coordination, yes, I have that in abundance. The courage bit I'm not so sure of. I did some crazy things; at twenty-seven I decided to learn high diving. Looking back, I don't think it was courage. To a great degree it was a sheer disregard for my life! I've had it always; took my first overdose of valium at seventeen years old. (Can't write about that yet; hurts.) It really is only in the last few years that I actually started to value my life, I lost it again with Malcolm – maybe another reason I didn't leave. Ouch! I've only just thought of that! A sort of suicide? I'll have to really think about that one! I was mulling over the word prism as opposed to prison, very similar – a prism takes light and shows it in a different direction. Mmm – that has possibilities. Now my life is very precious. I sometimes think that prison has saved my life, I wonder if I could have coped with the guilt and trauma of Malcolm's death if they had only given me probation?

I'm getting teased a lot by the girls – and even my English teacher on Monday night, 'Ah so you do love him, I knew it weeks ago!' So smug. I tell you how bad they are – Martina is putting together a brochure of DTP samples. Guess whose names are on the wedding invitations she's done? I nearly died!! Don't worry, George – I have a loathing of marriage, never ever again. Of course, they are chuffed – it's very unusual to actually fall in love with someone you meet *after* being in prison unless of course they are prisoners themselves. So once again I'm breaking newish ground!

I guess for them it's like a fairy tale! They really do love it. Even one of the officers said to me Tuesday, 'You've got a letter from George!' I remember your first letter: Tracey opened it, read it, then passed it to me, saying, 'Read this one, it's special!' Your handwriting took my attention straightaway. She was right, it was special – *you* are special and I really thank God for bringing you into my life. Nagging doubts – whilst I'm in prison – that you'll have an accident on your bicycle and I won't know for days and days. God forbid! That you'll get frustrated and angry, and seeing that, I'll stop everything. That you will meet some woman who will bowl you over and then be too scared to tell me – but – I'll guess anyway, and I *hate* deceit. If I get out early, that my high spirits will wear you down. In Coventry I used to drape a beautiful red bedspread over two washing lines and sleep underneath, pretending I was Cleopatra on a barge going down the Nile. So you see . . . I'm not normal. You'd probably get tired of me. Having been locked up – how hard would I find it to cope with freedom again? If someone asked me what I was going to do on release, expecting a reply like, get drunk, eat a steak, spend money – I'd merely say, 'Go to bed with George and be left alone for a week.' Would you understand that? You, me, Sibelius, Neil Diamond and a jar of olives, tuna fish sandwiches. A mango, beer and candles – I've grown to *hate* electric light in here – we have it always, no sunshine. I'm not afraid of other men, I know myself – I know what I want. Others seem shallow now. Tough shit, Delf – you're stuck with me. I want to walk on the fells, for miles, sit in comfortable silence, make love to you, wake up in the night and feel you there, wash your back, sit on the bath while you shave, talk, listen, learn, teach. *Debate*, plan, hope. Love – yes, keep coming back to that one, the thought of making love with you is almost too much to bear, but I too can hope, can't I?

When I went for trial, I said to Billi, whatever happens, I want one day to look back and say I was proud of the way I behaved. Even when I was sentenced: 'Take her down . . .', no officer had to carry me. I held my head erect and even bowed slightly to the judge, thanking him. Then I turned and walked out as everyone looked, more like the queen leaving the Royal Box after a command performance. All the way to the holding cells the officer kept saying, 'Cry, love, you must cry.' I did of course, the thought that hammered and hammered in my brain, 'I won't see Luise till she's twenty-six years old.' Yes, Daddy trained me well didn't he?

Stiff upper lip.

What do you want me to do with my hair? I won't have it streaked; everybody does in here, it's awful. I won't dye it. I worked hard for these grey hairs. I once read about a woman who had the world record for the longest hair. After having her head shaved in a concentration camp, she swore she'd never cut it again. I know this isn't Belsen, but . . . I'm wearing it up at present because it's at an 'awkward stage'.

I hope I get a letter from you tomorrow. I hated Saturday – no letter, made me miss you all the more over the weekend.

It's not just *my* justice, George – I told you that, it's for *all* women in Britain. As for politics, you do *not* become embroiled in those here – too much of that already. Reading what you wrote about children on scrap-heaps – I would have gladly lived on a scrap-heap if I had had some love from my parents.

Stop comparing me with Simon, we are not siblings. Do your sons know how lucky they are? I love you – have a good weekend. I'll write more tomorrow and give this to you Friday. Some things are private – oh to be alone with you! Sleep well, you beautiful man.

With love, *Sara*

Dearest Sara (that sounds a *bit* better),

What happens when a topless woman falls into a bottomless pit?: first question on your exam paper.

Here's another bird for you:

> A robin redbreast in a cage
> Puts all heaven in a rage
> *William Blake*

Seems suitable for a topless show-off like you!

Talking of Indians, Shakila has just phoned. Was calling from Glasgow – a woman there has three years' *probation* for strangling her husband. Society has made you pay a high price for your unusual vitality and 'cockiness' – so let's make society pay a high price for listening to your story and letting you go.

You get on better with men, and I get on better with women – is that why we get on? I love you, whoever your God is.

Saying of the Year: '*I don't think I'm an easy person.*' I wouldn't love you if you were. We're both difficult, I think. I suppose it's easier to recognize 'freedom' in its absence than its presence. For me, the poorest part of my life has been the freest. See you soon – Toe the line! I love you.

George xx

Dear George,

Got your letter this lunchtime, very welcome – I missed getting one on Saturday.

I hear all you say, and will, in due course respond. However, your line, 'Please never make assumptions about time regarding us' is, to put it mildly, puzzling.

I haven't made *any* assumptions regarding us – I am quite aware that the only time I have to offer you is an hour and a half per week, plus, if you are lucky, three to four letters. I know that won't satisfy any man for long. I know I am facing a maximum of fifteen years in prison. How on earth do you think I am in a position to make assumptions? I thought long and hard about even continuing this friendship, once I realized what was happening. I don't want to hurt and disappoint you, neither do I want to be hurt. It's difficult enough without you writing things that leave the meaning beyond my reach.

Let me give you a warning – Some men can only love what is unattainable, i.e. a woman serving a life sentence. What you can't quite have is very tantalizing, isn't it, George? As a young girl, the best guava was always at the top of the tree. Once I reached it, grabbed it only to be badly stung by the hornets I didn't see.

How typical of you as a male of the species to promptly start laying down rules as soon as I find the courage to tell you I love you. Your very existence in my life makes my sentence even harder to bear, my imprisonment doubly frustrating, my reasons for early release more personal, selfish. Don't feel sorry for me either, pity I don't need. I'm not brave, I'm just trying very hard to understand why I'm here, what went wrong, can I ever make it right?

As to falling in love with your letters, maybe I should design you some of your own notepaper: 'George Delf – writer, postal love affairs offered, yearly contracts only'? Some of the girls here choose to write to men who are serving sentences of a similar duration. They promise everything, undying love, marriage, eternal devotion, quite often to someone they never meet. It's all quite shallow, but very flowery and romantic. Maybe I should do that, play the little games – I feel tonight as if real life hurts too much. I love all of your letters but that one line I keep returning to like a tongue worrying a broken tooth, till it gets red and sore. I sat in the shower crying bitter, angry tears – *you are hard work, but I won't give up.* All I want is a chance to know you, learn, understand and maybe show you. Who needs marriage, George? You sound like a geriatric judge!

Your letter put me in a bad humour. During supper some supercilious sod from the Board of Visitors was wandering around. They never introduce themselves. I think they feel their imagined halo of charity is visible to all prisoners. He asked us stupid questions. When he was leaving, I said, 'I hope your conscience doesn't prick too much tonight!' 'Oh, not at all,' he replied. 'Then why do you come here?' I returned. Won't see him again.

I can hear it raining outside. I haven't heard a weather forecast for this week, is it bad? Will I see you? You owe me 3,000 hugs, and appropriate kisses.

Here's another bail story:

Just about five weeks before Christmas last year, I was burgled whilst I spent the day at V.'s shoe shop. Thieves got in the back door, took all the jewellery, electrical stuff, over £2,000-worth. I hesitated, but eventually called the police. A fingerprint man came out the next day. He took my prints and stayed quite a while drinking Earl Grey tea and talking. Three days later he appeared at my door again. No, they had no luck with fingerprints, but he was returning mine. He thought they might be of interest. (Some people liked to show them to friends; good party piece, etc.) Could he come in and have some more of that delicious tea? I soon got rid of him, an amorous policeman I did not need. Party piece? I'd love to have seen his face if he had bothered to run a check on the computer, and found out that the pretty lady was currently on a charge of murder! It would have served him right if I had played his silly games. Yes, life on bail is a ball!

If you want to call it quits, first give me a couple of weeks of gentle hints, so that I won't be raw and vulnerable. I'm very bruised emotionally – I love you very much, but I'm also starting to love me. Take care and keep warm.

Sara x

Dear George,

I finally finished the essay for Faction Films [*Dispatches*]. I've been working on it for nearly four days. Doesn't serious writing drain one? Did you find that when you wrote your book?

It only amounts to one page. I haven't gone into detail about my case, but used the suggestions in your letter – and built around that. Like my letter to the *Independent*, I have tried to be purely factual, not elicit sympathy, though maybe empathy. If they want to make *any* alteration, or require further info. – they are to contact you. Is that OK?

I still feel angry over the way I was treated before and after Malcolm's death. Writing today, thinking deeply, and trying to be as honest as possible, made me sweat, shiver, and feel slightly sick. At lunch time I came to my room and wept again. (One day I might write a letter without mentioning tears?!) Another reason I'm tired, I think, is due to a certain pint-sized Kraut waking me up at 5.30 a.m. with a loud rendition of 'Here we go, here we go, here we go!'

The heating is on – Hurrah! Maybe my plants have a chance of life now.

I hope yesterday's letter didn't hurt too much. Maybe I'm just not ready to love anyone yet. Your little owl is looking at me from under a red carnation. His facial expression reads, 'Stop feeling sorry for yourself you stupid woman!' He's right, bless him.

Lots of love, and hugs and kisses and cuddles. *Sara* x

Dearest Sara,

Oh you out-of-reach guava, protected by squadrons of hornets! I'm stung by your misunderstanding of my brief comment about *time*. It was very innocent, a shorthand way of saying – by all the averages

43

of nature, I will be dead a long time before you. That is all. I love your comment, 'you are hard work but I *won't* give up'. Please don't. Nor will I.

My notion of 'God' is that we are each agents of Creation, the product of millions of years of life and death and if we fail to add something of value to what we find, we are just a dead weight.

If our love fails to create anything new in us, it won't be worth anything anyway. For me it already has.

By the way, I liked the threat of being 'kissed into submission'. Better by far than being stung to death.

I laughed at your visitor's fob-off. Why don't you give them something useful to do? Give them really tough questions requiring research, etc., and look very solemn and earnest about it.

Re: your idea that maybe I love you *because* you are out of reach, how come then I have never loved any woman before like that? I want you *out* of there soon. What happens after that, I haven't the faintest idea.

As to being a 'geriatric judge', my language fails. I'll sentence you to love . . . How many geriatric judges do you know who cycle up hill and down dale to see a stinging guava?

Hugh MacDiarmid, the Scottish poet, wanted as epitaph on his grave: 'A disgrace to the community'. I rather like that.

I'm *glad* you love you. If you didn't – I'd be loving a cripple.

I'm keeping my fingers crossed that Hate Men Week has come to an end!

I love you, *George* x

My Darling George,

Being with you today did something strange. I'll write it as best I can. I hope you understand.

When I left you, and returned to the wing, I had the weirdest feeling as if for a time with you I wasn't in prison. When I walked on to the flat, I had to 'focus' myself back into prison. Spiritually and emotionally during our visit I put a foot back in the outside world. I felt so alien to H-wing – yet when I returned from hospital I felt as if I was coming home. *You* are setting me free. The physical bit is to a degree beyond us, and many inmates still feel emotionally caged even after release. The hard part is setting the spirit free – you are my key. I love you, George Delf!!

Book outline! Well, what can I say, it's very good. I feel both humbled and honoured. You used my favourite word, 'vital' or 'vitality'. I think it might be worth considering some part about Luise, how Billi had to (after sentence) drive back and tell an eleven-year-old child that her mother had just been sentenced to life imprisonment. The children are such an important part – do you agree?

I can't sleep – so many thoughts going through my head – so you keep my letters! I don't know why I am surprised. You were so intense this afternoon, I was just bewitched, bewildered and bemused. Do you feel that we were communicating on two entirely different levels? I have to dig to recall what you said. I just remember your voice, the touch of your hands – I may never wash my left foot again. I had to keep an intensive block on my reactions, physically it's very hard.

Chris read your synopsis, she's placing an order for the book and two dozen boxes of tissues. It made her cry. Martina is very approving, thinks it's wonderful! Won't show anyone else, green-eyed monsters lurk in every unsuspecting corner.

When I come to stay with you, could we have one day a week which will be dedicated to silence (except for moans and groans) so that we have to write down what we want to say. I love the written word and I don't want to lapse back into everyday mundane conversation.

Very abrupt ending to our visit, *not* quite what I had planned. How did the return journey go? What are you going to do in dead of winter? Will I have to endure snow-bound weeks of utter loneliness?

What if on a visit you suddenly realized – don't like her now! Silly I know, but such is my emotional insecurity at times. Mummy once said that she wished she had adopted two children. I barricaded myself in my bedroom. She took no notice. I then stormed out and sat in the tack room (off the stables). Three hours later hunger forced me in, but stubborn me, I climbed up the drain pipe to the *third floor* toilet. Mummy never knew how I got in. George, the next day I felt that drain pipe, it's a wonder I didn't kill myself. At parts it was coming away from the wall. Billi, bless her, sneaked me up food. To this day, we both prefer our food cold and think nothing of eating out of a can.

I Love You! *Sara* x

Dearest S.,

I really earned the hot bath. Had a slow (in fact, accelerating) puncture halfway back – had to stop every few hundred yards to pump the damned thing. I told you it's hard to get away from you! So maybe you're right and we're 'stuck' with each other for ever and ever, amen.

What on earth went on in your mother's childhood/background to turn her into such an avenging fury? These things seem to cascade down the generations, don't they? Sounds to me as if your mother was inwardly demoralized within an outer shell of social success. You're doing OK – she was imprisoned in 'freedom' and you are free in prison!

I hope Martina will send me one of those wedding invitations so at least I know who I'm marrying.

Was there any sense in your childhood that your father really wanted a son and you tried to fill that role?

I promise I'll do my best to stay on the bike (when it works) – I won't get angry with you (except in *very* small doses encased in love!).

With a Pacific full of love, *George* x

Dearest Sara,

I've looked at your report for Channel Four again and it's *really* good.

Yes to candles. Candle-lit baths are good, too. And as for being 'stuck' with you, I'd put up with that, too – even being stuck *to* you.

If your high spirits did 'wear me down' it would be because you were very careless with them, or because I was too stupid to be inspired by them, or both. I hope there's a lot we can learn from each other. Stiff upper lip? Hmm – can't say I'd noticed. Seems fine to me.

Your father's gullible swallowing of the 'liar' image of you is truly horrible – he sounds an emotional cripple. I sometimes wonder if this civilization is simply dying and going hollow – I've come across so many men whose social/career *success* is matched by inner decay.

Reminds me of a weird sight in Crete a few years ago. An olive tree covered with shiny silver shells of dead cicadas, clinging to branches and twigs. A kind of cicada cemetery.

Love is really the heart of life, isn't it? 'God is love' has become meaningless because it has been used so glibly and cheaply by people whose lives are starved of real love.

You are very lucky being able to cry about all the hurt, etc. – it will free you to grow. The real problem is blank indifference and frozen pain.

A lot of love and hugs, *George* x

George,

I can't think of an endearment that is appropriate to the way I feel. Do you know how I feel? I was shaken by my response to you on Friday, on every level. I don't understand how, in such a short space of time, and with the various restrictions we face, but I am deeply in love with you. If any drug made me feel the way loving you does – I'd soon be addicted. Everything seems brighter, clearer. I feel almost invincible. I'm trying very hard with mere words (all that is available) to be honest. These are not the gushing protestations of a teenager on her first date, but the heartfelt feelings of a woman who is somewhat bewildered but utterly grateful. If you sentence me to love, then I can only hope it's a life sentence – no short tariff, please! And I refuse to appeal. It's not something I feel I want to say in a prison visiting room either – I'm always so conscious of the lack of privacy, of where we are! (I think I've done this pen in, too. The Geller effect!) Writing this to you gives me a sense of peace, too. I want you to feel happy and secure in the knowledge that even if I do verbally fly off the handle – I love you very much! I can be a caustic bitch sometimes, even if I count to 100.

Humanizing Hell (*The Law* v. *Nuclear Weapons*) – I think is great! Seriously, I got to the end. I *don't* understand what happened. I never heard of it (or you) before. I would have thought a book with that stark frightening message would have landed you on every chat show in the country.

I can just imagine you in court trying to pass an indictment on Thatcher. Bet you didn't look like a tramp!

I'm glad in a way that I didn't know you – I would have been intimidated and far too scared to fall in love with you (or even tell you so frankly I did).

My Grandfather was a magistrate in Atherstone – he was on the bench for fifteen years. He was a devout Mason. I used to write up his minutes and he'd take me to 'Ladies Night' when I looked after him. I was always the youngest 'lady' – and the most irreverent. I just used to get drunk in order to pass the evening quickly. Often I was caught without wine for a special toast when Grandpa and I had to stand up alone. Once I bribed (or tried to bribe) the 'waiter' to leave a bottle of wine by the table leg. He did, but I found out later he was my bank manager, dressed as a very Junior Mason, with a chamois pouch at his waist.

Got through church without crying! Malcolm Palmer is leaving – this was his last service. He's the one I vented the last of I Hate Men Week on Friday morning. As the service was finishing, Mic the Vic said, 'Don't forget to say goodbye to Malcolm!' I asked, 'Can we kiss him as he's leaving?' 'Of course,' replied Mic. 'Go to it, girls!' I shouted. Malcolm is a bit of an infatuated girl's dream, very good looking, and separated from his wife. There was a stampede! We had a rather pompous visitor in the shape of the Minister for Northern Prisons or something. I wish I had seen his face! He preached quite sincerely about redemption. It was spoilt by the fact that he never looked at us, but at some spot quite high on the back wall, way above our heads. His gaze was at times so fixed I couldn't help but turn my head to look. Naturally, everyone else turned to look at what I was looking at. Me, disruptive? Never. I just hate pomposity!

It's only Sunday, and I miss you so. Are you coming to see me this week? Do you still love me? Did you write to me Saturday? Will I have a letter tomorrow? A day with no letters is an empty day – A Delfless day.

All my love, *Sara* x

October

Dearest,

Jogging with A. – she said, 'Sara, you are different from the other girls – you are . . . alive!' Hallelujah – someone noticed! Majeeda made me a samosa tonight. Yum, yum!

Prison is full of stupid rules, e.g. we are issued with tweezers after supper which have to be returned and signed into a book by an officer. Yet all of us have razors in our rooms! If we are eating in our cell, e.g. bedrest, we have to have the most awful plastic plates, yet we are allowed pottery vases, etc.! Archaic. I'm sure the officers get as fed up having to enforce these rules as we do abiding by them.

Do you notice my letters to you are full of 'yes's? OK, I'll go for wrestling, winner goes on top, eh? Bet you'll cheat there too – does your aversion to aggressive women extend to love-making? Answer that, please!

Have you heard anything about *Dispatches*? I think between us we've probably raised their viewing figures over the last three weeks. Everybody I know is watching and waiting!

I'm at a dead end regarding Mummy and Daddy. I think Billi's comments have stopped me in my tracks, I'm very curious to see Daddy's reply to my question of happiness.

I feel as if I don't have a friend in here at the moment, yet I don't feel sad or lonely! What a puzzle I am.

I think I have figured out why the Pope always falls to his knees when he disembarks from a plane – he's pissed! We've got a 'framed blessing' from the Pope downstairs, courtesy of Algy. Maybe I should write to him. Anyway, how long does a framed blessing last? I'll bet it's stale now!

I love you and feel lonely already at the thought of you being so far away, physically. Be careful, don't talk to strange women. They may be relatives of mine.

Lots of hugs and love, *Sara*

My Wonderful George,

Your question – Did your Father ever want a son? – bullseye! I remember all sorts of things – Daddy told Billi's mum (Joyce) that if her baby was a girl they wouldn't adopt. Joyce refused that stipulation. How I never really felt good enough for Daddy. All the things I excelled at – gymnastics, horse-riding, swimming – never ever good enough! You know, I think I'm quite an accomplished woman. Yes, you are right. I never had a chance, did I? I was the wrong gender – completely out of my control. How tragic – if only I had somehow learnt this when I was younger, I would have saved myself a lot of heartache.

I have, as you know, been very quiet about release/Appeal, sentences etc. Today, talking to Mr Hicks, I blurted out that I *want* justice, I want the impossible. A Solomon to say, 'Malcolm's death will cost you X number of years in prison.' I thought I would get that from my trial. I was really quite content with my life sentence, you know. I knew the judge would give me an appropriate tariff. But as we go deeper into it, it isn't justice, is it? It's all a game – 'getting away with it'. I could well be released *not* because the courts feel I've been punished enough, but because the prosecutor said the wrong thing. That isn't justice either.

I'm in such a turmoil tonight. Anyway, Mr Hicks says he wants to meet you. I gave him your phone number. He also gently pointed out that legal visits are not personal visits – then wished us both the best of luck! Amazing – we (the girls and I) are really very lucky to have such an understanding Wing governor. I think he is marvellous.

Regarding conjugal visits, if you think I'd marry you for your body, forget it! Seriously though, I'm totally disillusioned about marriage.

Mummy had an eventful childhood. She wasn't abused. On the contrary, she was terribly spoilt. Her extravagances and bad behaviour, which everyone catered to, were legendary in our family.

Mummy was a very sickly child. She was packed off to school in Switzerland at an early age (it wasn't till she had me they discovered she was allergic to cow's milk). Asthmatic, she couldn't live in England. She returned and at a boarding school had an accident in gym. It wasn't treated, as a result she got osteomyelitis in her big toe! She was seventeen. They removed the toe joint, and saved her leg – but it was touch and go. Then at Dublin (Trinity College, where she met Daddy) she contracted polio. As a result she was paralysed down her right side. I know her litany of accidents, dreams and misfortunes, because everybody always felt sorry for her – and she became an evil, bad-tempered woman who could – in the eyes of my father, grandmother, grandpa and her brother John – do no wrong. I hated her! That feeling has passed now, but it all still grieves me.

I still can't eat or sleep – does true love have to be like this? Ah well, a small price to pay. Please write me lots of letters this week, George. I sometimes feel as if I am almost falling into a pit of complete despair! Three weeks since my last bout of depression.

Had a letter from Billi today. Luise is worried that everyone is worried about her, and not worried enough about me. She can't say or write the word 'prison' and has started to talk more about me, Malcolm, everything. She also draws lots of walls.

Are you coming in this week? What happens in dead of winter? Will we have to endure weeks of snowbound separation?

A Pacific Ocean of love to you, *Sara*

My darling George,

I'm in bed – finally my body said enough! Don't worry, I'm OK, just a touch of bronchitis. I haven't been eating or sleeping, I guess I've got run down. Yes, do come on Friday. As it's a legal visit you had better hire a suit and bring a *briefcase* – for God's sake don't touch me – just a handshake and *don't* forget to call me Mrs Thornton! The last few days (and nights) have been very painful. I've cried for my past, my childhood. It really has been an emotional battle. I could only have done it alone in the physical sense, but your love and letters have helped more than I can ever say. As you said, one must do it with the support of love. So you see Truth and Love are a package deal. Knowing the truth about me, I will love myself (finally), and in loving myself I love you and I can tell the truth. I had a rotten life till now. I picked up dregs of boyfriends – because I didn't love myself. But I'm beginning to understand it all now. So, if I can finally start to love myself, I can ask for my freedom. It's all tied in. Started on Sunday, this journey has been frightening – but I'm nearing the end.

I'll be able to stop punishing myself, because I'll realize I wasn't always wrong (or bad).

Writing to Daddy last night was a major step. I've never written to him since I was convicted – he never wrote to me either. I think all this is what I am supposed to preach about. I'm not sure yet.

Mangoes I adore – let's have a bath with candles, wine and the mangoes. They are so deliciously messy. I could never love a man who didn't like mangoes. In Fiji we ate them all the time; guava, sugar cane, water melon – I could live on fruit! (I can. All I ate yesterday was an apple!)

In Fiji, when we had a hurricane, we would rush outside during the 'eye' and frantically collect the mangoes – green ones for chutney.

During my vegetarian stage, it lasted seven years, then I lapsed with Malcolm, Luise ate so much fruit I half expected to get up one morning and find her hanging upside down asleep (like a fruit-bat). That's what I used to call her – my little fruit-bat.

No, I'm not a puritan – and you'd better believe I'll prove that to you – but, give us a week, alone: no phone, no post, no visitors. Just a whole week alone. I throb thinking about it. After that we'll get married. I don't know why we have waited five letters dropping subtle hints – that's the truth of it, George Delf – I've known it in my heart since the second visit.

You say that our writing is dynamic because our situations are. Don't you feel that we are both dynamic people anyway? That's why we've sparked off so quickly and love each other so much. Nobody says it's going to be a bed of roses, but you're my destiny. Simple fact.

I remember the letter I wrote, you should have received it today, telling you how much I loved you. I was in an agony of indecision as to whether to send it, yet today I can write all this quite clearly, calmly and with no fear at all. I wonder how many lost opportunities occur because we don't know ourselves well enough to see what we want. I know I want you. I adore you, but you know that already.

Love, *Sara*

Dearest lovely woman!

Maybe we're both at last really beginning to believe in our love, and not always in fear it will suddenly fly through the window and we will wake up to a dreary old world? You are so incredibly honest and brave with your emotions (that's why everybody dissolves in tears . . .) that I struggle to keep up. By daring to face the complete truth of your 'crime' you have joined the ranks of the falsely imprisoned.

An example of our togetherness – you say in your letter we must set aside a day for letter-writing. I was thinking exactly the same thing – we must relate to space and presence and absence with care. I feel you are a companion and partner and a lot else, already. I love the *way* you write, as well as *what* you write.

You know, at first I tried to fit you into my world. Now I realize I need a whole new world for you!

I'm trying to fix my bike today – you ruin pens and I ruin bikes. I hope we treat each other better! Don't worry, if the bike doesn't work I'll get a bus.

All my love, *George* x

Hello Darling,

Gosh, it's a whole six hours since I last wrote to you. I've read your letter again and again.

I have been thinking this evening about this wonderful love we share – what a miracle it is. You know, if by chance I had met you when not in prison, I can tell you exactly what would have happened.

I would no doubt have jumped straight into bed with you, then your inquisitive mind would have started to try and unravel the complex crazy character I had become. I would have put up a shield – and after a while you would have given up in sheer exasperation. Doing it this way (after all it's how Eliz. Barrett Browning did it), we are getting to know each other in our writing – a true courtship, don't you think? I've always written far more honestly than I have spoken – Billi says she only feels the real me in my letters. I don't let my guard down very often. On the outside, you would have stood very little chance of getting through. I find we 'feed' off each other's letters. You mention an idea, we grow it. I mention something, we analyse it together. I find it a great source of comfort to read your letters. To me they are your hand and your heart, brought in by the postman. I can honestly discover and tell you facets of my character because I'm totally secure in the knowledge that you'll still love me. Aren't I lucky?

I'm so glad you have the empathy and understanding to have seen fairly early on the sort of woman I am. What you call vitality is translated by most as 'weird'. What you call perception – others call nosey. Before, I was kind because I desperately sought approval. Now I can be calmly kind – because with my new strength I feel it's just what I am.

Mr Hicks came to see me this evening. I complimented him on his bedside manner – he called me cheeky. He stayed quite a while, he explained that a person on bedrest has to be locked in or they could faint or slip when they run around the landings.

Mr Hicks laughed when I told him I had a legal visit Friday. 'Well, make sure it is legal,' he said. I think he's going to 'have a word' with you when you arrive. I told him all we did last time was hold hands and kiss each other at the start and end. He says that's tantamount to sex. I think we'll have to reward ourselves with a VO visit, don't you? Maybe next week, then if you want to kiss me, you can.

I'll never find true justice, George, leastways not in a court. Justice means the truth has to be told. It wasn't in my trial. Truth hurts people, they don't want to hear it, so these lawyers just play games and call it justice. My justice is in the hands of the Lord.

I love you, *Sara*

Hello again, wonderful man.

I have been contemplating for nearly six hours. I'm at the end of my journey, here is the last piece.

When I was sentenced and locked up at Risley, that first night, I was in utter despair. I had prayed, been what I thought was a good Christian, and yet he still gave me 'life'.

The next morning I saw Sister Jill. We talked, I cried, then we prayed. As a result and the wonderful way I had of adapting and twisting facts to hide the truth, I decided to become the perfect Christian. Of course, this would take hours of prayer, I would study, scrub floors with a smile on my face, brave the insults of the officers and inmates, and after a suitable number of years, God would see me released – a good martyred Christian. When I came to Durham (having prayed for Holloway because it had a swimming pool), I was genuinely aware of domestic violence and its problems. I was aware that I would do something. Seeing that article, I wrote the letter, when people started to reply saying *I* should be freed. Almost in panic I wrote back saying it was not for me, but *all* women. I prayed for God's love and strength. I think I did get it to some degree, but I was sinking fast into a spiritual quagmire. I lashed out at everything, police, Church, AA – I am right about their culpability – but for the wrong reason. Then into all this confusion cycles one slightly tarnished knight in armour. Your letter with, 'The sooner you are free the better,' terrified me. But you were so close. Best see you and put you right as to my motives, especially as your credentials were good. You were not a lost, confused fan. You knew what you were doing. I thought I kept you well at bay, but looking back, I see that I wrote, 'What is it about this man?' However, I was still on safe ground till my Appeal was granted. I wasn't counting on that. I'm sure you can remember your confusion at my not wanting to fight for myself. Marilyn's statement last Sunday, 'If you don't get released on Appeal, then none of us have a chance,' the synopsis of the book – all drove me so desperate that, to survive, I had to go on this journey. I have hated myself, been full of anger, jealousy and bitterness, so all the genuine love I did feel was twisted. I couldn't understand. But when you asked that question about Daddy, it unlocked the gates. I've done some awful things that I've had to face up to. I think the hardest is that, in seeking honesty, I was only twisting the truth, so my hate of myself was hidden in a noble charade. Now I can be a good person, but for the right reasons.

The hardest thing I have had to face up to happened about eleven years ago, just before I cut my throat. I was looking after my uncle John's house whilst they were away on holiday. The day they were due back I ransacked the place – nothing broken, but I stole some of Gilly's jewellery and put it in a drain. To this day, I have never been able to understand what drove me to do such a terrible thing. Of course, Gilly was almost sure I had done it, even had me dragged down to the police station, where I was forced to admit it. But nothing was ever done, I told people I had only admitted to it because the police threatened to take Luise away from me (true, they did). This event caused a terrible rift. Poor Billi – poor everyone. I managed all these years to practically convince myself that I didn't do it. Last night it hit me, this event. I cried, and shouted, no, I can't admit that. But I have, and in doing so I understand something of why I did it. But that was not enough, George, as I wrote yesterday, truth is a package deal with strength and faith. I found the strength to write to John and Gilly last night, admitting what I had done all those years ago, and explaining a bit about what I was going through. You see, John has his own private demons. John knows the truth and knows why I hated myself so much. He will be able to forgive himself for never helping me. He is my Godfather too. No one (excepting perhaps Billi) ever thought to ask themselves, 'Why should Sara cut her own throat?'

If my formula of Truth=Strength=Love=Truth works, then admitting this awful deed should bring us all together again as a family. I have my doubts about Daddy. I have spent today searching my memory, to see if there is anyone else I have hurt who needs my truth. But I can't think of any more except Malcolm. Basically it's *me* I have hurt. I need to love and forgive myself. I'm getting there. Knowing all this, you can use the word 'maybe' in relation to our love? Only in loving myself can I ever acknowledge anyone else's love for me. I think what has happened to me is a most wonderful experience, I've been on a roller-coaster, fast and terrifying. I feel reborn. Behind your love and my love is the love of God.

I need to write to Luise. You see, I always felt that I was an awful mother, so I was very glad to see her go to California. I've never expressed any desire to have her back, because then I didn't want her – I often heard my mother in the way I spoke to Luise. I was terribly afraid I think that history would repeat itself.

Do you forgive me for lying to you, too, all these weeks?

With love, *Sara* x

Darling S,

Your 'revelations' may be the best possible 'medicine' – but please *eat* something! You're not (quite) Eve, munching forbidden apples of the Tree of Knowledge. An apple a day, and nothing else, makes you fair game for serpents and doesn't amuse God either . . .

I think what's happening to you is that you are being *sick*, psychologically and emotionally. Just throwing up all that mess of hurt and anger and bitterness and betrayal that you have never been able to confront. You feel, and cry, and express your pain – laugh and love – what if you were silent, frozen, shut in, like so many?

Marriage? In one letter you hate it and in the other you accept it! In the most basic sense I feel married to you already – as for social rites, let's leave that till there's an obvious need for it?

Bring the criminal procedure book along please, Mrs Thornton. And if you touch me I'll ring the alarm bell . . . If you don't I'll ask for a longer sentence (love)!

It's pretty clear from your description of your mother that she was insanely *jealous* of you – she was *crippled* – and she probably made sure your father was kept far from you. She had to knock you down to make her feel more whole.

I love you – all of you. *George* x

Dearest George,

I got about four hours' sleep, was woken by a terrible nightmare. One I've had since I was very young. It's *so* vivid and *so* frightening that I can remember exactly when I first had it. It was in the Gilbert Islands. I was about six or seven, I guess.

I'm in a room (the rooms can vary) and something is coming to the door. Something so horrible, so terrible, that if I look at it, I know I will die. I search frantically around the room for somewhere to hide, not so it can't find me. I know with ineffable horror that 'it' will always find me. I'm looking for somewhere to hide my face, so that I won't be forced to look at 'it'. But I *know* I won't be able to resist a peek and then I'll die. I don't think this has any relevance to looking at one's 'true self' as I've been doing. It's too pat. Maybe it's a memory from very early childhood which became distorted somehow. Needless to say, I always wake up just as the door is opening.

I hope they let me go to work tomorrow – Ella is concerned I could get very depressed locked in all day and night. I think she has a valid point.

I feel a desperate need to be 'one' with you; relief in dreams and visions of the future are blissful but empty. I don't know if you have a hairy chest? You don't know if my tummy button is an 'n' or 'u'. (It's good to laugh!)

I think I've mentioned before that 'caring' has for long been a word exempt from prison vocabulary. Anyway, just to prove me wrong (and make me feel humble) Chris and Bridget came to give me two oranges. They are like gold dust. I said no – maybe I should have taken *one*. It's hard to remember that there is pleasure in giving – I love giving – but it is selfish to not let others give. I'll ask Bridget for one orange for breakfast.

I do hope you don't stop loving me over my last revelation about John and Gilly. Having got rid of all this anger, I feel like a vacuum. I need your love to fill it. Where's my faith? I feel so raw, so vulnerable, still remnants of worthlessness remain.

There is something I must write to you – nothing bad. In the film *2010* – as the monolith is engulfing Iona and turning it into another sun, Dave (the star child) says in a thick heavy voice, 'Something wonderful is about to happen!' It does, Iona exploded into a sun, giving new life on Europa and two suns for earth. But the best part is that knowledge of a higher intelligence seems to stop the cycle of war and destruction between Russia and America. I love that film, for its message (Arthur C. Clarke) – and that is how I feel. 'Something wonderful is about to happen.'

I love you lots and lots. I think I'd better try cracking a few jokes tomorrow – situation is getting desperate and *I'm* in danger of turning into a quiet, normal person!

See you *soon*. Remember how *much* I love you! *Sara*

Darling George,

You posed some interesting points in your letter today. Tomorrow we'll have too much to discuss, so I thought I'd reply. I've not read much of Shelley, or much of the greats come to that. I must start. Can you advise? As to his body being burned on the beach, I can think of no better way, being reared so close to the sea. I love it and respect it hugely. Ideally, I'd love to be cast off in a pyre on a burning ship, Viking style. A waste of a good ship – the beach is fine. You wouldn't need to rescue my heart, you have it already! (How maudlin I'm being.) I like your description of me as a Spitfire – though I hope you'll one day amend that to a Fokker!

I've eaten today, a piece of meat pie, and . . . an apple. I was brought some stew at tea time – yuk – I couldn't eat it. I think part of the problem too is that the prison fare has become so boring – I will never eat mushy peas again. I used to fill up with toast and jam, but one day a few weeks ago they found a mouse in the toaster. Make great traps these antiquated toasters! Prompted quips like, 'If you are vegetarian, don't eat the toast!' We were afraid they would just take the toaster away, then bring it back as 'another toaster', so I scratched m-o-u-s-e-s on the side with a pin.

I think your first letter of 2 October, beginning 'dearest, lovely woman' is one of the best. Emotionally, it caused +10 on the Richter scale of my heart! Thank you. Don't for God's sake feel that the honesty with which I express my emotions is forcing you to 'keep up' or divulge something you aren't ready to! If I thought that, I'd clam up completely, and my letters would be shallow trivia. Don't forget, I'm new at this honesty of the heart bit. It's like suddenly finding you can run after only stumbling for years. I've always been able to tell people how and what I think of them pretty easily, sometimes at a cost. Believe me, writing and telling you just how I feel took some guts, but loving you gave me the courage. It's so fragile me being in here, you out there and with no understanding or vision of the future (i.e. how long will I be in prison), I felt the only way to give our love a real chance and enjoy a certain peace of mind was by being honest. I love you deeply. So there! I also honour you.

No reply from Daddy, thank God. I'm sure it will be a thoroughly nasty reply – in fact I had already decided *not* to read it, merely staple it up and hand it to you. I'm so raw that any evil things Daddy says would still wound me. I can't take that chance! Any man who can say to his only daughter on the eve of her trial, 'You're evil and you're a murderer,' then put the phone down, thereby effectively stopping any denial, is going to need a lot more than one letter to change his views. I tried to tell Professor Brandon, in the foyer of the court, 'I'm sure my problems relate to the relationship I've had with my Father.' He told me Defence witnesses shouldn't talk to the accused. Closed book. I'm ashamed to say I wouldn't be reconciled with him now anyway, though I've been scared he'd die whilst we are estranged. Contrary woman, I hear you say!

There's so much about you I don't know. Frustrating! Have you only been married once? Owl is looking quite stern tonight. He sees everything.

I wonder, will you be so reserved tomorrow? Will you whisper 'I love you' – or act the part of a proper legal adviser? Your eyes say it all, and the touch of your hand. I'm very happy with it the way it is. I think if I did really start to kiss you, I wouldn't be able to stop. We'd end up on the floor being dragged apart by officers, alarm bells going everywhere. What a delicious, funny thought!

I hope you don't think I look too awful tomorrow. I've been told I look thin and drawn and pale. No gym or fresh air for one week. All the love in my heart for you George.

Sara xx

My darling George,

We've been locked in since 4 p.m. – staff shortages, we are very lucky, hardly affected by industrial action, unlike the men. In fact, if one of the officers hadn't volunteered to work over, then we'd have been locked in even earlier. Now there's dedication and compassion.

I've felt so full of love today, burst out of my cell like Superman does when he changes, and greeted a generally unhappy officer with all the love and joy I felt. She was very taken aback, probably thinking I'm completely off my head! Never mind.

Your last letter, so beautiful, so heart-warming, George, it's the most beautiful love letter I've ever had in my life. We must tell about our love, that's the story, it's a love story in *every* sense, how lack of love and blind desire to find it took me to where I am, how I *did* find it, here in H-wing with all the girls, with you and with God.

It doesn't matter how many journalists M. brings in they are always going to continue the 'Thirty most dangerous women' bit. Bad news sells newspapers. Bad news and glorified 'evil'. So we must, between us, create something of true beauty and *make* them see we aren't evil and dangerous, just a bunch of women who, for reasons known only to themselves, committed one awful 'crime', which has incarcerated them for years.

Tracey, in response to my desire to kiss you – 'I think, no imagine, that when you two kiss, you will mould together, and become one big, inseparable blob. Won't that cause problems?' Hello, fellow blob!

I wonder just what I would have accomplished if I had been brought up in an atmosphere of love and encouragement? Still, I have my chance now, and I have you. That has to be worthwhile. Did you ever stop and think that *one month* of your love and honesty has healed what thirty-five years of absent love did to me? Awesome! And you wonder if I value your love?

No food can be brought into the prison, darling. I love your idea of the mango and olives, but food can be injected with drugs. A sensible rule. Anyway, when I stop smoking, I'll be able to spend my wages on fruit, instead of tobacco. Another good reason to stop.

Please don't ever think of curling up – unless it's with me. I wrote you a letter ages ago, pouring out my love for you – I remember it was a Saturday night – anyway, I tore it up. I just didn't feel you were ready to hear it. I do remember though that I wrote, 'Are you a shoot-ing star who will light my life brightly, but briefly, or are you as I am afraid – a meteor, ploughing into my world, and changing my orbit totally?'

My love, *Sara*

Darling gaol-bird,

I try to reply to the points and questions you raise but some get lost in the flood, so please repeat anything you feel I have ignored. Your comments on this 'courtship' are very true – a strange truth, in the circumstances! The only risk of course, is that we'll get *too* used to letters for our own good, but there's no choice at present.

One problem with letters is that you can't see the smile on my face, sometimes, when I write something. I'm not really afraid of you zooming off ahead on your truth trip. We've got different insights to offer each other, and in any case TRUTH has a short shelf-life and needs constant renewal (like love).

I hope you get a reply from K.J. [barrister]. The sooner your defence team is fired the better. You must have someone really competent for this Appeal. If you send a VO I'll aim to come in Thursday p.m. I'll only come if you promise to give me a 24-carat kiss (everything short of rolling around on the floor scandalizing the onlookers).

'Friendliness is not the abolition of distance but the bringing of distance to life' – Kafka (and love, too) – and Kafka's description of his father's methods of upbringing – 'abuse, threats, violence and irony' . . .

Yes, please, back massage anytime – I'll return the offer.

See you soon. All my love, *George* xx

Darling,

Church this morning was a fiasco. I felt so full of love, I couldn't stop laughing. Father H. came in. He didn't have a clue. At one stage, before we started, I looked up to see him robed in a long white smock affair with a hood. He looked like a little pixie, and I burst into giggles (I'm laughing now). Mr Mogg had to tell me to stop, half-heartedly.

God keep you safe.

All my love, *Sara* x

Darling George,

One of the girls is going for her Appeal in ten days – guess who her barrister is? Yes – I've told her to tell him, 'Mr Buchanan, Sara Thornton says you're fired!' No word from anyone. Your suggestion of sexual assault. I sat and thought, but honestly I don't remember a thing. I was told by someone who was sexually assaulted from an early age by a brother, that she used to close her eyes. That way it 'never actually happened'. She related easily to my nightmare. We'll probably never know.

Did Billi phone you? What is it that Billi remembers that makes her so angry? I'm scared that she'll tell me something terrible, thinking I know already. I need you! I'm scared sometimes. Mummy fed a puffer-fish to my cat, Clockwork, to see how poisonous it was. Clockwork died. I was six years old. In all my spiritual journey I never recognized the betrayal I felt all my life. You pointed that out.

I love you – be careful. *Sara* xx

Darling,

I've just been told that I'm 'toeing the line' tomorrow. Will you be my crutch, Thursday?

I kept my radio on all night last night. Woke several times as certain music caught me – it was a strange night. 'Let It Be' – that woke me. And the awful news about the Israeli shootings. I'm rushing to get this written and out for tomorrow. I'll be fine, really. I'm not nervous. I just wish his scalpel could slip and he could take half an inch off my nose too!

I'm sorting out the papers from solicitors. So, bring a briefcase, and you, and lots of kisses and lots of hugs. But be careful on that bike.

I love you. See you *soon*. *Sara* x

Darling,

I woke up this morning to a beautiful light show on the hill outside – I lay on my bed and watched as the low-level sunlight lit up one group of trees and then another, with dark-grey cloud behind. The leaves are gold and green. And then a woodpecker landed on a branch opposite and began hammering away for its breakfast. Question for you, like the odd socks, why don't woodpeckers get headaches? Wish you'd been with me, just to be wrapped up together watching silently (no sex, please, we're birdwatchers!).

For God's sake tell Tracey I'm not at all 'wonderful'! She'll be totally disillusioned! I'm an explorer, that's all – and your lover-in-waiting. I'm so glad you had a wretched childhood and awful marriages! That was the only route to *us*!

Blob – the fusion theory – sounds very primordial! The start of life on earth was a kiss – that's a good idea. Better than Genesis or Darwin.

Part of our 'miracle' is our laughter, thanks to *you* mainly – not stupid jokiness, but real laughing. Golden plus for Sara!

Wish I was wrapped up tight with you.

All my love, *George* xx

Darling graftee,

I hope the sculpters did a good job on you – I'll sue them if they touched your nose. And I hope it doesn't hurt too much.

You are irreverent, so am I. When you write 'I felt the Lord in my cell last week', my question is, did he feel good? I hate that word, I'm afraid. Lords in England are to do with feudal male power. Lords of the Manor, House of Lords, Bishops, etc., etc. Why translate all that nonsense to the sky?

Ninety per cent of the mass killing in Europe this century has been backed by 'God'.

Don't we need to keep a sharp eye on our appalling ignorance as well as our brief moments of real insight?

Enough for now. What I really want to do is curl up with you!

I love you, *George* xx

George,

I was looking forward to seeing you today, I couldn't understand why you hadn't booked a visit? I've been worried!

Don't object to my relationship with God – it happens to be very important to me. I do *not* see him as some vague, syrupy comforter – neither would I ever do something bad and then absolve myself from responsibility because I did it in His name. I'm really pissed off with the world and all that's in it. Maybe it's for the best you can't come today. See you tomorrow. I love you lots, I promise not to bite – just growl a little!

Sara x

Darling,

Wednesday night, once again your favourite fiend reaches out to you – somewhat woozily, but I know you're there. I took your letter to hospital – I didn't go till one o'clock, and spent all morning in the workroom. Two officers and a nurse came with me. So engrossed in your lovely letter, I hardly saw the surroundings, but I did blow a mental kiss at the Swan and Three Cygnets.

Once at hospital, I was directed to a day-room and stripped for bed. The usual questions re: allergies, etc. – at one stage I said Sara Thornton without an 'h' – so the nurse spelt Sarah Tornton! I was quite happy, not at all nervous.

I was talking to a trainee officer tonight. I asked her what she felt she could offer the prison service in her new role. 'Dunno,' she replied, 'never really thought about it.' I pressured her, asking if she came with the view that we were 'locked up', i.e. a prison, or whether we were 'helped', i.e. an asylum. 'Well, you're here 'cause you are dangerous, ain't ya?' George, this is recruitment material!

Q. WHY DON'T WOODPECKERS GET HEADACHES?

A. BECAUSE THEY'RE ASPIRIN' HEAD-BANGERS!

You are, in all probability the only man I could fall in love with who would help, no, work with me for H-wing on my release. Most people want to forget prison. Very, very few prison friendships exist after release. I love you so much, you really are my soul mate – I honestly feel as if I finally belong. It gives me a lovely sense of peace, knowing that finally, after all this time, I have 'found my man'. The peace partly because I'll never need to struggle to make you understand anything about me – do you realize just how attuned we are? Quite frankly, it's amazing. And partly because it feels so good and I know *with you* there's little we couldn't accomplish! A certain sense that if someone as 'wonderful' as you can love me, then I'm not all bad. I just adore you.

Had fun in hospital, refused a pre-med. Got on great with the anaesthetist, Mr B., and laughed all the way to the theatre. They must have been short staffed – a blood-pressure belt was passed quickly through the theatre door by 'a hand'. 'Mmm – still warm from the last body,' I commented as it was positioned on my arm. I had pads for electrodes positioned to my chest, the nipples on them were better than mine! Invited all the theatre staff to H-wing Christmas party – now we'll have to have one. Miss B. says, in the recovery room I was lying flat, still asleep, when I suddenly jack-knifed into a sitting position and demanded that Mr B. kiss me, in the name of compassion. He was still chuckling as I passed him later, breaking the speed limit in my wheelchair. A fun day for all!

My last words as the 'milky way' was injected, in response to B.'s 'For God's sake, give her a double dose!' 'You can't keep a good lifer down!'

The only thing 'throbbing' is my toe. The anaesthetist, Mr B., asked what I was allergic to, I replied, 'Phenergan, penicillin and rude doctors!'

Oh George – guess what else I bought today? Olives and a small piece of Brie – we can feast during the visit!

Please do write about nature, anything – I do miss it, but feel it's only 'on hold'. Do you get crossfinches here – or are we still too far south? I really do love birds. Used to spend the Spring hand-rearing them. Mummy helped, but I was never allowed to cry if they died! I remember one blackbird. He was a flightless baby, I kept him in the conservatory. I had to go out early mornings to find slugs and snails for him, and worms. I always heard his hungry call as I came down the stairs. One evening I found him a really long worm, which he ate in slowly satisfying jerks! Ominous silence next morning. He was dead. An autopsy revealed the worm had contracted and split his gut! I cried and cried but never again gave live worms; always cut up tiny! I've reared so many birds. And hedgehogs! (Mummy objected to the fleas.) Here in H-wing, I taught the girls to save bees. I love them – they crawl all over me, never sting.

I wrote you a shitty letter, I'm sorry. I was in a rush to write and send it off with a VO. As it happened, they said they would phone. I guess they did, because you're coming tomorrow. I *so* wanted to see you today – maybe it's better I didn't – I've not been on my best form.

Didn't sleep much last night and from 5.00 a.m. onwards I was in awful pain. I could have quite cheerfully cut off my foot. I couldn't walk, the pain was making me sweat – awful! But it's OK now, it's where they took the graft from.

I am really dying to see you. I love you. I want to touch and hold you *so* much it's almost a physical ache, yearning.

I wanted to fill pages and pages with stirring romantic words that would warm you over the weekend – all that's stirring is my hunger – (for you) and a piece of brie cheese sitting on the window bars. I'm waiting to share it with you. If I put it in the fridge – it'll be nicked. It's hard to feel romantic with a period and a ruddy great bandage on my foot. I do love you so – please don't doubt that – sometimes being imprisoned can make me angry. Especially when I or others are suffering.

Tomorrow, tomorrow, I'm just going to hold you, touch and kiss your lovely face, listen to your voice and feel your arms around me.

I put an app. in tonight for a potty on my visit. Ella is having a visit with her Mother. IRA – so Cat. A – the room will be full of officers, I'm afraid. Ella is terrified I'll use it. 'Please Sara, my mum's from a tiny town – she wouldn't understand.' After looking at her today, now imagine she has another twenty years to do! Ella is now studying for a Ph.D. in Eng. Lit. What a waste, she's a lovely dear lady and friend, and it sometimes breaks my heart to think of her locked away for another twenty years.

I can almost imagine kissing you – tomorrow it'll become reality. I can't wait.

All my love, *Sara* xxx

Darling,

Maybe you had more underlying anxiety about your toe op. than you realized? It would be strange if you didn't. Without fully realizing it, I think I was anxious about you and on edge.

Our situation is so finely balanced – it either works perfectly or not at all, rather like my racing bike!

I reacted sharply to your Lord-speak because I felt you are starting to write about it like a drunk/addict, all fervour and no thought. This alarms me because I feel we have to function at the highest level (all of us, brains, imagination, feeling, intuition, etc.) if we are to change the situation. Sorry if you felt it was too sharp and not understanding enough. Just tell me how you see it, please.

Modern life has been torn apart by collective personal fear and greed, hasn't it? We have to start afresh, at the roots! I dream of living with you in an old stone farmhouse, with chickens and vegetables and trees and a lot of very simple practical things to do, as well as recreating the world! And you?

With all my love, *George* xx

Hello you wonderful, lovely man,

It's late, after ten o'clock and I confess I've done nothing since lock-in at eight o'clock, except lie in bed, and think of you. Of our last visit, of Saturday, of the future. If I'm like this when we are apart, how can I ever hope to accomplish anything living *with* you? All I want to do is lie in your arms – and eat. Did you notice? My new hobby? What a glutton you must think of me. I scoffed all that cheese and the olives – you never got a look in. Tracey says she's never seen me eat like that. 'Real food.' I love cheese!!

I wanted you to walk in on Friday and find me, like the good patient I am, sitting quietly in a chair, with my foot 'elevated', following nurse's instructions. Mrs Kerr pulled the curtain off its rail, what could I do? She couldn't climb up, and we need the curtain for privacy. Ella and Martina hadn't come in by then. I figured it would only take a second, but the damn thing was tangled and the fan was blowing hot air right in my face. I didn't even hear you come in, I was so embarrassed and flustered – too flustered to kiss you properly – blew it again, George! I can see the funny side, but at the time I felt like a kid who'd been caught with my fingers in the jam pot! I was so overjoyed to see you. I felt drunk with happiness, quite content to sit and just be near you! Can you feel all my love for you? Believe it!

Goodnight – *Sara* x

My Darling Man,

As always, my first letter this weekend is for you, just as every day my first thoughts are of you. I have so much I really want to try to make you understand – on two subjects, God and Marriage. I don't want my ideas of what God is to cause friction because you don't understand. And, I've had enough friction over marriage to last a lifetime.

I see God as a God of truth and *Love*. One cannot exist without the other. I do not, cannot, believe in or worship Christ – not on a cross. If you read through my letters, you'll see I make no mention of Christ. It is still all an enigma to me, the thought of worshipping someone who died through one of man's worst traits, mindless violence, sickens me!

Love is the story – how lack of it in my childhood turned me into a warped, emotionally crippled woman, who hated herself and everyone else. How *your* love, honest love, made me want to return honest love to you, and thereby face up to everything. Until I went through those 'revelations' last week, I would have been no earthly good to anyone – you, Billi, or all the women I want to help.

Believe me, I ponder often about God. Will he test my faith by denying me physical freedom in years to come? No – I don't see him as sitting up there saying, 'OK, today I'll give Sara Thornton an A-level test on faith!' I do feel He has given me the chance to do a lot of good. That is to try and help change the image the public have of H-wing from a prison of bars and rules and anger, to a sanctuary of love, support and guidance. Because that is what it has been for me, I know it can be that for others. I am living proof.

I know you will understand, darling, I've been trying so hard to understand myself, and in doing that have probably written you pages and pages of garbled warblings on love, truth and faith. Here endeth the first lesson. This letter is written with *All* my love for *you*.

Sara xxx

Darling love,

It was very good to see you both yesterday (I can still feel the warmth of your hand). I like Tracey a lot, she looked great – and give her a big hug from me (and both of us?) for saving the day! I so very nearly didn't come (and very glad I did – reading your lovely letter made me realize how easily we can be trapped in this correspondence time lag). When I got your note of anger Friday morning I just sat and stared out of the window for an hour while all the energy (and hope) drained out of me. I now know what space rockets on the launchpad feel like when they spring a leak at the last moment and tons of high-octane fuel have to be drained out! Luckily the red squirrel was dancing about on the grass opposite, collecting food for the winter, and very slowly my spirits revived. But I still felt I couldn't go – the idea of meeting a new person, as well as trying to find out what had happened to us, seemed impossibly confusing. I almost reached for the phone to cancel the visit, but something stopped me.

Tracey is right. Mark any future letters 'high explosive' if they are filled with anger. Don't not send them. I'll do the same. We have to be angry and fed up sometimes, especially in this tense situation of minimum contact. You're too brave and stiff-upper-lippish! You should have told me how much your foot hurt – after all, it's not long since my heel and ankle were giving me hell. I know what it's like.

I'm learning about you all the time – I've decided you perform in public. You're very like a Fool at a medieval court, jumping about and fooling around trying to rouse a smile on the face of the solemn king! Maybe that's what you had to try with your poor father? Have you read *King Lear*? The Fool was very important and touching. You're *my* Fool now, and I am smiling! I love you very much.

Look after that blue foot, please. *George* xx

My Dearest Love (That's you George!),

I got your two letters this morning. I felt sick reading the first page of No. 1. I didn't realize how much you loved me. I'm so sorry for causing you that pain. Thank God you didn't cancel, I'd have been beside myself – in utter despair. Please, please promise me you won't *ever* cancel a visit without a valid reason. Even now, the thought of what I did to you sits in me like a cold lump of fear and shock. I'm truly sorry. My anger, which stemmed from the pain in my foot, sheer tiredness, worry (over Daddy), the desperate need to see you, and the incompetence of census in forgetting your VO was just directed at you and your scathing remarks about God. What do you mean, 'If I still love you'? I would just give up if you weren't there for me, my soul would wither without you. I don't just *love* you, I *need* you, I can't be without you! I can't imagine what my life would be like without you, how could I have ever been content before I met you? As I once wrote, you have altered my axis, no other man could spin in your orbit again. It's yours and yours alone!

Your second letter (well, all the rest) was lovely. I had three brown envelopes today; your two I recognized and read first (I'm greedy for you!). I even went to see Hicks about some charity work in DTP, before coming back to the third. I didn't really recognize the writing on the envelope. Out spilled a letter from *my mother*. I took one look, and was sick. Physically ill! My father sent *arsenic coated in syrup*! Did he really mean to be so cruel? Does he know the fear that my mother's handwriting would cause? I can't believe it, even though I know she's been dead for twenty years. I am sending the letter to you, I *don't* want my mother's letters in my room near me. Clever Daddy got Juliet to write the envelope! The two letters he sent date from Millfield [School], all the girls got 'chatty letters' once a week.

At first, I thought, 'God – I am mad, I've imagined it all.' I can't begin to tell you how I felt but slowly I calmed down and remembered Billi's last letter. She felt sick just writing his address. If ever I needed you, and if you hadn't come on Friday . . . I think I would have cracked. He also enclosed a prayer on the back of a religious picture of the Archangel Michael with one foot on the devil!

I've always wanted to fire a barrister. I'll write to the Registrar and tell him.

They have amended census rules, only 10 per cent of letters to be censored and 10 per cent of each letter censored to be censored. Not a popular decision, I feel! I wanted to go up to census this morning, hand in ten letters, and say 'Which *one* are you going to censor?'

I feel sick with worry, George – I think I knew that Daddy would reply with poison – though not so sugar-coated – that's why I've been so uptight. I couldn't, just couldn't do it without you, your love and support! I love, love, love you – don't forget that!

Came down to breakfast this morning, said to Tracey, 'Give us a puff?' 'I wish you bloody would,' she said, and they proceeded to tell me how horrible I've been. 'We want our laughing, caring Sara back.' So, my darling, I had a puff. I've smoked three cigs today, so sorry, but I feel this is just not the right time to give up smoking. When I think how I could have lost you, I could cry! Dammit, I am. Too much! They won't let me in the gym till the stitches are out, so I've all this energy!!!

As I said, I saw Hicks today. 'How are you?' he asked. 'Fine,' I replied. 'No you're not, you're too thin, you're drawn and pale.' He says I'm doing too much, he knows I won't stop the campaign, and admires it too much to want me to.

I didn't tell you about my foot because I cannot reveal pain. Throwback from childhood. I once broke my arm. Mummy made me ride my horse up and down a hill, then drove me to hospital. She was so brusque, the doctor didn't believe anything was wrong, and none-too-gently shoved me against the X-ray plate. An impacted fracture made him apologize; so did Mummy! She never had an ounce of sympathy. Her favourite expression was, 'Stop crying or I'll give you something to cry about!' She would, too, a smack across the head. Had a really bad dream last week, I awoke to find myself kneeling on the bed, banging the wall with my fist, the tears pouring down my face. My cries alerted the night staff who came and turned on the light. I have a funny feeling that Hicks is getting reports of all this – hence his concern. I don't know! I can't remember the dream – I was locked up somewhere – I awoke feeling frightened, but more angry and betrayed than anything.

Guess what, darling – on Wednesday I will have known you for two whole months, *August 17th*, a Friday, I first met you. Wonderful, marvellous day! I think I started to fall in love with you then. I look back and see I wrote *two* days later – 'His spirit touched hers briefly and she knew they would be best of friends.' How's that for perception?

I thought you were married – I'd have settled for pen-friend, hussy, slave, fan, disciple, anything. I adore you! I wish I could take your letters, pin them all together and make a cover to sleep under. As it is I always put your last one or two under my pillow.

So you think I'm a performing Fool, eh? I think you are quite right. Certainly a performer. Maybe that's why A. & Co. were so scared for me to be 'myself' on the stand? I've always been a better 'doer' in public. If I could not perfect a gymnastic move in practice, we were sure I'd get it right on the day.

Love you, *Sara* xxxx

Darling,

Kathleen O'D. asked me in her letter to give her love to you. I feel like telling her that you are drowning in love, cascades of it pouring over your head all day long! Her letter was friendly, despite my comments about husbands.

You have a very complex and difficult personal/emotional set-up there and I will try to understand that better. Whereas you walk downstairs to see me, I cycle for three and a half hours plus (there and back) to see you, over countryside no sane person cycles over! I realize, too, that the way I expressed my feeling about your religious statement was pretty crude. There's something ironic, isn't there, about our love being disrupted by a 'God of love'?

If God works through us, as I believe (and it is after all only the human mind that can formulate any concept of God), then 'he' is us and we are him – there is no meaningful distinction. Thus it becomes impossible to say (as most religious people do) that God did this, or that, and wants me to do this and that. Nobody is more 'God' than anyone else so nobody can realistically stand up and say 'God commands me to love these people . . . or attack and kill those people', etc.

I feel with you and want to be together, close, warm, supportive, challenging – eating olives, making love, going for walks, chatting, sleeping and so on . . . ! Tell me what you think, please.

I like the idea very much that we are working towards a penal policy which is about asylum and therapy (love) not punishment and apathy. A long hard road filled with pot (ass) holes.

Sleep, eat well, *love you. George* xx

Darling George,

You're coming tomorrow, so I can spend all night scribbling at leisure. Loved your letter this lunchtime – heavy, man! Strange that we should receive each other's thoughts on God on the same day. Don't you think that it isn't God at fault, merely people's interpretation? There's always a leader (don't I know) and leadership gives power, which can so easily be abused. If one truly loves God, then one wouldn't abuse any power. I think that because our churches are so obviously hypocritical and out of touch, people will follow anything different merely to be given the chance to see God as they want. I finally believe that my relationship with God is a very private matter. People, I think, tend to forget that God has a sense of humour. Laughter heals, brings people together.

Do you believe in telepathy, etc.? I do – and I feel that again it is only achieved through love. After I was sentenced, I was only angry with God for twenty-four hours. Just think, if I'd been given probation of two years, whatever, I never would have met you! What an awful, awful thought! I love you so much! One night when I was ill, very late, I was just lying on my bed, drained. I'd been crying and praying and soul-searching, and I lay in bed, not really thinking about anything very much. After a while, I felt as if my body was very heavy, being almost pushed into the mattress. I thought I was going to leave it (that's how it used to start sometimes) so I kept my eyes *open*, thinking that would prevent it. I was getting scared as the pressure increased. I said, 'God what is happening here?' I couldn't move. Suddenly I was enveloped in such a feeling of love, so blissful that I can't explain it. Only 'heaven' can aptly describe it. I *knew* I was loved, honestly George, the sheer intensity of it left no doubt in my mind. I don't know how long it lasted, it wore off very gradually, but left me very calm, and very peaceful. I slept and the next morning the doctor pronounced me cured! I didn't refer to it in my letters to you as I didn't want census reading it. Got the nurse to change the bandage on my foot this evening. The swelling has gone down, and I was able

73

to take a really good look. It's unbelievable. Imagine my last two toes. He has sliced my toe away from my foot to get this corn out! There has to be at least 20 stitches on top and on the sole putting it back on. Gruesome! It's healing beautifully though. I'm getting complaints about my garlic odour. You never told me – do *you* like garlic? I put it in everything from eggs to toast. Oh darling, if you don't like garlic we are going to have problems! Scorn my God, my marriages, my childhood, but please not my garlic!

When we lived in Fiji – 28 Statham Street, Laucala Bay – a man (seemed old to us) would push a trolley with bells on the handlebar around the streets. This Indian's goods were heaven for Billi and me, we'd save our pocket money for packets of his curried peas, dahl, noodles, etc. When I returned to Coventry (after M.'s death) I started to go to an Indian shop in Foleshill, to buy their samosas, curried dahl, peas, etc. When Billi came for the trial, the first stop on the morning after her arrival was this shop. They knew me pretty well, so they let Billi sample lots of sweets, etc. 'Must try the curried noodles,' she said. 'Mmmm! Taste just like the trolley man's in Fiji.' 'Fiji?' asked the girl behind the counter. Billi explained about the trolley man, and she became very excited. Of course the noodles tasted the same, he had emigrated to England, bought this shop, and his daughter now cooked everything from *his* recipes. Sadly he'd died, but what an amazing coincidence. Next time you talk to Billi, ask her about the Indian trolley man! I love Indian food.

I love the tiger poem, why do you say Tessimond's is feeble! It isn't, it's *mild*! As an advertising copywriter he was probably too scared or reserved to ever 'let go'. I love all the things you send me – even your 'brazen hussy' bit. Don't stop please, it means you are thinking of me! I think of you all day, I thought it would settle down, that other events would fill your place, and I'd get my priorities right. But not so, you are in my thoughts *all* the time. If I'm not wondering what you are doing, or having an imaginary conversation, then I'm anticipating the next visit or letter, or writing one, or reading the last, or formulating some reply. Strange that my life would be barren now without you, yet I only see you once a week for one and a half hours. The sheer intensity of my love for you is something I've never experienced before. I've asked the other girls about their loves. They see it as a game, not expecting to ever meet, let alone live with their 'lovers'. But they also say, 'You're different, Sara' – and we are – unique. They can *see* my love for you, and yours for me – they see my happiness and joy. I love you, darling man. I was asked yesterday if I planned to write about H-wing. 'What about H-wing?' I asked. 'Oh you know, bitchy stuff!' 'Why on earth should *you* need to worry, Miss, you know I'm not bitchy. I just endeavour to tell the truth.'

That's a point. You get a gold star!!! You never mentioned another lover in your last letter. Hang on, let me check . . . What's up George, surely you can't be running short? Think of something. This is a joke (99 per cent). If bonking comes from a bunk, what do you do in a hammock? I'm beginning to wonder if I really want you to answer that question! I'm sleepy. What time do you go to sleep – wake up? Only so I can think of you!

I love you, be careful please. *Sara* x

Darling brown body!

All I wanted to do this afternoon was kiss that bit of exposed skin on your chest! I found it really hard – I ended up looking everywhere except there! In future keep yourself covered on legal visits please! Most distracting.

Did I tell you I had a letter from my Uncle John today? Full of forgiveness and remorse, how he felt, he should have been at my trial, etc. Six sides of sorrow. But no mention of my mother's part in all this. He merely confirmed that Daddy had an appalling childhood.

This evening one of the Education ladies came in, and on seeing my foot asked, 'What happened, Sara?' Poker-faced I replied, 'Did you ever read *Roots*?' 'Oh yes,' she said, 'by Arthur What's-his-name.' 'Yes,' I said. 'Well, do you remember that when Kunte Kinte tried to escape they chopped half his foot off.' 'Rubbish, Sara!' she scoffed, 'I'm not going to believe that.' 'Why not?' I asked in all seriousness. 'The man from the Board of Visitors did.' I've really been on the ball tonight!

Your face when I told you I had started smoking again was so full of disgust I could have cheerfully crawled under the chair. I even felt like terminating the visit, but I'm trying to tell myself you don't understand. I'm not as perfect as you. I do smoke, and have done on and off since I was seventeen years old. I chose the completely wrong time to stop. Waking up in the night crying and shaking from a bad dream is awful! So, Mr Perfect, I am trying to formulate a plan. One should stop when under as little stress as possible.

Your answer on marriage suits me fine, in fact I could quite happily leave it as it is for always, just as long as you don't reject the idea out of hand.

I love you, I thought you looked good today – can't wait till Saturday. I'll curb my pen, you curb yours, and with any luck we'll both be free to smile – and kiss and whatever.

All my love and lots of hugs and kisses, *Sara* xxx

Darling,

We were talking, saying what a beautiful afternoon it was, and what we'd like to be doing. M. suddenly got really homesick and said, 'I want to go home!' . . . I never feel like that – is it because all my 'homes' are gone, I've only got you to come home to! Isn't that strange? Did you ever think of that? Have you been to see your son at his musical venue? Do you have any photos? You must be so proud.

Harvest festival this morning. Mic the Vic talking about optimism. He doesn't know the meaning of the word. Optimism is when you are sentenced to life, thinking life means life, told you have little hope of Appeal, and *still* you are smiling and praying. We all agree, optimism is when someone leaves a pile of shit outside your door, and you think someone gave you a horse, but it ran away!

I Love You!! *Sara* xx

Darling,

Riches! Three letters and rude notepaper heading – I'll get my own back! Just wait . . .

Before I forget, can you give me back K.'s law article and I'll exchange it for another about domestic violence, etc. We need to take a good look at your Appeal (not sex, the other one) – I feel we haven't got to grips with it yet, the Registrar, new barrister, etc.

I had a long chat with Billi last night – very interesting. I like her. She said you could become quickly very enthusiastic and suddenly cold again – she said this with no hint of malice, so don't scold her, please.

In an odd and interesting way I now feel that your Black Friday letter showed how far you had advanced – instead of just cutting me off altogether you held your anger in check and ground out some love as well (between clenched teeth!) – I love you for that.

K.J. just phoned for over an hour, and she's very interested, very sympathetic and willing to help and act for you at Appeal. She may be able to come up to see you next week – I'll tell you all about it – she wants you to write to the Registrar and ask for a change of lawyer, etc. Let's discuss it. She seems really nice – she is just completing a book on this theme. She says *she* kisses some of her clients on legal visits, so . . .

Agree with most of your Godly views – I do love religious music, and the poetry of the O.T. – 'they sat down by the waters of Zion and wept', and 'he took the wings of the morning and went to the uttermost parts of the sea', 'where there is no vision the people perish', etc., etc.

I love you, to the uttermost parts of the earth and life.

George xx

Darling,

I was thoughtful, happy and hopeful about your comment on 'going home' when released – it made me suddenly very humble/protective to think of myself as your home (and vice versa?). I like the idea. Yes. And we'll quickly have to make a physical home with a roof on it, too, otherwise we'll both be tramps!

The real miracle for me would be just to wake up with you beside me and reach over and hug you and feel your lovely sexy, warm body against mine . . . no words, just silence filled with us . . . That's my dream and it keeps me warm and believing and loving . . .

See you soon, darling, I love you, *George* xxx

Darling Man,

Can I be a jester instead of a Fool?

Saw the MO this morning. I started to unwrap the bandage to help, but was told, 'Leave it Sara! We'll go in the other room and you can climb on the bed!' I replied with, 'Best offer I've had since last week'! Sister G. smacked me on the head. He seemed impressed. 'Ah,' he said, 'a neat dorsal flap!' So that's what it is. Now I can say, 'My dorsal flap is really itching' and everybody will understand, won't they? He's not taking the stitches out till Monday, so if you bring the pneumatic drill in Saturday I can smuggle it on to the wing in the bandage! My *Roots* joke has backfired on me – someone said today, 'Tell that Kunte she owes me some sugar.'

I had a truly heart-warming letter from K.J. Made up for a Delfless day. Sod you, I think I'll marry *her* instead – and I'll kiss her when she comes on a legal visit. I want you to come in with her, we are a *team*!

We have laughed and laughed all day. It's just been a happy day. Had yet another meeting with Hicks over the business of being in DTP. He really wants me to stop using my brain. Doesn't he realize that all this creative energy needs an outlet, and not in machine-stitching cushions?

I briefly mentioned Clive in my last letter, he owned a business behind my house in Coventry. Badly wounded from a very cold marriage, he responded to my gaiety and caring by falling in love.

After I was convicted, he and Billi came to see me in the cell. Shocked, dry-eyed, almost too choked to speak, he held me whilst I told him to go home and drink all the champagne. 'No,' he said, 'I'll put it on ice till the day you are freed.' 'Don't bother, luv,' said a middle-aged, fat, peroxide screw. 'By the time *she* gets out, you won't be able to find it in the ice.' She cackled at her humour. I saw for the first time, I think, what life in prison would really be like. In place of gruel and water, bitterness, and companions totally lacking in compassion. Prison as a punishment should mean merely that you are denied your liberty, too often it means you are also denied the basic everyday responses of a caring society. Kindness, compassion and understanding. I'm glad to say it isn't at all like that here in Durham, but it certainly was at Risley.

Darling, I must stop – like a drunk driver I'm 'over the limit'.

Kiss me! *Sara*

Darling,

So 17 October was our anniversary, was it, and you refused to kiss me! Hmm . . .

Yes, getting your mother's letter must have been awful. Poor you.

Yes, I love garlic too, so we'll smell awful together! You said once, almost in despair, 'I *won't* give up'. I loved that. Don't, and I won't!

Someone said recently that in reality Beethoven could compose easily but chose deliberately only to work on what was supremely difficult. Because that was the best. He fought with his own devil in public, via his music, and transformed it into something beautiful and hopeful – that's what we're doing, isn't it?

You wrote a lot about your love for me and I value nothing higher – but it's time to put your mouth where your words are and give me a proper (or improper) kiss on Saturday! I shan't speak to you otherwise.

See you soon. I love you, *George* xx

My dearest love,

I'm lying in bed, it is so cold – they are doing something to the boiler, so the heating is off. I've got four blankets on my bed, and one round my shoulders. I must look like an old Granny. I *hate* the cold. Will you take me somewhere warm to live, please? All the bones I've broken ache, even my re-designed foot hurts! I wish we could blob now.

B. lost her Appeal. She left here forty-eight hours ago, a bright woman full of hope, deeply in love, and has come back dejected, demoralized and broken! I *hate* them for what they have done to her. She's a human being not a pawn for their legal games. BASTARDS!

She sat in the dock of the Appeal Court, high and barred, she says, with the public gallery full. For two and a half hours she sat silent and immobile, while psychiatrists and lawyers tore what little moral fibre and dignity she had left into shreds. Personality disorder (where have I heard that phrase before?) which does not allow her to feel any deep emotion. I've seen the deep emotion that woman has. How dare some half-baked psychiatrist ruin her life with a diagnosis obtained after five half-hour consultations – which took place whilst she was still in shock! I *hate* that term 'personality disorder'. Don't they use it often? Basically it means this person is psychologically sick, but I don't have the time/money/commitment to find out why – nobody else will bother – so let's leave it. 'Severe personality disorder.' An umbrella term, if ever!

They refused to let her see her mother before she was driven back to Holloway. The doctor at Holloway also discovered that she's anaemic due to a year on Phenobarbitone. A common side-effect.

I learnt all this in fifteen minutes. She appeared at my cell door, hesitant, then flung herself into my arms and sobbed.

All my love, *Sara* xx

Darling,

Don't be angry with me over the smoking – I was very mildly sorry about it, and not at all disgusted! I know how stressful your life is. Retract your claws, please, I love you.

A heavy parcel thumped on the doorstep – from V. Makes me feel sick reading it [trial depositions] – I just want to hug you until you finally leave that nightmare behind.

Wealth and childhood don't seem to marry well. The richest people I know had the worst childhoods, and people like K.J. talk of their fathers and mothers with great affection. Less pretence, perhaps? Less to hide? And rich people always try to buy off problems instead of solving them. Long live the poor!

Now that at last you recognize that I am 'perfect' I expect you to do everything I say – sarcastic so-and-so!

I want (need) a kiss please. All my love, *George* xx

My Dear Love,

I wasn't going to send the last letter, it's so depressing, and I feel as if I've hurt you enough lately. But, I decided I would *only* if my spirits and mood raised enough to be able to write you an antidote. Happily, I feel much more positive today. I don't want you thinking I'm happy, boisterous and utterly confident all the time. It also includes some revealing insights, I think, as to why I feel so insecure when I have no need to, and my writing is the only way I have of letting you get to know the real me. In future, if I do feel like that, I will always send the letter (suitably titled) with an antidote. Because I don't want to hurt you. I still think of that letter last week with an awful feeling, remembering the desolate response I had.

I spent some time before going to sleep re-reading your past letters last night. I especially enjoy the one where you wrote, 'Don't you realize yet that I love you?' I feel again the resulting joy and disbelief that I felt on first reading those words. I love you too.

I don't really know if I do want to be a psychologist now. I just love people and want to help.

It is said that to make love on the astral planes with the one you love is the ultimate, your bodies literally fuse and become one. Personally, I'd be happy just to achieve physical fusing – even a kiss (with you, none other)!

Had an awful thought this afternoon, what if I start to get 'fan mail' after the *Dispatches* programme? You'll have to handle it.

I slept all last night, no nightmare that I can remember. No bandage either. I took it off. Will do the same tonight. Stitches out tomorrow, I think they'll hurt a lot.

This afternoon I decided you have a strong, noble face, very noble, I love it.

I love you *always*, Sara xxx

Darling,

The only fantasy I can imagine is putting those pompous judges and lawyers on the stand, and morally stripping them!

Thank you for your letter today, the officer in census told me that since the 10 per cent rule, they don't bother to read your letters any more.

I agree about your nudity theories, I see nudity as freedom rather than sexuality. Making love with a thin shirt or top on is often much sexier than nude. Naked is such a rough word, nude is smooth – agree? Just do not expect me to start wearing a bra – never, never! I love thermal vests though, and longjohns, and I have them here, so you see that rather validates my point on sexuality versus freedom!

As regards blowing hot and cold (Billi's statement), I think she's right. I used to set myself impossibly high goals and standards, then give up in depression and failure when I didn't achieve them. Now my goals are much more realistic, and I hope and strive as opposed to demand! I hope to be released on appeal, I hope to enable other women to get a fair trial. I hope to show that women can be understood and healed. I hope to be with you forever! I'll strive and work towards all those goals, but a setback in one will no longer mean that I'll admit defeat on all fronts. I *won't* give up, because I know I can win! With your love and support, everything is possible, because now I'm not doing it alone. Before I was (or felt) alone, one against the world. Don't get angry, get even!

Sister A. asked me tonight when I'm going to start settling down into prison life. 'You mean say, "yes, miss, no, miss," and walk around a zombie?' I asked. 'Not really Sara!' 'Well what then?' 'Just settle,' was all she could say. 'Never!' I shouted (well almost), 'I have a healthy disrespect for authority and I'll never change!' If I do, I'll have my food tested for Valium.

Here is your weekend letter and all I've done is moan – I'm sorry darling.

If we get on well (you and me, I mean) then I am going to ask you if you'd like to come back tomorrow afternoon, just the two of us, to kiss and cuddle all we like.

I suppose by now you are having a cosy evening with D.C. [literary agent]. I am jealous. If I get any hint of intimacy between you two tomorrow, you will see the razor in my eyes, its cutting edge on my tongue. Caustic – you won't know the meaning of the word!

Of course we are writing the book together, much of it is *our* story, and without your love, there would *be* no book. Yes, we are partners! Together or not at all! When are you going to realize how much I love you?

Have a good weekend, I'll send you waves of love. Till tomorrow, I'll dream of kissing you.

I love you. *Sara* xx

Hello Darling,

I'm restless, restless, restless. We've been locked in since 4 p.m. – I spent till seven just lying in bed, dreaming about you, going over the visit with you and D.C. Still didn't kiss you, but got to touch you, your hair was soft like a baby's hair. Your dear sweet face, your neck and a bit of your chest. Loving you in tiny physical doses. When I found myself trying to burrow into your shoulders, I realized how foolish I must look and managed to control myself.

Now with all those depositions at your fingertips, my fears are doubly intensified. I'm miserable. Logically, I tell myself, of course he loves me, and I think of all the big and little things you do for me. But my heart asks, why doesn't he kiss me? Why should he love me? I'm really not as confident as I make out, am I? I'm still, at heart, a terribly insecure little girl who feels that she's not good enough. Will I ever feel any better about myself? Shit, now I'm crying.

I also wanted you to stay behind today, I know you squeezed me when you said, 'No', but it still hurt.

Anyway, if K.J. comes this week, I want you to see her with me! I'm enclosing a VO with this, because I need to see you.

I feel very isolated, very aware that I only see you for one and a half hours a week. I feel you talking, planning, writing with others and I'm not really included.

'Come to Durham jail and see this strange, loud fool of a lifer I've met!' I'm *not* moaning or telling you off, I'm just trying to help you understand how I feel, and why I feel so sad!

Billi says she remembers that Mummy had this conversation with her. 'The vicar says you are a lovely little girl. But the vicar doesn't really know you like I know you, does he? I should tell the vicar what you are really like, then he won't think you are a nice little girl any more. You are a deceitful little girl. I know.' This took place in Cumberland. She was twelve, perhaps.

That sort of thing represents much of our childhood and it helped me realize why I always feel that you will suddenly decide that Daddy is right and I'm just an evil murderess.

I don't know if I'll ever forgive her! I *will* post this letter, but I'll mark it, distressed jester – albeit a Fool.

Sara xx

Darling,

I hope you enjoyed that visit as much as I did – five stars! A Blob Opportunity Scheme . . . It was also a great relief to be so close to you after all these fatuous stand-offs.

Your back is/feels lovely (I'm sure the front does too . . .) – very clever wearing that loose pullover. I love your nose – I hadn't had such a close view of it before, and there was a small white mark on your right eyelid – I was dying to touch it to see if it would come off or was part of the fixtures.

Truth is ultimately poetic, a magic conveyance of all that's best in us, and best expressed via love – isn't it?

We are searching for truth together, aren't we, not throwing bits of it around like hand-grenades in a battle?

I want to live with you, for years and years, in a kind of loving I have never yet experienced – as light as a deer floating over a fence.

We've proved we're pretty good at touching each other, haven't we, in many ways, on many levels, in many places? What more can we want? Just to be together all the time.

Maybe see you with K.J.?

I love you – and can feel you still. *George* xx

Dearest love (I hope you enjoyed using that form of address as much as I enjoyed reading it!!),

I have some misgivings about the letter I posted today and its comments – I just hope you can feel the love which underlines the criticism.

I entirely agree about all the 'personality disorder' hogwash. Reminds me of a woman I know well. She's sensitive, interested in poetry and probably the most interesting person in the village. She was officially classified schizophrenic and told me about a ludicrous session with a young doctor who was totally out of his depth and relying on similar empty jargon. It is often the people who prattle about personality disorders who themselves lack real emotional contact with others, including their clients.

By the way I had an interesting letter from an old friend who said she totally understood your 'bizarre' behaviour after stabbing M.: 'If ever I am distressed or panicking about something I always throw myself into cleaning and cooking – it's a sort of anti-hysteria measure. I think a lot of women do the same and I am sure it is how they cope with a crisis, better than men in some cases . . .'

Be a jester if you prefer, but jesters are just idiots with bells on their shoes!

Fools with a capital F are clever, brave, impudent, full of insight and poetry – a better class of jester! Read *King Lear*! You are *my* Fool whether you like it or not. It's a life-long career with a pension.

You know, of all the millions of things you've written (apart from love) to me there are two which I value especially – when you said: 'I *won't* give up' (about me and us) – and when you said, going to the hospital first time, you had seen these 'summer' children and 'could have scooped them up' in your arms. Lovely woman.

This week is the last I can do an afternoon visit by bike – gets dark too soon. I'll need a balaclava. Just imagine if I turned up in one of those! 'He doesn't look like a solicitor or behave like a solicitor.' . . . Thanks be to God. What a compliment!

See you soon. Keep remembering what it feels like, *close*.

I love you. *George* xx

Hello my Love,

It's cold! I'm tucked up in bed, footloose in every way, fancy free? No, I wanted to play, 'This little piggy goes to market,' to celebrate my newly designed toe released from captive bandages, but nobody would play with me. Will you?

How has your Monday been? Not too black I hope. It will be if you keep wading through those deps [trial depositions]! The thought of you reading my diary, all those personal feelings, still scares me, but I'm glad now that R. included them in the deps.

I am amazed and proud at how well I have reacted to your criticism. A month ago I'd have told you to F— off. I love you!!! Sometimes I can be too flippant about things and I hurt people. With D.C. it was quite deliberate, I'm sure, though done without conscious effort. I suppose I felt she'd spent the night telling, pouring out her heart's troubles, you with a sympathetic ear or shoulder, and I felt quite left out. I just wanted to widen the gap.

Please try to understand. Falling deeply in love whilst on a life sentence has got to be *scary*! Loving you brings me great joy too, and confidence, but sometimes I just feel very insecure and vulnerable. Do you? Smack my hand!

Write me a love letter, darling, I feel bruised!! *Sara* x

Darling slightly aggrieved author,

Knowing it's Monday, and you're feeling 'S'less and perhaps slightly worried about your 'bollocking' letter, I thought I'd write a reply, to save you any worries.

I'm laughing and I love you so. In some ways you're so right, in others so wrong. I was taking the piss – I'm glad it irritated, now you know how it feels.

As for D.C., you're right, I felt very much an outsider, she knew so much about me – I knew little about her, and didn't have *time* to learn more. And I felt that to a degree I was being treated like a child! I must watch that with her. Do you realize how terribly vulnerable I feel with this constant baring of my innermost feelings and fears and *love* for you, to someone I've never met?

I can't help but feel a little defensive – she was, and you can be a little patronizing! Enough. I'm just not secure enough in our love yet, hardly surprising considering the circumstances! I *love* what you wrote in your last letter . . . 'a kind of loving I have never yet experienced' – I knew *I* felt like that, didn't realize you did too. Wonderful, wonderful.

I've had my stitches out, very painful, Sister D. held my hand, and I breathed deeply (like giving birth).

Gym on Wednesday. Whoopee, I feel very flabby and unfit!

I promise not to do any more digs/jokes – you only have to tell me if they hurt, or irritate, stupid. I am like a child who has to see how far she can go – you must tell me to stop! I love you so much.

How about coming in on the VO and we'll just talk about whatever we want? Don't you think there's a danger of always talking about the book, appeal, H-wing, etc., and never just *us*?

It's time for work. Flocked noses, here I come. Write me some more – especially about how much you love me, I'll *never* tire of hearing that. Never, ever.

Bye Darling, Love you! *Sara* x

PS I'm laughing at *us*.

Dearest love,

I hope you're feeling at ease with life (and me!) again. We're in mid-ocean and can't always be on top of the same wave at the same time, can we? It's hard, sometimes, I know – for both of us.

I don't just love you, I love especially your struggle to recognize and tame your inner demons. I can imagine you 'breaking in' wild horses, with courage, patience, skill and affection. Let me say it again, I'll never abandon you unless one day you want me to.

It's a partnership, and a companionship, and a well-made Ship of Fools sailing on a voyage of discovery ... I don't mind being a Fool!

I had to smile when I read your, 'Why don't you ever say anything good or nice about me?' You've got a good memory! Count the times and ways I've told you I love you. Here's a summary for doubting Sara: I love you, your face, your eyes, nose, eyebrows, hair, your body, breasts, legs, etc.! I love the mole on your neck, your feet, the feel of you, the sight of you, the sound of you, the sparkle of you – I even love you when you are depressed and pissed off – I love your spirit, your impudence, your contempt for authority (except when it spills onto me!). I love your concern for others, your insight, warmth and I love your laughter, I love your courage, I love (I'm half-ashamed to say) your love for me, I love the way you fight your demons and try to turn them into pussy cats, I love your love for Luise and Billi, and for children in the street, and I love your 'performances' when they don't drown out *you*. I am sure you are not bad, in fact you have all the ingredients of a truly remarkable, creative woman. I love the way you write. I need your love, and your sharp perceptive mind.

Good enough to go on with, darling doubter?

I love you, more than ever. *George* xx

My darling man,

Bliss, you're coming Thursday, so I can spend two nights scribbling to you and save stamps. That is if they don't search me thoroughly following your '*faux pas*' over the diary! And I thought you had brains . . .

I went up to census this morning, after putting in my letter to you. There's a half door (like in a stable) and I leaned on it and watched Mrs M. read *all* my letter to you! 'Marks out of ten?' She had the grace to blush!

You asked about the Monks. They come in from Harsham Monastery. Brother P. is the favourite, very dishy. All the girls swoon (except me!!!). He once asked me what had happened to the tables on the flat, I told him in all seriousness that they had escaped! I find the concept of Buddhism very attractive.

I went right back to the beginning, trying to figure out just when you started to love me. One month after meeting me, third visit, you wrote, 'Dear lovely Sara'. I remember my heart skipping a beat! I can still see you, waiting to go out the main door, whilst I sat with my head on my knee, watching you from the legal box. I winked at you, I thought you were the most wonderful man that had ever walked into my life. I glided back to the wing, a foot off the ground. How I loved you. Daughter indeed!! My life for you!

Hicks has been harassing me again. At lunch I went to see him, told him I felt he was doing too much, and I was scared he was cracking up. I *was* being sarcastic but he didn't see it, and started to talk about the problems on H-wing.

It's my father's birthday, 2 November, I think I'll send him a card. He hasn't remembered my birthday for over ten years, bless him.

T. told a very funny story about a couple who were into very kinky sex. The wife was handcuffed, hands and feet to the bed, while the husband climbed on top of the wardrobe, dressed to the waist in a Batman outfit. When he jumped he broke a leg (hip) and couldn't move. Neither could the wife, so she had to scream for help till the neighbour phoned the fire service and ambulance and police!

I do agree that we should try to iron out every problem now, like who is going to wash up, make the beds, empty the trash, etc. Let me know your preference. I love you so much I'd do them *all* and with a smile and joy in my heart if it would make you happy. Somehow I think that you are a sharer, am I right?

I love you so much. *Sara* xx

Darling,

'Send me a love letter,' sez you! They all are, aren't they, or I can't tell 'a hawk from a hand-saw'.

I'll tell you about K.J. and her call last night – maybe you've heard from her already. Mixed news. I was a bit taken aback by her change of tone. First call, in the afternoon last week, was relaxed and casual, friendly. Last night (with kids in the background) she was brisk, businesslike, almost rude. I think she's 'riding with the hounds and running with the hares'. One moment the liberated feminist and the next a part of the legal establishment.

Don't worry about the K.J. hiccup. It will be sorted out. It's just a learning experience for both of us. I think she's a good person but also part of a very stuffy, ossified, mainly male cartel. Just keep your sharp wits about you.

I'll try out the socks when I get back, maybe I'll wear them in bed until you're there to keep my feet and a lot else warm.

I *love* you and miss you already. *George* xx

My Dearest George,

What a wonderful visit, darling, now that's what I call a kiss! A glimpse of life with you, sheer bliss. I hope we never run out of things to discuss. On looking back, I had to smile, one minute we were sitting in quiet silence, then kissing, then disagreeing about Northern Ireland. What a pair we are!

It's been a wonderful day, all due to you, how did your journey home go?

Nothing from K.J. – do you think I should write to the Registrar and explain why I wrote to her home address, or just leave things? If I don't hear from her, by Saturday, then I'll take the bull by the horns! I keep thinking they can't do much more to me – can they?

How much I loved you today! Did you feel it? You must have done. What a power. I came upstairs and said to the waiting girls, 'Do I look like I kissed him?' They burst out laughing. I didn't realize I looked like the wreck of the *Hesperus*! Why didn't you say? Hair everywhere, mascara smudged. I looked pleased! In every sense of the word.

Now you've seen my muscles! What do you think? All the better to *squeeze* you with!

Did you feel snuggled and kissed? You are right about my mother. One of the ways I realize how cruel she was, is by comparing her behaviour to me, in relation to my behaviour with Luise.

I miss her so much, that's why I don't talk about her much. I can't open the box, it's hard enough carrying it. Remembering how much I love Luise and how I *showed* it makes it clear how my mother didn't love me. Contemplating our life (Mummy's and mine), I realize that she was one of the unhappiest people I've ever met. She seldom laughed. There was no joy in her at all, just angry, determined *will*. Of course she made Daddy's life hell!

I love you so much. *Sara* x

Darling,

Your lovely letter to keep me warm and buzzing for a while.

The 2 per cent [Appeal] success rate is an outrageous insult to your, my, anyone's intelligence! Can you imagine aircraft engineers, for example, sending in detailed reports exposing flaws in aircraft design and function which had a 2 per cent 'success' rate?

So why is it that high-paid lawyers exposing faults in the administration of justice have a 98 per cent failure rate? The suspicion must be that the Appeal system is not serious. It is cosmetic, a source of easy money designed to soothe the public conscience and help control prisoners. I think part of K.J.'s curtness may be due to her belated realization that your case is a deeply serious human as well as legal problem and that she feels personally uneasy at carrying out this 2 per cent charade with you.

I think the raw humanity and feeling of you (and me) make her quite uncomfortable. They are used to life at arm's length!

All that stuff about the Registrar's hurt pride is just a smokescreen, I'm now sure. Let's discuss all this on a legal visit next week. Any refusal to go along with the Appeal procedure would have to be part of a much wider campaign. We'll reform this lousy system yet!

Yes, dear lovely Sara, I can remember winking at each other. It was the first time, I think, I really felt at home with you. A good moment.

We've come a long, long way haven't we, in such a short time?

Yes, I'll share. I wash up, one of my few skills. And I'll share everything else, except you. And if you still think I'm reserved, at least it's for you.

I love you, all over, and miss you.

George xx

Darling,

Kisser-in-chief . . . I laughed at your description of the H-wing response to your mascara smudges.

I wonder what you're thinking about the Appeal puzzle?

Sometimes it is better in life (!) to refuse crumbs and demand a loaf. Your public image, too, would be greatly enhanced, I think, by leading a reform crusade to go along with your personal demand for release.

These Appeals are like printing money for lawyers. If I decide to do this talk at the House of Lords I'll start by referring to your case and the disgraceful mess the law has made of it so far.

I'm still mulling over this Appeal problem – I think we'll get the right answer in the end. You know, it's the classic English élitist method for keeping the 'great unwashed' at bay and sedated, to offer them titbits now and then to make them feel they are not totally left out of heaven. The Appeal system (in line with the psycho report) seems exactly this sort of pompous con.

Back to reality and my love for you.

Very real! *George* xx

My Darling Tramp,

Had a good day – stole another Catholic this morning, thereby swelling our congregation to the need for extra chairs, and reducing Father Algy's to three. It's *not* a war, just that he preaches death and sin for an hour, then leaves the girls in despair with no comfort of any kind!

He's a supremely intelligent Jesuit but no empathy for women, especially in here.

Father Algy has cassettes. You know, I often jokingly enquire how he can fit 200 male voices into such a tiny room – you hear them and then look in to see three people.

I'm glad you have small feet, I can nick your socks – I used to pinch Luise's (I think she was secretly proud).

Ella got engaged officially on Friday. They passed a new rule that the girls could have their engagement rings, worn on a chain (stones on a finger are a good weapon). I wrote to K.O'D. I read her last letter – in it she writes, 'My students gaze up at me like hungry sheep. I want to run and hide. One of my colleagues is having a nervous breakdown because his wife wants her freedom – or the key to the prison door.' Strange thing to write, isn't it?

Yes I do feel bonded, well almost, if you know what I mean.

No, you are not reserved. Cautious, I think, but I like that. Love you! Hands off on the legal visit, that will be hard.

See you soon. *Sara* x

Darling absentee,

Did you ever see the Japanese film *Ran*? It was on TV last night (kept me up late). *Ran* apparently means 'chaos'. It's a Japanese *King Lear* set in the middle ages, with three sons instead of three daughters. It's highly stylized and beautiful, meticulously organized, with warring armies with flags, horses, etc. Very dramatic in parts, and the old King had a real Japanese Fool! 'All my life I've been his nurse,' he says of the dying King, and sits crying. 'You're the Fool now, I speak the truth ... Man is born crying. When he has cried enough he dies.' The King (c.f. your father) repents of his life-long militarism at the end and begs forgiveness from his sons, 'If only you can forget my cruelty to you.' The Fool shouts up at the skies, 'Are you so bored up there you crush us like worms? ... Men prefer sorrow to joy, suffering to peace.' You see, the Fool ends up with the wise statement.

It seems to me that M. had given up, inwardly, ages before he met you. You were two suicide risks clinging together in a vacuum – saving a drowning man is hard enough, especially if you're drowning yourself. You escaped, just in time.

I want to get on with a proper Free Sara Thornton Campaign, by TV, books, etc.

I hope you do write to the Registrar as I suggested, re K.J. and it being entirely your choice.

I'll try to get over Thursday or Friday for a 'legal' session – I will miss kissing, hugging, touching you – but I'll *look* at you.

I love you, *George* xx

Darling,

Thank you for your lovely letter – made my day! I love you, wish you were here.

As for Tracey I hurt her the most yet I love her the most, it's not fair. She's trying so hard to shelter me, smooth away the rumpus I cause with my unwarranted venom, and instead of appreciating her efforts I'm just mean. I don't understand myself at all – and I don't think anyone else does either. I'm so angry half the time, little things annoy me. I don't like me at the moment at all and quite frankly, I'm very scared.

To do anything else but accept the condemnation and sentence of a court full of men, leads to heartache, despair and fear! How easy it would be to just say – OK, hell, forget it, and do a quiet well behaved sentence, with all emotions frozen within. I wrote that a murder trial was one of the most frightening experiences a woman could face – shit, that's peanuts. Disagreeing, and trying to fight for justice, that's far more frightening, because as you search deeper for help and allies, you are forced to see the hypocrisy and shallowness of our system of justice. Others, too, are reluctant to shatter their fragile illusions of a fair and honest legal system; so to protect themselves, pour their energies into stopping me. 'You can't win Sara!' or, 'Leave it, Sara, you are making yourself ill!'

It's hard for the officers too, they have to lock us up – so they have to convince themselves of our guilt or their conscience would overcome their work.

I'm very angry with K.J. for seeming to play games with me. Talking to M. she cannot understand why K.J. should be upset by a minor fracas with the Registrar over using K.J.'s home address.

First she writes a letter full of hope, saying she's coming to see me, and we must 'champion' my cause. Even if I do lose the Appeal, 'let's be in touch', etc., then, after one curt phone call to you, leaves me high and dry. It really has knocked the wind out of my sails, I mean she is, as you put it, a woman, a mother, and a very well-respected barrister, yet I don't feel that I can now rely on her support.

What started off as a fight to ensure that victims of domestic violence receive the help and protection they warrant, has grown into something much bigger, deeper, wider, hasn't it? Will we ever find a core of truth, honesty, or will maggots continue to spill out? Is there, in this whole land, one judge or barrister or QC who is willing to risk his bread and butter and say, publicly, the system stinks and is rotten to the core?! I fear not.

Where's my faith, hope, courage, strength when the going gets rocky? What a hypocrite I am sometimes. I've been let down and it's knocked me for six. Maybe I saw K.J. as an angel of mercy, who would stand up in the Court of Appeal and say all I wanted said and see justice done.

My angel of mercy appears to have feet of clay. At least through all this, I know *you* are there, quietly loving me, supporting me, and trying to understand my written ramblings of fear and self-hatred. It says much of my character that I saw K.J.'s behaviour as a fault of mine, that I wasn't good enough for her to champion. As there seemed no other explanation at the time, it was an easy conclusion to come to, and it started another train of self-doubt, recrimination and hate. Hence my real and to a degree justified anger.

But to a degree anger can be a creative force. I now feel even *more* determined to show the whole thing up for what it is. I must remember that I am not a lonely frightened little girl any more, riddled with doubt and loathing. I'm a loved, strong woman, treated unjustly, and asking only that the public and society recognize that, and acknowledge it.

Your love still wanders round my soul – keeps me warm and strong. I love you. *Sara* x

Darling,

I'm in self-imposed exile; at lunch-time I told the nurse I had a headache (true) and thought it even flu (false). I asked to be locked in on bedrest – she complied.

Even your marvellous letter failed to cheer my spirits – refused lunch and on coming upstairs I found nearly all the gifts I've given Tracey piled up outside my door. Childish but more hurtful than I can say.

Emotional savages the lot of them. I've got as much chance of turning this place into a caring community as flying to Mars. I've cried buckets this afternoon, with the sense of utter betrayal – I feel as if I gave her my trust and love and she has abused it.

I feel alienated, dismally alone, and emotionally dead!

Once I crack a joke I'll know I'm getting better!

Tuesday a.m.

The sun is shining. I'm starting to – but I still feel like an antibody.
Sara xx

Darling,

Perhaps both of us are still a bit startled and overwhelmed by the revolutionary quality of our love – nothing will be the same again! Old landmarks disappear and new ones arise. Don't be fierce, be gentle!

In some respects you are braver than I am – *heroic* (is that what made you 'cry'?). It's a word I've never before used of anyone – I hope you're flattered.

And I hope you're feeling better. I worry about you, all the time, but also smile.

Maybe some of the inmates are scared that you know too much about them – more than they know themselves. That can be frightening for them because it gives you a certain power – 'it's good to have a giant's strength, but tyrannical to use it like a giant!' Maybe you're responding to their fear?

Here's a nice Irish view of the law (17th C.) – Charles Macklin, actor: 'The law is a sort of hocus-pocus science, that smiles in yer face while it picks yer pocket; and the glorious uncertainty of it is of mair use to the professors than the justice of it.' Like it?

Ever heard of Lord Gifford QC? A Labour peer and quite left-wing, from a very upper-class background. He was on BBC TV yesterday p.m. (he's written a book, *Where's the Justice?*), says judges are 'arrogant and out of touch', 'narrow in every sense of the word', 'fail to see injustices going on under their noses', 'different body language when a judge talks to a policeman and a defendant', 'should be taught what fairness is about', 'lawyers frequently only see client on morning of case', 'courtroom is an extraordinary ritual, very intimidating', 'uniforms mystify and hide what's really there', 'judges don't get any real training at all', 'very little understanding of the effects of sentencing', etc. Good man. Maybe we should get him?

See you soon,

All my love, *George* xx

Darling,

I've just been told that you are coming in to see me tomorrow, a legal visit, and so I won't get the cuddle I so desperately need. Still, it will be a tonic to see your dear face again and discuss with you the fears I have. They have gone now, but you won't have had the letter I sent today – so you'll be thinking I'm still maudlin. I'm not, darling, just on the up and up, especially at the thought of seeing you again.

We've had a High Court judge and his clerk visit the wing this evening – Judge Ottley, I believe his name was!

I looked for him, but too late, he had gone. I wanted to say, 'If you want to see a life sentence being carried out, why not go to our homes, and see the children, broken by untimely separation from their mother? Why not come at visiting times and see screaming young children being dragged out after their one and a half hours every fourteen days with mum – whilst inmates weep and officers block their ears? Why not come after 8 p.m., and tiptoe round the landings to hear women cry tears of guilt and agony alone behind locked doors?' Because he doesn't want the truth, he wants the platitudes he delivers, and receives from us! I was so cross with myself at missing this golden opportunity that I sat and wrote a furious letter to him.

I *wish* I could have shouted what I've written above from the second or third landing. The effect would have been electric – and would in all probability have started other women off. Instead, like justice itself – it was all a charade! No doubt he now feels, after one hour in H-wing, well qualified to dish out life sentences left, right and centre.

I've decided that on domestic visits, if you talk too much I'll just kick you, effectively shutting us *both* up and affording us a little bit of silence.

Let me tell you what little M. told me about Saudi Arabia. Contrary to what you think, he wasn't indifferent to the barbarity. M., once only, witnessed a stoning to death. Saudi Arabia is high-tech now – they buried the man up to his shoulder, then tipped rubble from a dumper truck on him till he no doubt suffocated. Sober, M. would tell tales of the barbarity and injustice in S. Arabia with jollity and wit. Drunk, he would weep. Malcolm told me that his second wife, Anne, who was a nurse, hid a young unmarried Arab girl in the geriatric dept. of Aramco's hospital. But when she had her baby her father found her, took her and the baby to the desert and shot them!

I want to remember M. with love, I have precious little else to remember that's good.

When I get out, you can kiss all my other moles! It's 12.25 a.m.

All my love, *Sara* xx

Dearest Love,

I'm climbing out of the pit; this morning when I went for my vitamins, Sister asked me if I was going to work. 'Only if I can be locked up if I start crying,' I replied. 'Oh don't be so silly, Sara. If you are not well enough to work, don't go.' It seemed brutal at the time, and tears of self-pity followed again, but I got myself to work. So many asked how I was, Chris gave my shoulder a sympathetic squeeze.

Mrs H. tickled my neck till I grabbed her hand and kissed it with abandon. So much care and sympathy, it just drove the hate and anger from me! Bless them all. I sat talking with two girls, and we discussed depression and how we deal with it.

Something good has come out of this, the girls are realizing that if bubbly Sara can be struck down then depression is a real issue, a tangible result of being parted from our families. The guilt at the pain we cause them.

Told you I was better and I feel such *love* for you.

Miss you so. *Sara*

Darling,

'Disgusted of H-wing', your letter was so dismal I just had to laugh!

H-wing is a high-pressure, emotional cauldron full of trapped feelings, so the kind of things you complain of must be there all the time. Single sex groups = regression. Do you agree?

Don't worry, I'm not going to go off and write biographies of 'obscure composers'! Why don't you tell me some of the things you'd like to work with me on? I just want to find the best way of keeping our love alive and fresh and stop it becoming stale and riddled with habit. I don't even want to look back on this first stage as a golden era.

I want you to understand more about me. In fact I want you to understand all about me. What a hope! I'm greedy.

You'll read this after I've seen you! I love you, *George* xx

Dearest Man,

Lovely letter today, *thank you* – I can really feel the difference getting my letters makes to you.

Don't please ever brand me indifferent! I'm just a slow starter when it comes to 'doing things'. It's only since the publication of my letter to the *Independent* that I've become assertive enough, and confident enough to voice my opinions. Due in no small part to you! It's still scary for me, so you'll have to be patient. I've read your comments three or four times, but still I get the feeling you are saying I'm not good enough for you. I'm sure that's not what you intend at all.

The British are so callous with their children, too often I've read of the upper classes giving their children a lovely nanny (I had one – I adored her) then at six to eight, sending the child off to a boarding school that has no love, care or emotional security. Brutal! I suppose a large number of our judges and lawyers started life that way. No wonder the judicial system stinks.

My mother always seemed to be whispering or muttering about me (and Billi) to Daddy. I knew what she was saying was bad. I also know she only told the truth if she felt it would hurt me more! I still hate her terribly. She's not a woman yet, just a shadowy entity of threat and evil. My grandparents adored her, she didn't have a good reason to be bad, and worse, continue to be bad. I'm terribly afraid that her cruelty was genetically passed on to me. I feel such anger, and as you say, cruelty too.

I know she hated sex – in fact, I never saw her cuddle Daddy (or me or Billi). I wish Daddy would help – his insistent denials that she was anything other than the angel he's fabricated don't help at all!

This letter was to be full of love to keep you warm and buzzing; instead my mother's crept in again. Tomorrow after I've seen you I'll write a real love letter to cheer you through two S-less days. Your comments on rain – same in Fiji. I rain-bathe in this country, too. Once, in summer, Luise and I went swimming. A twenty-minute walk to the pool. When we finished, it was pelting down, so we stored our clothes in plastic, and ran home in our swimming costumes. Nearly caused a pile up!

I miss you too and love you so much. *Sara* x

November

Darling Mole Catcher,

I felt very tired but very peaceful after seeing you. I've turned off K.J. completely. Unless she comes up with a good reason for not writing to me and for being so curt with you, then we might as well forget the idea of having her as my barrister.

All my love darling – *Sara* xxx

Dearest Mole Maker,

I love it! It's sitting on the mantelpiece, between two tall African figures of a warrior and a woman. Where are all the moles on you? I've only seen one so far. I want a map, please.

I feel our approach to your 'release' is still very disjointed and disorganized. You say in your letter that I should be more patient and we must wait for the Appeal, etc. Maybe, but: (a) the Appeal issue is not yet settled, is it? and (b) time doesn't stand still, for Registrars or anyone else. If months and months go by and nobody is doing anything but waiting, they are *not* likely to spring into action suddenly next Spring! Maybe what we need is a relatively low-level campaign now and a much higher profile campaign – if the Appeal fails?

The House of Lords talk is not talking to rows and rows of sleeping, snoring, dying and dead Lords – just a public meeting at the H. of L. But I'll do it and see what happens. I will refer to your case.

Do you realize, darling woman, just how unusual our communication is? Talking to you, reading your thoughts in the pub, and your letter at home. I wonder if there are any couples who make so much effort to reach each other?

I love you, deeply, longingly, smilingly and thankfully. *G* xx

Darling,

I have an apology. I'm a fool (the stupid kind). I've just woken up to why I've felt so uneasy and confused this week – like my comments about us not really listening to each other, etc. I had thought, naively, that you could explore all this debris from your childhood and stay calm and rational. I couldn't understand why you seemed to be so disorientated and angry and regressive, but now I do. Exploring that early hurt, angry part of you, dragged you back to a replay of the past and you became to some extent what you had suffered. You *had* to be like that, otherwise you would have learned nothing useful from it. A lot of what you have been feeling is a left-over part of you, isn't it? It's terribly difficult for you to handle the past and the present at the same time. And I've probably made it harder by trying to get you to look at the future as well. The best and most useful thing I could offer you is probably endless supplies of hugs, and you're out of reach.

Interesting, your comment about forgiving men but not women. That reflects your attitude to your father and your mother, doesn't it? Real forgiveness is very hard work, isn't it?

One of my favourite films is on TV tomorrow night – *One Flew Over the Cuckoo's Nest*. Do you like it? Brilliantly acted, I think, and directed. Quite sad too, and funny.

Keep warm and well. I love you. *George* xx

My darling George,

No letter from you today. I knew I wouldn't get one, but still there's hope, isn't there? I skipped gym this morning (hurrah, common sense, I hear you say), also skipped lunch. I feel so sad, all this injustice being forced upon me, makes me wonder *why* people have never done anything. They all say, 'But we knew the system stinks' – and to my question, 'Why didn't you do something?' I get the standard, 'Can't beat the system, Sara!' I need something to happen, things are too quiet, like the eve of the storm!

I've put a stop on confessions and counselling, one result of hearing people's worst secrets in here is that they then avoid me afterwards, even though I tell them it doesn't change the way I feel. As a result, I'm fast becoming a recluse.

I love you, and I miss you too. I wish you were here. See you soon my darling. Man of my dreams, you are too!

Sara xxx

Darling Sara,

From Shelley to you, via me.

> The fountains mingle with the river
> And the rivers with the Ocean,
> The winds of Heaven mix for ever
> With a sweet emotion;
> Nothing in this world is single;
> All things by a law divine
> In one spirit meet and mingle.
> Why not I with thine? –
>
> See the mountains kiss high Heaven
> And the waves clasp one another;
> No sister-flower would be forgiven
> If it disdained its brother;
> And the sunlight clasps the earth
> And the moonbeams kiss the sea:
> What is all this sweet work worth
> If thou kiss not me?
>
> 'Love's Philosophy'

Like it? I do.

George

Hello Love of My Life,

Guess who I spent all weekend with? Me! I have been alone, in my cell. I slept most of yesterday, the onset of a very heavy period knocked me out. I loved every minute of it. I looked in the mirror, winked and said, I love you. How far I've advanced, six months ago I couldn't look in a mirror.

Gosh, darling – are you still awake? Well, I'm not so frantic, calmer. Maybe I too have finally realized that I can be free? Full steam ahead.

After lunch, I came upstairs, lay on my bed, and went for a walk with you. The wind bit my face, we were well wrapped up, and walked for miles in silence, just being together with the elements. I turned to kiss you and felt the cold tip of your nose press against my cheek as I pushed myself longingly into your arms. Then I woke up, but I could still smell the weather. Strange what a physical prison can do to your senses.

How did you know that the dolphin is my favourite creature? Well, dolphins and whales. I think one of man's worst deeds is teaching dolphins to plant bombs. Dolphins pair for life. They 'punch' sharks with their noses. Never been known to hurt man.

See you soon. All love, *Sara*

Dearest Mole Dispenser,

A lot of my frustration stems from the temptation to want/demand quick solutions to problems which are as complex as life itself. I doubt if two people have ever faced such a varied challenge.

The squirrel has vanished – I've long thought hibernation a wonderful process – imagine being wrapped up snug together and waking to the sound of ice melting and birds chirping. We'd be well and truly bonded then, wouldn't we?

One of the many things we are having to learn is when to take a step back from full engagement and ask for 'time out' for a while to refocus our energies.

You once cited your mother's will-power – yes, it can be a destructive force if not tempered with love. You and I both have traces of this problem, don't we? We can be a bit ruthless at times.

The prisons publicly advertise their policy of making prisoners good citizens. Let's make sure that they swallow a new and more human and creative definition of a 'worthwhile life'.

We must get the Free Sara Campaign on the road, even if it only travels in first gear to start with.

The only offer so far on accommodation to rent here is a shared house with the local hairdresser! A young woman. At least my hair might improve! Don't worry, it's fizzled out – I want somewhere nearer Durham.

Hope you're chirpy . . . and full of brilliant ideas and love.

I love you, *George* xx

Darling Man,

I've just had a very illuminating twenty minutes with Dr Foot. She asked how long I had suffered heavy periods. When I told her they started at aged seventeen, and that I had been put on the pill to stop it, she became *very* interested. She noted how thin I was, and that my neck is slightly swollen. She thinks I could be suffering from an overactive thyroid gland. Too much Thyroxia causes manic depression. She's ordered a blood test. If it proves positive, this could be a very useful point at the Appeal! Let's discuss it.

We will be together, always. *Sara* xxx

Dear Disorientated Love,

Why the hell are *you* disorientated and confused? *I'm* the one that's been suffering! I love you, I guess my behaviour and writings must have seemed strange, all this hurt and betrayal, sparked off by K.J.'s behaviour, I think.

I was working in soft toys, really not my forte, I'm slow. I'm going to call my efforts 'after-life' cushions, I take so long to make them. I said in despair, to Mrs H., 'I'm really no good at this you know!' She replied, 'You're lovely, so it doesn't matter!' Bless her.

Maybe Daddy's letter has sunk me, I've got to be honest about it. Sara, the aware logical adult, sick. *But* there is still enough of the child in me, the fearful, insecure little girl, who is no good and feels terribly afraid that Daddy is right, I am no good and I did make Mummy and Daddy very unhappy, therefore I fully deserve punishing for ever. I'm scared that I am going to crack up, George. The nurse said that a bad thyroid would explain why I go 'over the top'.

So how was London? I'm so, so looking forward to seeing you. Things are quiet here now. I've nearly completed my first cushion in soft toys – a miracle!

I will be fine tomorrow, don't worry – I won't crack up. Far too stubborn for that, and I couldn't bear to let either you or myself down.

I LOVE YOU. You are my antidote to everything that's bad. *Sara* xx

My darling Shadow!

You a shadow of me? You're as little shadow as Durham Cathedral! Great to get your double-jointed letter, complete with dyslexic 'rionic'! I love it!

There is a sense in which your 'girls' are right to be apathetic, isn't there? Stick a tiger in a cage and it will snarl and roar and claw at the bars. Keep it there for months and months and it has learnt a new 'life' of confinement, tho' deep down there is a glowing ember of old instinct. Aren't people the same? All you and I and anyone alive can do is fan that ember into life – blow on it with care.

An additional point, aren't women *doubly* punished in prison? Prisons are in fact designed by men, for men – men instinctively band together in defensive/aggressive groups (army, Masons, clubs, public schools, teams, etc.), so prison is not so strange for them. But women instinctively fall back on home, children, family, relatives, community; so going into a single sex, childless, authoritarian 'male' prison is a *perversion* as well as a punishment. Isn't it?

I love your dream walk – let's have lots and lots of real ones, with cold, hot and warm noses . . . Do you think we would ever be silent for long?

Must post this, along with a mass of love – I love you, *George* xx

Darling yo-yo (do you know there is a Japanese musician called Yo Yo Ma?),

I'm glad you're on an upswing. It's time, darling woman, for your campaign train to leave the station. Or should I say, being a plane-o-phile, it's time for the plane to move out to the runway?

'True forgiveness' is also to do with recognizing the 'lost child' element in the other person, as well as experiencing fully one's own pain, isn't it? We are haunted by people we hate and fear – you know all this. Shut up, G.D.!

I don't agree that the nurse in *Cuckoo's Nest* was so awful. In fact, the more I see the film, the more I realize the underlying subtle level of flirtation between MacMurphy and her. In fact, the strength of the film lies in the balance between her efforts to keep the system afloat and his efforts to sink it. The final lobotomy was the system taking over, brutal and ruthless and interested only in control.

I love the Mrs H. quote – she is the voice of 'God', isn't she, not all these posing priests. Can't you imagine telling God, 'I'm really no good at this life, you know,' and 'She' replies, 'You are lovely, so it doesn't matter'? The ultimate answer.

I'll sponsor your silence, but only while you're kissing me!

Funny to think of thieving in a prison – rather like stealing *inside* a supermarket! A closed shop. They must be addicts. 'Judges who steal, themselves give authority to thieves.' I wonder if stealing is a kind of hangover from babyhood? Demand feeding.

I love you. *George* xx

Darling Love,

The thought of having an over-active thyroid gland keeps buzzing in my head, as the full implications hit me. If the test is positive, I'd like to see the complacent psychiatrists who stood in court and quite calmly tore me apart in front of my sister and half of Atherstone. Why did none of them think to do a test? It's quite apparent, as I'm sure you'll see on Friday. It's made me cry with anger, all those years of terrible sadness. I'm having the blood test tomorrow morning, I don't know how long the results will take to come back. It's terribly important to me.

I feel very alone sometimes, and often feel that apart from you, I don't have an ally. I'll see you in less than twelve hours, wonderful, I want/need lots of cuddles, I probably won't let you go.

I want out of here, I only feel alive when I get your letters and see you. I know I just won't be whole (never really have been) till I'm with you all the time. Our love gives me such strength! Wrestle with you? Can you take it if I win? I once beat a man at arm wrestling, and felt very ashamed at the humiliation I caused him. I want to do everything with you. Let's get me out so we can show each other, tell each other, love each other. Always!

Sara xx

Darling Sara,

I've got a nasty feeling that religious bigotry is going to be one of the negative trends of the 1990s – a kind of mob psychosis where millions gang up together around a few over-simplified 'truths' and hate everyone who won't join in.

I feel very cut off from you and would give the whole of Finland to see you now. No wonder people who are badly hurt/traumatized, relapse into blank indifference. Indifference is the ultimate self-protection. Nothing matters. Life or death seem the same. Caring about someone creates pain as well as pleasure. *Loving* someone is the ultimate high-wire act.

I'm no saint, but I can promise one thing, *you* are my first priority (including your right to your own decisions, etc.).

A lot of love, *George* x

Darling haemogoblin!

Yes, good news if it's your thyroid which has been ruling your life, tho' I hope the treatment won't take away your lovely spirit.

We'll need de-briefing (in every sense!) and de-compression, for weeks probably, after you get out. Do you know that quite a few people died soon *after* getting out of Nazi concentration camps, from eating normal meals too soon? I'm sure we'll work out the right way of doing it.

This whole experience has taught me how many people feel *they* are in prison, in their own heads and hearts. Almost an epidemic!

Most of that set-up depends on the supposed inferiority of the prisoners for its own imagined superiority, which is why you are both a threat and an attraction.

We have a long way to go in our religious discussions, don't we? I will only criticize your beliefs if I feel they have a negative effect on us or your life – please do the same. Often it can be the words that get in the way of the meaning.

If Hicks says 'No' to everything why not go in one day and say, 'Do you really want to keep me here?'

Cheeky woman! I've had bank accounts since before you were a dot in the Pacific.

When they privatize the prisons, I'm thinking of putting in a bid so I can turn all you scallywags loose!

I woke up this morning wishing you were merged with me like scrambled eggs.

Hope you enjoy reading *Walden*. Thoreau is what I love about the States – thinks for himself, hopeful, non-pompous.

Can't wait for the kisses/hugs – hope you can still feel them when you read this Saturday. You're lovely!

I love you and miss you, all the time. *George* xx

Darling Lovely Man,

What a visit. Did you feel my sadness and loneliness? I didn't want to let you go! It's never ever enough is it? I think the situation is getting bad – at least this morning when Ann stuck her fingernail in my nose – I truly felt *no* violent retaliation, just shock and sadness. So *I* know, I am not a violent person. You felt so good today, I can remember the touch of your hands, and the feel of your face.

I've got a blinding headache and I'm tired – started *Walden*. I love it, and will probably finish it by the end of the weekend.

All my love, *Sara* xx

Dearest sweetheart,

A million things to tell you, as always. Firstest and mostest – how much I love and miss you. I suppose we have to thank prison for one thing at least, scarcity value! One and a half hours per week is a drip torture, in one sense, but in another it does underline our value for each other, doesn't it?

I'm proud of the way you are coping; restrained, but not giving in.

The more attention you get from outside and the less they get, the greater the gap and the bigger the target you become.

Please give that toe some mercy. It will never heal if you punish it all the time. (I should have taken it away with me.)

I think our campaign is cranking up, don't you? The fog is beginning to lift.

As for arm wrestling, if you beat me I'd apply to the nearest

Sunshine Home. In reality, you can't ever win against me because I'm too good at inventing excuses!

Did I tell you a robin has 'conquered' my little garden and sits on the gate post guarding its territory? Your spirit . . . Look after yourself darling.

I love you. *George* xx

Darling,

I had a good phone talk with Billi. She has finally stopped having her awful headaches, but is plagued so badly by panic attacks whenever she tries to remember our childhood, she is going to have hypnosis.

Luise has started to play volleyball, and told me that yesterday she went to the ocean and chose a rock to send me – so I can smell it! Haven't I got the most wonderful daughter? She says she is happy.

My love, *Sara* xx

Darling,

Were two people ever so bonded who had not yet slept together? I doubt it.

A story about Beethoven to prove he was human as well as a genius: a pupil of his was playing one of his own (the pupil's) compositions on the piano at a recital, before playing Beethoven's work. The audience (very posh) were told he'd played something of B'hoven's and cheered loudly. When Beethoven was told, he was disgusted, so he played a trick on them at the next recital, by himself playing one of his pupil's pieces and pretending it was his. They all clapped as loudly as ever, so he told them the truth!

Sibelius on the radio (Fourth Symphony) – reminds me of fir trees and you, sleeping bags and you, and lots of snow and you, and olives. I wonder if you will like his music – it has the most distinctive sound of any composer I know. Impersonal, very atmospheric, brooding, just right for huge empty magnificent landscapes. That's why I want to listen to it there, where it was written. Coming?

When I go through Durham tomorrow, I'll blow a kiss to you from the station, at about 11.48. It's possible to see a chunk of the prison from the station.

I'm going to sign an alliance with your toe against *you*! Look after it or you'll be the only one-legged gymnast in England. Just off to the capital ant-heap. See you Friday a.m.

I love you, *George* xx

Darling Tramp in Shining Armour!

Lovely letter today – Oh boy, did I need it. Someone got very cross about something I had written. Their anger was such that they barged into my cell and started to choke me as I lay on my bed, dozing. Only lasted twenty seconds or so, but I've been threatened with death. It just goes to show how much we need real, active therapy in here.

I was called up to census and handed two letters, one very thick with Daddy's writing on it. I started to cry. I knew it was not pleasant, I suppose because I asked too hard a question in my last letter. This letter beats them all! He says that if I continue with these lies he cannot morally support me, just as morally he couldn't support me when Malc. died. He says my mother was unhappy because *I* made her so, till her illness did.

As yet, no test result. I went and checked this evening, but the sister says it hasn't come. She also said I'm becoming obsessed with my mother, I should forget it, she's dead and I won't find out anything. I tried very hard to explain how important it was to me – to understand *why* she treated me so cruelly at times, in order to forgive and let go.

Send me lots of love and good thoughts this weekend, darling – I need them more than ever. Did you really doubt my gymnastic ability, you louse! In the olden days I would have done a handstand – just to show you. But I know now I don't need to prove anything to you! Time enough – *à la* Batman, I could always do a full twisting back somersault off the top of the wardrobe! . . .

I love you. Have a good weekend. *Sara* x

PS   Postcard from P.B. with a statue of Beethoven on it!

Darling,

The purpose of this letter is to fool the postman; by sending it second class, you might, just might receive it Monday.

Our favourite toys were bottles, any size and shape, we'd make dresses for them by cutting a hole in a strip of cloth, and placing it over the neck. *Voilà*, a doll.

So my darling man, hopefully this is your Monday epistle. 'And tell me, Sara, what was your main ambition in H-wing?' 'To get a letter to George on a Monday!' I'm so happy loving you – I'm anxious just to see you, touch you, hear your voice. Well, I'll get two-thirds on Friday, darling.

I love you, terribly, *Sara* xxx

Darling,

In your last letter you wrote that quite often our misunderstandings about God arise from the *words* and not the meaning. How true this is!

Yesterday morning Mrs C. called me into her office. She told me that she had read my exam paper, and thought it superb! I moaned about the lack of therapy – we discussed prison reform. She said I was so intelligent, with a 'brilliant wit' that takes her breath away and at times scares people.

I think our love is so unique and honest that nobody can deny it. Not one of the officers has ever made a disparaging remark. Maybe it's because they've read your letters, which are so beautiful. Mrs K. says she always enjoys her stint in census, just to read our letters to each other. I love you so, darling.

The Government could never justify all this phenomenal security for just two women. Martina and Ella are the only two Cat. A women in Britain.

The atmosphere this week has been awful. Last Saturday, no post was given out, no reasons why. When I saw E. in tears, saying, 'Sara, you are always telling me to try and understand the officers, but they are just bastards!!' I resolved to confront them.

Everything I do, I do with you, I don't suddenly think of you, I never stop thinking of you! Do you understand? I feel our love has gone beyond the whole question of marriage now – an optional extra. Do you know I adore you totally? *You* are my life sentence. Thank you, Judge and jury!

All my love, *Sara* xx

Hello my beloved Peddler of Words,

Raced upstairs, skipped lunch, and sat thinking about you, desperate to retain the image and feel and smell and aura of you.

Please try to understand how awfully difficult it is for me to take all this in! It seems that one minute I am writing a letter to a newspaper, then suddenly all these people that I've never heard of, never met, are talking about me, and now TV – millions of people? Wow! I *don't* want to be 'famous' and I'm only consenting because I feel it will achieve something. As you say, people cannot relate to generalities, they need a specific situation.

Don't you *dare* forget my birthday. One of the reasons I don't tell people when it is, is so that I have an excuse when they forget. Put aside your bloody principles and remember it, if you love me!

I hope you have a good weekend, can you feel my love? I was saddened when you told me how tired you were yesterday. I've never seen you tired, that's when Luise used to really show her love for me, getting me pillows, making tea, rubbing my feet. I want to see you tired, asleep, awake, angry, cross, bad-tempered, happy, sad, thoughtful, creative, silly, cooking, washing. Lots and lots to look forward to. I just want to be with you.

I love you, darling man. *Sara* xx

Darling,

We are public property till all this is over. You are a number in Her Majesty's cage. You must become, publicly, a real, fascinating woman suffering injustice, in a society which does not understand violence and woman's experience.

I tried some mind-over-matter stuff on the way back yesterday. It rained the whole way and a ferocious wind blew leaves and rain like hail in my face. Instead of looking at it as a dreadful, frustrating, wet slog, I added an hour to the normal time for the ride – told myself I'd enjoy getting wet. As long as I was cycling faster than walking, it was OK! It worked quite well.

Lawyers and judges and the rest are like pimps, living off immoral earnings. No crime, no criminals, they'd all be on the dole! Yet they behave like prima donnas, without either manners or respect.

I like these comments of William Blake:

> 'The Winner's Shout, the Loser's Curse
> Dance before dead England's Hearse.'

I can see your lovely, smiling face and it makes me very happy. I woke up loving you and I still do, all the time . . . Hugs.

I love you. *George* xx

My only Love,

You really did think that my mother was a man, didn't you? I'm enclosing two other photos.

By the time we got to Fiji, Mummy was permanently in trousers, don't remember seeing her in dresses! Her lack of clothes sense drove my Gran to distraction. Gran was elegant.

I'm not (nor ever have been) into bondage or violence. Sex, with love, is ultimately about pleasure, isn't it? There was a girl in here, who said that unless her man hit her she did not believe he loved her. True!

On our second meeting, at the end you stood up. I remained seated. When you bent forward, I reached out and touched your face. Cupped it briefly. For me that was important, it was the moment that a spark of love appeared.

How far back do you want these visual ideas to go? I have blanks, but I remember certain things very clearly. M. throwing his ring in the bushes, us staring at each other while the knife stuck in his belly, being told he was dead, being formally charged with murder by a sergeant in a solemn voice, who then asked, 'Beans on toast suit you, love?'

I miss you, and love you very, very much. *Sara* xxx

Darling scrawny owl,

I've been staring at that photo of you and your mother on the ship – it really puzzles me. There is only one thing about her that looks slightly feminine – her hand! Smaller than you'd expect from a man. Hair, face, expression, flat chest, clothes, all seem to me more masculine than feminine. Unless the photo is a very poor likeness (and you didn't say that), I should say she had a severe identity problem, sexually. Is it possible that a lot of her cruelty to you was rooted in her insecurity within a female personality, and that she envied and hated your natural femininity? All that love of power and obedience seems like a crude imitation of male values – interesting that in the only letter of hers that I've seen, she thinks it funny when two corpses are muddled up!

If there's any truth at all in this suspicion, then I can see how much of a threat to her fragile identity your high-spirited femininity could be. Just by being YOU, you would expose her psychological cover-up, so she retaliated by accusing *you* of cover-up, lies, cheating. Am I wrong?

My Irish friend has phoned to say there's a room to rent at Brancepeth Castle in a rather quaint little village about 4 miles from Durham. Brancepeth means 'lair of the boar'.

It would help me in dealing with your trial if you would give me notes and comments on as many different aspects of it as you can remember – e.g. Prosecution case, Defence, judge, cross-examination, etc. Split it into days if you wish.

One day, darling, we'll shut out the world, lock the doors, draw the curtains, light some candles and retire for hours and hours into each other's arms. I just want to listen to you breathing and hear your heart beat and find your pulse. A silence filled with our love. TV cameras and books and 'public opinion' will be totally forgotten. Your love for me is so wonderful and unexpected, I pinch myself and hope I'll never 'wake up'!

Eat something, sleep *with* me, I love you. *George* xx

Darling Man,

I've just been listening to wonderful music – Paul Simon's latest CD, *Rhythm of the Saints*. Absolutely superb! You must hear it. Drums, life, rhythm – pulsating! I half expected two or three African tribal natives to appear. Some of the tracks sounded Polynesian. I *love* Polynesian music.

It's all very well K.J.'s friends saying she's over-committed, but where does that leave me? As time goes on without further word from her, or the Appeal Registrar, I get more and more disgusted. Don't you? We want more than just a change in domestic violence laws, surely. We want women to be treated with honour in a court.

Saw Mogg today, briefly. He said that lots of women here don't want therapy. How on earth could they not want what they don't know exists? I didn't want you before August, I didn't know you were there, and now I want you terribly, in every way.

Sara xx

Darling,

Your comment about your mother wearing trousers in Fiji. If ever there was a place to wear a skirt, you'd think it was there. Even Fijians wear them!

My friend M. says, 'I am dizzy at the heights you and Sara are travelling at.' She means that she also probably thinks we'll crash. She'll be right in her fears only if we fail to express our deepest feelings as well as aims. Right?

I told M. that I only function fully when I'm facing an 'impossible' challenge. It's true. *You*, and your situation, and us are stretching me to the limit, and it's very good for me! Keep that brain of yours sharp, too, sweetheart, not just for backchat, but the path ahead of us.

Yes, I do remember you touching my face. Lovely gesture.

I've heard of snow-blindness. You are toe-blind, darling! If I'm a tramp, you are my trampoline. Why are you so merciless with your toe? What did it do to you, except prop you up? You should apologize to it for taking it into prison and depriving it of grass!

See you soon, darling. I love you. *George* xx

Darling Man!

I've just written to K.J. I feel the time is right. It's over a month since she wrote to me, and you are right in what you say – I don't want her to represent me! Let her explain it to the Registrar of Appeals. I hope we are not making an enemy, but I feel that we are 100 per cent correct on this issue.

Living in the Light, by Shakti Gawain. Have you ever read it? You must. I've only just started it, and quite frankly, I'm dying to get back to it. She writes, 'I believe that on a world-wide level we are being challenged to let go of our present way of life and create an entirely new one.' 'The old world was based on an external focus – having lost our fundamental spiritual connection, we have believed that the material world was the only reality. Feeling lost, empty, we have continually sought happiness through external things – the new world is being built as we open to the higher power of the universe within us, and consciously allow that creative energy to move through us!' Her book is telling people what you have been writing me so beautifully in your letters.

I feel better for having written to K.J. With my luck, I'll get a lovely letter from her tomorrow. Run out of space again, I am dying to see you. Yes, I too awaken loving you, and go to sleep loving you, and LIVE loving you.

Sara xx

Darling traveller through my mind,

The bit about the story of Jesus that always gets me is the crucifixion and eternal life. I believe in reincarnation, devoutly so. Surely this didn't start merely because Jesus died on the cross. In a way, I feel Jesus committed suicide, perhaps because he felt that only by dying, and in such a brutal fashion, would people remember him. After all, he was the ultimate psychologist. People only say and remember good things about you when you've either died or gone away for good! Maybe that's one of the basics about a suicide – perhaps thinking that someone will say good things *or* be made to realize finally the good in a person!

I have to say that I love *your* idea of God too, in many, many ways you are as much, if not more, a 'Christian' (i.e. someone who lives by Christ's teachings) than anybody I have ever met. You do try to 'love your neighbour' and you do try to love God with all your heart, mind and soul.

Until people can really see the good in themselves, they cannot reflect those qualities in a 'good God'. As a race, humans just love the bad, as opposed to the good.

I love you, more than I can say, and *yes*, I *do* sleep with you every night.

Did gym this morning, a workout. Tracey said, 'When you lie down, you really do look like a boy, there's nothing there.' 'Thank God George won't see me lying down till it's too late!' I replied. Giggles.

Yes – it's time to start writing about the trial, what little I can remember.

I think there's one thing you must remember when trying to visualize me going through this – above all, my greatest feeling was one of intense curiosity. I wasn't scared on the outside (but I was inside). I was affable, cool, controlled – a lady – (I think I wore a very smart wool, purple culotte suit). Tigger [Buchanan, defence barrister] did say he noticed the admiring glances of the bank of barristers there to defend other clients. I was surprised at how modern the courtroom was, one expects surroundings like the film clippings of the Old Bailey. It was so relaxed, I came away thinking that 'it's not going to be so bad after all'.

It was my turn – I stood, walked sedately to the box, and said, 'Not guilty' in a firm voice. Bail was once again granted, and it was over!

Tigger, A. and I had a meeting. This was the occasion when Tigger said, in response to my query if he thought I'd go to prison, 'A woman of your calibre will not find prison a problem.'

We get visitors to the wing – they make a beeline for me – and the others get jealous. It's the power of attraction that comes from being so *alive*! Domination is something completely different. Mummy tried to dominate – but *why* she felt she had to, I don't know. Until I do, I can't release her.

It's funny, three hours ago I didn't want to see you at all, now I'll count the hours and minutes till I can be in your arms. I just want to be comforted, to crawl on to and into your lap and hold and be held.

I take it for granted you'll always understand me and my motives. You won't. How could you? I don't always understand myself. For example, my toe – why do I have the need to overcome the pain? I think I feel that to give in to pain is weak.

All these days with no letter from Registrar or K.J. Soon it'll be Christmas. Dead, the whole bloody country goes dead! Shit, I'd forgotten that. Now *I'm* panicking. No, I won't. I refuse to panic.

I've never ever experienced a 'bonding' like I have with you, or ever loved anybody like I love you! So stop being a shit! I'm trying so hard to understand you, can't you see that is a measure of my deep love for you?

I hope I feel in a better mood tomorrow morning, able to finish this with something loving that I *mean*. If you've troubled me into a depression, I shall refuse to kiss you!

Later

Still can't sleep – it's all I want, long for – I feel as if someone just pulled the plug, like a balloon you let go, whizzing round the room in a fury, then lies empty – dead – a fraction of its former self.

With my love, *Sara* xx

Darling lawyer-destroyer,

Good for you! It will do K.J. no harm at all being pushed aside, by you. You must have a lawyer for Appeal that you like and trust.

There's an important question here I want to ask you – it concerns men and women in relation to creative action. Male creativity is easily identified by a woman as a rival 'woman' and 'lover' – after all, artists refer to their 'muse', etc. Thus there is a paradox. Women inspire art and civilization, but can also conspire to destroy/sabotage it. In traditional, practical terms, a woman (especially with children) needs protection and security – the last thing she needs is high-risk experiment and exploration.

What do you think, scrawny owl? Your Shakti sounds sensible, but Indian thinkers are good at abstractions – my concern is why people are trapped in materialism and non-creativity. Not because they lack ideas but because they are really trapped, by depression/fear/self-loathing. How to get out?

Collectively we are still in the slime of mass murder (world wars) and the phoney materialist cover-up. By feeling smaller than they are, human beings try to be bigger than they are, by dressing up in giant's clothing.

I'll show you some of the notes I wrote in September after seeing you – you can read them while I kiss/stroke/touch you. It will distract you. Seems such a long time ago in some ways, yet like yesterday, too. Did you know that 'eternity' means outside time, not endless time? I think love = eternity, don't you? It's as if time is entirely different, longer, shorter, different. The more we love the less we are prisoners of time. 'Doing time' in prison is the exact opposite of love, usually. We've reversed the process. We're not usual, are we?

Take care, darling. I love you. *George* xx

Darling,

Well, at least I'm not crying. Had an awful dream – something invading my body – I felt its fingers, terrible screaming winds roaring in my head.

I just feel quiet and lonely this morning – I hope you can heal this sadness in me – I spent half the night trying to really imagine life without you. Just felt bereft! I want/need a cuddle, love, kisses, hugs, lots and lots of love.

I love you. *Sara*

Darling,

Just home from seeing you and what do I do but write to you? Please smile, darling, I love you. I'm very sorry you were hurt by my comments and hope they seem to you now as relatively trivial as they really are. When I see you hurt I feel awful and guilty. I'm so glad we had that chance to hug each other.

I don't think we would have so much energy and strength together if we weren't difficult people, and complicated, as well as full of a lot of positive love. Please don't stop believing in us.

I don't know if you'll like it or not, but one of the first things I noted about you, early September, was that you were like a 'thoroughbred horse that's been maltreated when young; nervous, insecure, with a vicious temper when threatened, but basically wonderful, warm, unusual, intelligent and good-natured'. Is that far off? We're worth a lot. Let's prove it.

I hope our motto is: 'Only the Best'.

I want to say something about your nightmare, about 'fingers'. My first response is that it aroused thoughts about sexual molestation, maybe a deep, long-ago repression? Linked, perhaps, to the 'domination/power' issue – is it possible you developed a need to 'dominate' in order to be able to suppress that fear in you?

I shared every step of the agony and anger in your letter. Your hurt anger was so real it hurt me too. I don't mind. As I said, it made me love you more. I really do love your spirit. We can both fight. Let's help each other fight more effectively.

Darling, if anyone I know ever takes your letters or ideas as 'entertainment' I'll be merciless with them. Don't you know yet, I'm as good as a guard dog for you? All I need is to be stroked occasionally, plus a few biscuits (more than occasionally).

By the way, it's a general 'truth' in psychology that extreme anger and/or distress are rooted in areas of repressed energy. Rather like hitting a 'gusher' in an oil field.

Another spark between us – we both referred to 'eternal' in our letters. What does 'reincarnation' mean to you? I like Shelley's idea of a world-spirit.

Have you ever thought that your 'suicide' attempts may be a direct by-product of your childhood tactic of trying to defuse your parents' quarrels by running away and forcing them to re-direct their energy and concern to you (e.g. a 'posthumous' concern)? A desperate attempt to win parental affection?

I'll do all I can to make up for all that devastating loss of love, darling.

How can I stop you 'misbehaving' occasionally? I couldn't in a million years. Miss Behaviour 1990! I don't have the slightest control over you.

Your free-spirit, Robin, is feeding off my bird-table. It looks very well, plump, Christmassy. Keep warm.

I love you. *George* xx

Hello my fellow spirit,

I've been reading *Living in the Light* again. It answers so many questions, I just wish we were reading it together. It says, when a person actually becomes truly in touch with their spirit for the first time there is great joy, euphoria, then that person will usually retire to nurture the feeling. On passion: 'Passion in a partnership is true intimacy with each other – to experience *real* passion, we must first be true to ourselves, and then honest with others!' That's why I've never fallen in love like this before. In the new world, when a man is attracted to a woman, he will recognize her as his feminine aspect, and vice versa. 'Falling in love is actually the powerful experience of feeling the universe move through you.' You did that with me didn't you! You see, I've always been able to recognize that without *your* love I would not have been 'reborn'! But, I also knew God/Universe/Spirit was involved, the trouble came when I tried to reconcile the two. Now I understand why when I've seen you, I feel more energized, recharged. Our spirits really are one, darling – believe it.

My angry outburst last night *was* therapeutic and necessary. That line about you acting inappropriately? That was no dream, George, that was a memory! No wonder I couldn't sleep and felt sick. I didn't realize till this afternoon. The roaring noise? An adult's tortured heavy breathing in a child's ear. But I am beginning to feel the pain and release it. I cried this afternoon. I told Sister A. the dream tonight – she winced! Then I said, 'It's a memory isn't it, not a dream?' 'Probably, Sara, yes, I think you might be right!' She had other 'customers' so I left.

The energy of the universe just flows through a person when one is giving aid. That's why you feel *you* only work at peak when facing this 'impossible' challenge. Agree?

Darling, I feel that's all – nobody at my trial was called to say good about me. You must! I *love* you – feel it! See you Tuesday?

Sara xx

Darling barer of teeth and much else,

How are you? I've decided to type out a 'defence case' for you, based: (a) on the existing Appeal: and (b) on the law regarding self-defence and provocation. I've been looking at another book on criminal law. It will at least be good enough to show a lawyer so he/she will have to respond in detail. The more I find out about it, the more disgusted I am with your so-called Defence team. Duds.

Has there been a group decision there, about 'evil' and what it means? Very important, I'd have thought. It's an interesting concept. Describing someone as evil is basically a confession of one's own immaturity and lack of comprehension. I remember when a Governor of Kenya publicly called Jomo Kenyatta 'a leader to darkness and death'. Utter crap. He was describing his own myopic view of life and African politics. But I do think negative energy exists and can become very concentrated. Nuclear missiles, after all, are highly concentrated negative energy. Prisons are focal points of negative social energy, which is why I hate them! Society's attempt to evade the consequences of its negative energy.

Keep your nakedness addiction for yourself, darling! I like clothes, most of the time. Don't they mention 'stripping off in public' in your psychology course? They should do. It's a recognized syndrome! Maybe it's a Genesis complex? A regression to babyhood innocence? One certain thing, it's not at all sexy, so keep those clothes until the last stages of . . . !

I'll tell you something about trees – An ancient survivor of the Mayan tribes in Mexico said, 'if you cut a tree down and don't ask its forgiveness, a star will fall from heaven'. I like that, don't you?

Cold, wet, horrible, but a good fire, good music – wish you were here. See you soon. Lots to talk about.

I love you. *George* xx

Darling,

Please write a *loving* letter, to hold through the weekend. That and the memory of your dear face is my armour.

Yes, I did say I wanted to see you angry – but I think I would be very frightened if that anger was directed at me. One thing I've learnt in the last twenty-four hours is that I'm not very good at handling anger, am I? I'll have to learn, I've spent so many years either suppressing it, or turning it against myself!

When I get upset, I seem to lose all appetite. It's an effort to swallow food. Beware of making me happy and contented, I might blow up like a balloon!

Have a good weekend, think of my scribbling, I'll just think of you, and love you – all the time.

Sara xxx

PS I miss you already – it's never long enough, is it? Oh for days and nights alone! Just to feel love, joy, and no pain, hurt.

My 'lousy' lover?

Something occurred to me whilst I was writing, Daddy's attitude to Mummy was nearly always cringing, cowering, apologetic. It wasn't love, it was subservience!

After writing to Billi, I started to look at Shelley. Yes, I do like the introduction by Mary. But, leafing through his poems, I found *you*. I spent a lovely hour or so reading all the parts that you had marked, and felt very close to you, darling!

Thank you for your 'humble' letter today – I wanted so much to hug you in return. When I get out, I just want you to hold me, and hold me. Even when I'm asleep – I want to wake up to feel you holding me! Promise? I've eaten like a pig today – actually had a pudding tonight (I rarely eat sweet things).

Hope I'll have seen you by the time you read this.

I hug you to my heart always! *Sara* xx

Darling absentee,

One nice human thing to report. My landlord came round and we discussed my move. He couldn't be more helpful and friendly – and then he phoned later to say his daughter had told him I can take anything I like with me, except cooker, chair, carpets – I can take crockery, fridge, bed, etc.! I don't really need extra stuff but it's a typically generous gesture.

I miss you, very much, and want to give you a hug and apologize for being such a surly grouch.

Ludovic Kennedy has just said on TV that there is no 'prisoner of conscience' in this country. *Wrong*! In Durham Prison today there is N. Wild, a young baker from South Tyneside, who refused to pay any taxes for weapons of war. He has just started a 28-day sentence. Why are people in England so smug? Nothing bad ever happens in Merry England. Oh yes it does!

Just read an article about a woman who had an op. to reduce her breasts. You don't know how lucky you are, darling – at least I do!

You'd laugh if you could see me now, surrounded by half-filled cardboard boxes, paper all over the place, but a good fire, and Mozart.

Thought for the day – Pro-creation: men fertilize women. Creation: women fertilize men.

See you soon. I'll bring *all* my love. *George* xx

Hello my darling fellow irritant,

Yes, you have been on edge, haven't you? Surely the partial cause of *my* anxieties. I felt much better after your visit, once again your presence healed my hurt.

I've written three pages to Court of Appeal. Said I wish to bring in more evidence on Appeal. Asked for clarification of 2 per cent success rate. Said, please, could he see how important it was for me to find own barrister. Thanked him for QC.

I love you and miss you! *Sara* xx

Darling,

I'm writing in blue – it suits my mood. I've cried all afternoon, skipped English this evening.

I'm getting to the stage where I have no time for me – if I don't write something, I feel guilty. Lay off. Just keeping my head above the sea of despair is difficult – one of the girls cut herself up at the weekend, ended up in hospital. Though first they put her in the punishment block.

I'm not Superwoman – why is it that the men in my life are never ever content with what I am? Starting with Daddy – I didn't turn out perfect – he can't forgive that. Don't expect me to be perfect, and stop pushing me! I don't look forward to your letters any more – they used to reach out to me, heal me, love me, now they urge, urge, urge! I don't think you can have any idea what it is like to be in a maximum-security prison over Christmas. I was warned that it is bad. It really is! You don't understand the pain. I want to do things at my own pace, please!

The people I'm *not* pissed off with. *You*, because I love you *so* much; only because I'm secure in your love, can I write and say you are pushing me. A tiny seed still inside says, 'That's it – he knows you aren't any good now – he'll stop loving you.'

I feel better now, I can only release anger and pain through writing. I've cried so much today, my cheeks sting! I'm very tired, have been sleeping with the light on – nightmares again!

Courtroom protocol at the end of trial proceedings, the judge granted me bail – but, in view of the evidence of suicide attempts, wanted to check I would not be alone. Judge asked QC, loudly, who turns and asks, loudly, counsel, who turns and asks A. A. trots to public gallery. Billi says, loudly, she will be with me all the time. A. trots back to bench and tells judge. Judge studiedly ignores A., till like a rude little boy suddenly aware of his station, A. retreats and whispers to barrister who whispers to QC who then tells judge. This took a few minutes. Ridiculous, as the judge heard Billi say, 'I will be with her all weekend!'

Did I tell you that I was, on the Thursday night, called up to hear the jury's verdict four times before they decided that they couldn't reach a verdict, and would be sequestered. One lady juror was in tears when she realized what being sequestered meant. She couldn't even phone her husband for a nightie! The judge forced them. If they had known fully the meaning of sequestering, they would have asked to be dismissed. I am certain of it! When they did finally return the verdict of guilty, one lady cried and cried! I would love to speak with her. I forgive them all, they were only doing their job – and I love you so much. When I think that only through having 'life' and being in Durham could I have met you – I could hug every one of them.

OK. Two hours later, I feel better. Love, love, love you. I want to feel those beautiful arms of yours, everywhere. And your lips.

I think one of the reasons (which you may not have realized) that I resent your 'nagging', especially about penal reform, is that I can't get away from it. I can't take a walk, or go to the pub, or make love or even sleep to forget. It's with me all the time! It all needs changing and I really don't know where to start.

They all agreed that I have to get out and tell the world that we are just normal women, who laugh, cry, feel sexual desire, love, play jokes.

I think the public feels we are stamped with a number, stripped of identity and given a lobotomy. Bye-bye, social problem!

Yuk – I look awful, I have a big red proboscis (like the monkey), my top lip looks like Ali hit it, and my eyes are shrinking from the world! I think I'll hide behind my glasses tomorrow!

I feel very much better, though very tired still. Will see you in half an hour.

I love you! *Sara* x

Darling,

Guess what I found in the wash this morning? A tiny, very drowned mouse! In two and a half years in this house I've not seen a sign of one. Do they come with the washing powder now? 'Daz with added Mouse.' Taking the Mickey, maybe?

A thought about your mother. You're right, she *did* look perfectly normal and feminine holding you as a baby. A very different and alarming impression when she was with you on the ship.

Do you think you could have been unconsciously trying to project, get rid of, externalize, her negative influence on you when you got married (especially to Malcolm)? e.g. you got yourself into an external situation of growing violent pressure which seems to mirror 'her' inner pressure. You half got rid of it, but became trapped because you couldn't 'save' Malcolm from his alcoholism, and then it all rebounded on you? Tell me what you think, please?

My thoughts, heart, feelings, everything are with you, darling, lovely shooting star! Slow down – I'll never catch you. Keep warm.

I love you. Hugs galore. *George* xx

Darling,

I hope you are radiant with creative universal energy. You'd better be!

Scribbling this in a tiny island of space, surrounded by boxes, papers, chairs, etc. Chaos. This letter will be short, but sweet. I love you.

Yes, be tough, re: scrapping Tigger. We'll get someone good.

I love you (and your picture). *George* xx

Hello Prince in Waiting,

Whatever you do – when you get to the castle – don't kiss any frogs, OK?

I've had a good day – finished yet another cushion this morning! Joined the drama class this afternoon – great fun. Played some carols on the piano – the girls sang. Can you imagine how I felt looking up at a sea of faces grouped around the piano? I've never been taken so seriously before as a pianist! I have perfect pitch.

More on my trial and after.

The journey from the court to Risley in a van – several other girls, though I spoke to none. I was in deep misery, every mile taking me further from all that I loved. The officers laughing and joking. Stuck in a traffic jam, they decided to put on their official hats so they could cut up the hard shoulder, at the same time instructing the driver not to go too fast. If we arrived after six o'clock, they got paid full overtime. Everyone was smoking like mad. Getting to Risley, we pile out, and wait in a reception area. Then we are searched (strip and twirl). A bath, then clothes from Deprived Prisoners Association; for me, jeans and polo-neck jumper. Handed a pillowcase with two sheets, a towel, soap and toothbrush, deodorant. Called by an officer, 'Don't sit on my desk, please, Thornton!' Very calmly informed that I am no longer, by law, allowed to hold a gun licence or carry firearms of any sort. Honest! I am given the only personal item I am allowed to keep – a brief letter Luise wrote to me the day before – though another officer queries this. She is overruled. I sit with a plastic plate full of stew. Ugh. The telly is on – some girls know each other – 'Hey Jerry – how are ye?' 'Did you hear about Pauline?', etc. 'Fuckin' judge, gave me eight months.' Sunk in misery, I sip the tea. The telly, high on a shelf, blares out. Yes, out there, so the news says, life goes on! For me it's just ended. The others are aware I've been given 'life', a sort of fear and respect causes them to leave me alone. I'm unusual because having been on bail, they don't know me.

When everyone has been processed, we troop upstairs dragging our pillowcases. Most have wet hair. I'm told I'll probably be put in the hospital. Hope flames briefly, maybe it won't be so bad. We queue at the door to an office. When we go in, 'Thornton, you have been given life – do you understand? Do not talk to anyone else about your crime.' I am then handed a leaflet, and led to the hospital. Hope dies! Behind a barred door, I am led to a bleak, single cell, with one bed, blankets, a commode (no container though), a desk and a chair. At least it is warm! I mechanically start to make the bed, as carefully as ever, hospital corners. My request for Vaseline (my face is very dry from tears) goes unheeded. I'm given Chloral, a bitter liquid, then after reading and re-reading Luise's letter, I climb into bed, silently cursing God and his world and sob myself to sleep! (Writing this makes me cry!) That's enough. Looking back, by the next day, after I'd seen Sister Jill, I had recovered my courage and humour. On the Monday I was kicked out of the art class for being disruptive. By the Wednesday I was kicked out of the hospital.

In the holding cells, I was taken to see Tigger, Barker, A. A. *was* upset. Tigger concerned – Barker didn't seem to give a shit. I said, 'It's OK, I know you did the best you could.' (I really believed that!) When I asked about the possibility of Appeal, Barker said they'd see, but not much chance!

That really is enough! It does hurt, very much. Though one thing I am sure of, Luise has inherited from me my courage, durability and ability to always look on the bright side. Bless her.

A reply to my query from my Great Aunt Rosie. She wrote, 'As you know, you were away for most of your childhood, so I have little first-hand knowledge ... I remember both your parents were extremely strict on inessentials. You started crawling on Gran's carpet, and were shouted at by both of them as if you were doing something terrible – your mother spent hours in the garden with the gardener and his boy. I don't remember any girls coming to play with you.'

I shall feel so much happier when you are closer, at the castle. I really do worry about you on your bicycle, you know. I like the idea of you being physically close too!

I've felt *good* today, I love you very much, seeing you yesterday did wonders for me. We had some lovely pineapple tarts the other day – I want to be *your* tart!

All my love, darling man – keep warm. *Sara* xx

Hello darling,

Stick to your guns and make sure Tigger and Barker QC are well and truly fired! Fired with enthusiasm.

I've been disgusted with the way *all* the media saturated the country with drivel about the Tory election of a leader. For days it was as if the rest of the world didn't exist at all, just these three stuffed monkeys – blind, deaf, dumb.

(Maybe you should change Tigger to Trigger, so you can fire him!)

Pity I can't use the removal van to come to visit you – I could say I'd come to remove a hostage!

You are lovely – All my love, *George* x

．

My Dearest Man,

What do you mean, 'if there's enough love left over, love me'? Don't you yet realize just how much I love you? I miss you terribly.

I talked to a few of the girls today. Their admittance to prison was very similar to mine, including the firearm warning! I forgot to mention that I also saw a doctor, after the bath. He asked me if I was on drugs, alcohol, epileptic. I answered all the questions, 'No!' Then he said, 'You're not going to do anything silly, are you?' My 'no' must have convinced him. It was over in about five minutes.

Do you remember me saying once, 'I'd love to put *them* in the dock!' And you replied, 'Why don't you write a play?' Of course, it's now 'we'!

There are some films of us in the Pacific. In one sequence, about ten to twelve months old, I was sitting in a shallow sea and fell over backwards. In danger of drowning, and distressed, Mummy grabbed my arm and sat me back up again, like a doll. I was crying yet she didn't comfort me. In fact, was laughing. Billi has a sequence of Mummy chopping up a huge marlin, obviously with relish!

I'm re-reading *The Winthrop Woman* – one line reads, 'His endearment sent a torrent of piercing sweetness through her body.' I know exactly what she means. I felt something similar the first time you wrote, 'Dear Lovely Sara'.

I love you darling, good luck with the move – I wish I was with you. *Sara* x

Hello my Love,

I'm looking forward to descriptions of the castle. And, I will need your telephone number there!

I hope your new 'home' is comfortable and *warm*. I wish I was helping you. Have you found anything whilst packing that you thought you'd lost?

I feel weary, played volleyball this morning, and then jogged over a mile. Felt the rain on my skin. Lovely.

I love you, keep warm my beautiful man. See you soon I hope.
Sara x

More on the trial

One of the most awful parts of the trial, for me anyway, was having to show the scars on my neck, to the jury, judge, and Prosecuting Counsel. I had to lift my hair out of the way. Tigger told me beforehand *not* to stretch my neck; tilting my head slightly made them look worse. I felt like a piece of meat, going from juror to juror as they craned forward to see. I just withdrew inside myself. The whole performance was repeated two days later with the scars on my wrist. A. was almost sure they would drop the charge to manslaughter.

Halfway through the trial, we had to move to a bigger courtroom. The public gallery was full to overflowing with curious outsiders and Atherstonians who had come to watch my destruction. That is no exaggeration. Not one Atherstonian said hello to me, even W. who I worked for, didn't look at me. I was already condemned.

One moving moment, when I took off all my jewellery, necklace, watch, bracelets, ankle chain, earrings, rings. I gave them to Billi. She cried. They might as well have tied my hair up and led me to the block.

Sara x

Changing Lawyers

Sara's change of defence lawyers was neither easy nor usual. The law in England is a foreign language to most of its citizens. Often literally so. The word TORT is French for WRONG, but lawyers prefer to refer to the 'law of tort'. No wonder most defendants drown in the jargon, often regarding their own defence counsel as beings from another world, many patronizing, most remote.

Even someone as intelligent as Sara played little part in her original trial at Birmingham Crown Court. Obtaining permission to change her defence team, from the Registrar of the Criminal Court of Appeal, was a legal obstacle course. She reached the winning post. Few even try. Fewer still get that far.

Letters

December 1990 – March 1991

December

Darling,

I've had a good weekend, thought about you very much. If they do offer bail, you'll have to stand and be responsible for me. I must not get my hopes up! But wouldn't it be marvellous?

Did my score card and spoof on poor Sean – after his sermon and prayer, I said, 'Can I have the marks for technical merit?' We all held up cards with '10' printed on. 'Now can I have the marks for artistic expression please?' Very funny, Jo called me 'a star'. Wrong, Sean was the star! I hope the church doesn't strip him of his zeal and fervour.

I like your idea of thinking of memories that act as triggers. In truth, George, I have few memories of my childhood – just a vague feeling of bleak unhappiness and constant fear. However, one incident did act as a trigger. We had my friend Jackie to stay for a month. This was in Fiji. Her mother, Maggie, who had matching orange lipstick and fingernails, was going to England for her divorce. The time that Jackie stayed with us was bliss. So much so that when Maggie came back from England and came to get Jackie, I went outside and tried to ram a large nail in the tyre of Maggie's car. Stupidly I thought a puncture would mean Jackie would stay just one more night. I gave up quickly, they lived within walking distance. I was just desperate for more peace. I felt, and was right in feeling, that the tirade would double in intensity in Jackie's absence. It did. My mother started the next day. She scolded me so severely, so unjustly, so loudly that I fainted. Just keeled over! It seems so petty as I write it, I can't seem to convey the sick fear, the disgust as her spittle hit my face, the way she clenched her teeth, and the dull certainty that she was right. After all she was Mummy, I was only a stupid, ignorant, lying, cheating child. Enough! How can we convey constant insidious, demoralizing treatment? If I was out on bail, I could remember all this and have the comfort of you and your arms to protect me from the nightmare. Oh Love, I adore you.

I'm going to play a little guitar to toughen up the fingers. I can play *Isa Lei*, the Fijian national anthem, and sing (mock) it all in Fijian. Some things you never forget.

All my love. *Sara* xx

Darling,

You will have guessed, I think and hope, how much I want to hug you after my fit of anger yesterday. It's just part of our long never-ending conversation, by letter and word and thought and feeling. I *was* angry because I felt you were being a bit careless with the urgent solicitor/lawyer problem. But I was also in agony (back) and tired. So I must have sounded like a bear (boar?) with a sore back. Sorry.

You can tell the Registrar you insist on a new team because you have no confidence in the old one. Be firm, be polite! I thought the R.'s letter you showed me was very patronizing and indifferent to your choice. These people are not used to dealing with prisoners with a mind of their own. Make him listen!

Love you. *George* xx

Sweet Prince,

You're angry – I love you, go on dish it out – I can take it! I know you love me too.

I cannot, in all honesty, envisage having my Appeal heard in January, darling. You must accept this. That's why I was so angry with K.J. Banking on her has helped cause this delay. I wrote to the Appeal Court that I needed time to find counsel I could trust. I don't want to rush this thing. I want a good psychiatrist to testify to the effects of constant abuse, I want to do it right. The rest of our lives depends on it!

A lovely letter from Luise, absolutely smothered in hearts and know it's a desperate attempt to tell me just how much she loves me. It's no use kidding myself, she's going to feel this separation at Christmas just as I will. I'd give anything to hold her.

How to show my stubbornness and disregard for authority. When I was in admin., DTP printed 500 video inserts for Mr Mogg – £70.

When he came in to get them I refused to let him take them. Rules, made by him, all goods *must* be paid for before being issued with a gate pass. I stood up to him, and told him that like everyone else he could bring his cheque book. Later, he sneaked in whilst I was in gym. He asked a teacher if he could take his order. She read the attached note and said, 'Sara says you can't have them till you've paid for them.'

'But I'm the Governor!' he shouted. No way. He was cross with me afterwards, but that incident gave many of the girls confidence. On another occasion I wrote him a letter saying that if he didn't pay his bill, I would instruct the staff not to serve him.

Just go to London and find me a good barrister. I have every confidence in your choice. I love you dearly.

Miss you every day, *Sara* xx

Later, 11.30 p.m.
More about my trial & A-levels.

Can you imagine it? After lunch break, court is sworn in, and I walk again to the stand. I'm reminded that I'm under oath, but before the prosecutor can resume his questions, which have gone far beyond my childhood – there's no chance that he can or will go back to the A-levels. I knew this, but felt that I must, as I've sworn to tell the truth. So, I calmly say, 'Excuse me, I must apologize but I lied about having A-levels!' Silence. The judge looked at me. 'I'm sorry, I didn't hear that?' 'I said, I'm sorry but I lied about my A-levels.' The judge, in disbelief, repeats this to the jury. I'm burning with shame, but resolute in my determination to tell the truth. The prosecutor jumps on this 'lie', asks me why I lied, and I explain. Billi was outside the courtroom. She told me afterwards that the prosecutor came out, threw his wig into the air, and said, 'Wow – I don't believe she said that!' Billi groaned inwardly and thought, 'Oh God, what has she said?' Buchanan later said if he had had time to have lunch he would have spewed it up there and then on the bench! He told me, 'I've never, ever had a defendant or witness admit to a lie like that. Rule one, if you are lying don't admit it!' Unfortunately, no one told me their perverse rules!

Darling Sara,

Guess what music is on the radio? Wrong! Sibelius's Fifth Symphony – we'll hear it in Finland. I've just been for a walk around the grounds and the woods – met a man with his dog. Very interesting. He lives locally and wanted to buy the place once, but the development costs were too high. Last summer (1990) his daughter in London got married and asked if they could have the reception in the Great Hall. They did and had huge log fires and a Glenn Miller-type band. Still want to marry, darling? Just imagine a real binge here.

The central courtyard is ideal for a medieval fair, with acrobats (you) and jugglers and Fools . . .

I've just released a butterfly that was scrabbling at the window – God knows how it got in. I took it downstairs and it flew up into the sunshine – a mid-winter butterfly. Hope it gets to North Africa!

Great to get your first letters to the castle!

Your sharp wits are going rusty, darling! 'Baby hugger' refers to you hugging Luise in the photo.

I love your letters, sweetheart. Whenever you don't understand why I've written something just think of the most obvious interpretation. If it still seems nonsense, it probably is!

Sing the Fiji national anthem for me on Thursday! You'll have to wear a grass skirt too, or am I confusing it with Hawaii? I'm conjuring up visions of you coming here on bail! It's a snug room with a coal fire. I'd keep you safe in a real castle – you'd never escape.

Surely they'd accept my 'surety' with this address. 'Yes, my Lord, I'll make sure she's kept in the Keep.'

See you soon. Lots of love, *George* xxxxxxx

Darling, I love your hair fluffed up!

Please don't be fed up or downcast because I'm not using the VO on Thursday. It's not at all, you must know, because I don't want to see you. Only that I'll have two VOs at most this month and I want to space them out with the other visits.

I love you more than ever – the possibility of you getting bail is a marvellous dream. But I know enough about this crazy system not to overbalance.

I've been thinking about your A-level confession in court! Why do you think it was so important to say it then, I wonder? Is it possible you were so hurt deep down by your mother's disbelief in you that redeeming a lie became a very important atonement, whatever the cost? You know now, I think, that 'truth' is very seldom a simple statement of fact. The most important truths are much more poetic than factual, needing a complex blend of accurate information, imagination, choice of words, and *awareness* of the person(s) on the receiving end. For me, poetry is the highest form of truth. The idea of 'whole truth' in a court is laughable – they can hardly absorb a tiny percentage of real truth in such a wooden setting.

My feeling re: Appeal, as you know, is that your defence was mis-handled. That is a major part of your accusation of injustice.

I hope you and I will build on this unusual inside experience and learn how to change the whole lousy system. There is a long, long way to go. Stay with me, and I'll stay with you. Don't ever let go of your fighting spirit.

All my love, *George* xxxx

Hello Love of my life!

I wasn't happy Wednesday. I promise I love you. Just that I wanted a bit of physical contact (7th heaven).

I received this letter (Registrar) today. As it was addressed to the Gov., there was a delay! Need I say that I am absolutely furious!!!!! I have replied stating the following:

1 He deliberately fails to understand I want to choose my own Counsel, i.e. barrister and QC.

2 Unless they are of *my* choice I see the Appeal and *his* part in it as a conspiracy to defraud me of a basic and real right of Appeal.

3 Asked once again how much I can bring in on Appeal. Pointed out *he* is acting as my solicitor.

4 That I find it frightening that he refuses to treat me with due respect, etc., and is making my Appeal hard!

5 That my appeal for bail still stands.

6 That he direct *my* correspondence to *me*.

7 That he spell my name right.

Let him put that lot in his pipe and smoke it.

After receiving that, I ranted, raved and then had guitar class. Having to settle down and play made me realize how petty this silly man is. I'll bet the Registrar treated that letter in the same offhand way he treated my other letters and requests. Thank God you are in London next week. How dare this man, whilst being paid to act in my best interests, treat me so badly! If K.J. is still willing to act for me, let's have her. There can't be a rule saying you can't change barristers or she would not have offered to help me. See if you can get in to see the Registrar.

I'm firing off all these angry, *polite* missives and I don't have a stamp to my name!

I was thinking about Luise today; did I tell you that in Coventry on bail, I heard her crying in bed? I went in, and hugging her I asked what was wrong. 'I don't want you to go to prison!' she sobbed again to me. I cried too, but we discussed it some, she knew there was a very good chance I would have to and we discussed our future with Billi, how brave we were going to be. Then she said, 'Averil [prob. officer] says that some children can go to prison with their mother.' 'Yes darling, but only babies, you're too old!' 'Maybe if I did something really bad they would send me to prison, then I could be with you?' 'Really bad? Like what?' I asked. 'Well, I could kill the Queen Mother!' she responded in all innocence. I cry just remembering that. I didn't answer her, just hugged and hugged her. She knew that I knew how much she loved me, and how loyal she was. I would like to write or put forward how she felt about losing me to the penal system.

This time whilst you are away, I am *not* going to get depressed. I felt your absence the last time you went to London – stupid as it sounds, I shall think positively of all the good things you will do whilst you are there.

Had a couple of pubescent priests in the workroom today. There's nowt like a trainee cleric for a good wind-up. I smile as they move in, show them what I'm doing then say in all seriousness, 'Tell me, how do you see Christ's teachings being used in the penal service? Where is the forgiveness? Have you seen any love?' They are never able to reply. These two were escorted by a nun – she was waiting on the wing. As I passed her I said, 'You'll wait a while for your lads, they are at the end of the queue hoping for a body search!' She rushed to find them. New visitors. Old wind-up. Never fails, though and we always laugh!

All my love. *Sara* xx

Darling,

Do you realize, my love, that we are approaching a landmark in our love? Sometime around Christmas you and I will have been together, physically together in the same room for one whole day and night – twenty-four hours. Isn't that amazing? Not many people can cram as much into twenty-four hours as we have done! 'One day, between August and Christmas, 1990 . . .'

I read somewhere recently that one of many hundreds of causes of depression is not expressing anger or criticism for fear of losing a friend or lover. So don't ever take that risk, sweetheart. Make sure you're angry if you feel it. I can take it, just as you can and do – real love puts anger (and everything else) in its place, doesn't it?

Take care of yourself, love, I'll be thinking of you all the time and hugging you . . . I'll come as soon as I can.

Love you, *George* xxxx

Darling,

By the time you get this, darling, I'll have reached London (or got stuck in a snowdrift between here and Durham!).

Even on the inside of this castle courtyard I can hear wind whistling around the windows – the draughts are speeding around huge stair-cases and corridors. It would be possible to hang-glide down the hallway. *Wish* you were here – hurry up with that bail. Ask Father Christmas.

Later

Snow in the courtyard – looks quite romantic against the turrets and walls. Maybe the train will get stuck at Nuneaton? Our lives are so symmetrical at present, it wouldn't surprise me.

I hope you were snug and dreaming happily. Keep close in spirit, dearest love. *George* xxx

Darling,

What a strange day yesterday was. Elemental, magnificent, old-fashioned! Human 'toys' were tossed aside by nature. Bus struggled through snow to Durham – electricity had gone off in this castle during the night, so breakfast in a cold gloom. The castle looked forbidding, a dark chunk of medieval fantasy stuck in brilliant white snow, with the wind howling. We don't have draughts here, they are winds! Luckily I have a lot of candles. Then at the station, chaos. All trains delayed, then cancelled. Got back here in a howling gale – still no lights.

The afternoon and evening here were pleasantly ghostly – white courtyard, whistling winds, coal fire, candles, no music, no TV, no reading, just sitting contemplating and watching the fire. A forgotten art. Wish you'd been here – we'd have loved it.

And today totally different. The lights came on with a flash last night – what an aggressive energy! The winds vanished. The sun shone.

That letter from the Registrar is a disgrace. Did you notice he doesn't bother to address you by name? No 'Dear Mrs Thornton'. Bloody cheek of these people.

The fact that there's a church next to this castle is typical of the way religion and power became allies in this country, resulting in a power élite which dresses up its privileges in fancy 'religious' ceremonies. A cosy conspiracy. I wasn't joking when I asked if any of those free-range priests in the prison ever challenge the system of prisons and punishment?

I regard that prison as little better than a torture chamber, designed to inflict pain rather than offer 'respect and humanity'. The minor concessions to 'humanity' only throw into sharper relief the cruelty of the rest of it – lack of privacy is lack of respect, lack of responsible choice is lack of humanity, lack of proper access to green grass, trees, etc. is sensory deprivation (a form of torture), separation from children (when not due to safety) is cruelty, restricted visiting is a violation of basic rights, etc. Insolent lawyers, bored psychologists, time-serving 'guards', fossilized judges, apathetic or vindictive public. It's a truly wretched system and you and I have a golden opportunity for doing something about it. You are unique and so am I. We've made a pretty good start, haven't we?

I hope you've checked the visitors' board and realize I'm coming tomorrow to give you a big hug. I think we both need it.

I love you, *George* xxx

Hello Happy Lover,

It *was* a happy visit, wasn't it? I enjoyed every minute of it, did you? One of the girls in there with us this afternoon said she thought you were lovely. Yes, you are. I felt (feel) very good after our short time together. We seemed to laugh a lot, not easy in here. I still giggle when I think of you saying in your best teacher's voice, 'And what's your excuse this time?' I felt absurdly like a pupil who has once again lapsed on an assignment. Great that I can laugh and not be hurt. I just love you so much, nothing else matters. I felt very relaxed, very easy with you. A glimpse of things to come.

I have high hopes of your week in London – something good will come of it I know. I shall think of you tomorrow at the House of Lords. I am proud of you, darling.

Living day to day with such petty, spineless restrictions is so very stressful, sometimes one feels that these rules are made for the express intention of denying pleasure and causing aggravation. Tolerance, my dearest love, tolerance!

I should write you some more memories but not tonight. The only memory I want to go to sleep with is the memory of you this afternoon. It was so *good* to feel you, hold you and laugh with you – I have to admit that sometimes I am a little in awe of you – perhaps a tiny bit intimidated. I think, 'What can he see in me?' You are so fierce sometimes! I love it, but it needs to be tempered with love. I can hardly wait for all the things we've promised each other, it's such a dream, a wonderful dream, I wonder at my courage in believing it can and will become a wonderful reality. Just to spend ninety minutes on our own is heaven. How will ninety hours be? I shall be drunk on happiness!

I love you, be careful. *Sara* xxxxxx

Mr darling Ambassador,

How is London? I'm missing you! Surprised? I didn't think I would. I said to the girls, I don't miss George – power of positive thinking! I'm not too clever. After supper I caught myself wandering around the wing in a rather aimless fashion, washed my slippers, strummed a bit on the guitar, but my heart wasn't in it. I felt so empty. I thought of what I wanted, not cigarettes, not a drink, not food, a workout? No, then it dawned on me that the empty feeling was because you are away. Anyway, one of the girls took pity on me, took me to her cell and made me a cup of coffee. She could see I was missing you. Can you tell? I'm missing you!

I fell asleep after writing that, slept the night through, great!

I fell asleep with my window open, I could hear a radio playing, it sounded like a night on the sea, my cell as a small cabin.

Don't get overtired darling, can you feel me? I love you very much.
Sara xxxxxx

Darling,

You'll never guess who phoned me this morning – His Master's Voice? Yes, none other than Registrar McKenzie from the Appeal Court!

He was *very* charming, said that he would write to me today, telling me to disregard everything that he has written so far. When I have chosen my barrister I must let him know so that he can grant legal aid. I said I didn't mind if my Appeal was delayed. He said he would leave me till mid-January. I asked about bail, he checked. It is being considered by a single judge. I asked about other evidence, he said, yes (i.e. Malc.'s state of mind), it can be brought in, but best to discuss all that with a barrister of my choice. He pointed out that he has over 8,000 cases to deal with, and he doesn't phone convicted prisoners. I only told one joke, when McKenzie asked, 'You have my address?' I replied without thinking, 'Engraved on my heart, Master McKenzie!' He laughed. I think he would have laughed at anything – he was trying very hard to be very nice. It wasn't till afterwards that I realized the full importance of what had happened. It's never been done before. Once again, I'm breaking new ground. I've been told how honoured and lucky I should consider myself. For what? Being granted what is mine by legal right? Bullshit about honours. Everyone conveniently forgets the tears and pain, etc. McKenzie has made me cry. But I'm smiling now!

I was tired again last night, so lay dreaming of you, then slept very well.

So your discussion is 'on'. Good. Basically, all I could add is that until we are seen in law as women with our reasonable standards, then I don't think that anything else is worth a 'fig'. Look at the struggle I have had with the Appeal Court, just to gain the right to take an active part in my Appeal? If women were treated with honour and respect due to them – then things like the domestic violence problem, would simply follow on.

When are you coming home? I don't want to be famous, just loved. I miss you!

Someone who shall remain nameless (male) said to Mr V. after the phone call, 'Well did he put her in her place?' 'No,' replied Mr V., 'he gave her hope.' It's true, do you really think they'll grant the precedent of bail? Dare I believe it? I told Master that I didn't know any rich people (he laughed).

Must go. I LOVE YOU! *Sara* xxxxx

Darling,

Two letters from you. Thank you, darling. You're lovely – and if you ever feel even a 'tiny bit' intimidated by me tell me to STOP being intimidating. See? The post must have been held up by the Christmas avalanche – too much snow, not enough reindeers.

I mentioned in my card the visit to the Registrar's office in London – a Dickensian odysscy. You must have packed a punch in your letter – the staff lawyer, Gibson, said the last six lines (he'd *counted* them!) were hard to take, or words to that effect. Good for you! It obviously galvanized Master McKenzie. I'd love to have your version of the phone conversation with him. I told G. quite a lot about the problems re: your defence. At least they now know how real both of us are – not cyphers in files. The Royal Courts of Justice are like the labyrinth in the story of Theseus and Ariadne and the Minotaur. Endless, endless, badly marked corridors, designed in a mish-mash of Victorian ecclesiastical/prison architecture – fairly shabby. About 10 yards of one corridor were decorated with streamers and balloons!

It's very important, I think, that the judges at Appeal know why you changed lawyers, as simply as possible. They will take note of it because it is so unusual to switch. Might wake them up. It's shocking how unused these people are to human beings having a mind of their own.

No fuss, no change! It's a question of choosing which battles are worth fighting, isn't it? I just hate the dehumanizing effect of tying people up in absurd rules. Kafka knew all about that. Have you read his *Trial*? The accused is never told exactly why he is being arrested or tried.

Take care, darling. I love you, *George* xxx

Darling,

I've just been to see the Sister to ask if pissing on my fingers will toughen them up. 'What on earth do you want to piss on your fingers for, Sara?' 'The guitar is killing them!' She's very interested in my phone call from Master McKenzie, very intrigued. Because Mr V. listened in to it, everyone is suddenly aware that bail is being considered. Up to now, I've treated the whole thing as a huge joke – when an officer walks in to the workroom I'll say, 'Have you come to tell me I've been given bail?' Very funny – they think I've cracked. Suddenly no one is laughing any more. Oh what a boost it would give the girls, George, especially the ones who say, 'You can't beat the system.' If only I could show them you can, that to fight may mean pain, anger and tears, but can be worthwhile. Just for that reason alone, I want bail! Of course I'm not entirely altruistic, there's a certain man I love very much that I'd like to see a whole lot more of in every sense of the word. I once wrote to Tracey, it's not hate that will get me out of prison, but love, and I'm right, aren't I?

I keep telling the girls, 'Relax, it's our carol service, let's enjoy it.' They keep saying, 'Be good, Sara – please – no Les Dawson!' Yesterday in drama I was playing piano, and as they earnestly sang carols, I slipped into the Les Dawson mode. Have you heard him do it? He plays it just wrong, very solemnly, it had them in stitches. I slipped into a jazz rhythm for 'Away in a Manger' and creased as they tried to catch on and catch up. I know I'm an untrustworthy sod, I just love their discomfiture – they take themselves so seriously.

You mentioned seeing a 'Rottweiler'. I saw the same one, same day, asked me for your address, so I said, Brancepeth Castle. Is that all? 'Well,' I said, 'you could always put King George on it!'

I'll post this to son Simon's address. Hello Simon – how are you – football freak – yobbo! I suppose the pair of you will go off to the match – do they play in winter? Probably. I can just imagine you in a crowd of shouting, abusive men, going wild when a goal is scored! I can probably say that every time I kicked a ball I scored a direct hit. Usually provoked a pretty wild reaction too.

All my love darling – come back soon. *Sara* xxx

Darling Sara,

Greetings from a cold, grey Norwich! But I'm warm inside. I hope you are, darling. Yesterday was Jason Day – I watched him play in a soccer match and he scored four goals – proud father listening to all the praise.

K.O'D. was at the discussion at LSE, in a very strange mood, mostly aimed at me! I was feeling quite cheerful and enjoyed meeting the people there. I did my best to be His Mistress's Voice! I read a bit of your letter about Master M. out loud – they were all very interested. I spoke to Andrew Nicol, barrister in K.J.'s chambers – tall, quiet, grey-haired, thoughtful, not at all pompous. I think you'd like him.

There's so much to discuss with you. I want to see you so much, you far-away and very close lover-in-waiting. I hope you're still bubbling after the Master's call – there's nothing you (we) can't do, either. I'm very proud of you, you're lovely, and brave.

Want to see, hug, kiss you. *George* xxx

My Love,

It's 11.30 p.m., a strange time to start writing a letter you'll agree. I've got hiccups, too, so every now and then the file I'm writing on jumps (it's balanced on my tummy).

I still haven't answered your question on the religious problems in the Middle East, have I? I don't understand how or why people can cause war in the name of God! Man, as a race, is so presumptuous! I've often thought this when I've heard people say 'of course there aren't any other beings in the universe'. It boils down to the question of looking inside yourself, doesn't it? When I do, I feel God (or the power of the universe or whatever you want to call it). It's such a *good* strong feeling, that all it prompts me to do is care, help, understand, comfort. No thought of violence or hate.

As far as God and presuming goes, it's so easy to fall into a self-righteous religious zeal! Remember when I nicked the Catholics? Well, one stopped coming and, angry, I was going to tackle her. Then I stopped to think, and realized that her happiness was not the root of my concern, but that I felt her defection reflected my ability to make her love my God. Very wrong, very dangerous. I leave them all now, to worship or not to worship as *they* feel they want to. A minor example, but I inflated *my* desires and gave them the label of God's desire. Yuk!

On that note your sage (and onion) will go to sleep! Good night darling man, just keep on being a living example of *all* that I love in a person.

Sara xxx

Sunday

Bad, bad day. Learnt in church this morning that one of the officers died last night. She was one of my favourites, everybody's favourite – divorced mother, two children; very sudden. I shan't go into any detail except to say it's strange. She was on duty yesterday. I linked arms with her and asked if she would censor and distribute the late mail. She replied that everybody was cuddling her today. Later I told her how pretty she looked with her hair cut. I meant it. She used to bring CDs in for me, I'll never hear *Rhythm of the Saints* without thinking of her. I cried so much someone suggested I go to see a Sister, but I replied it was my grief, and I needed to let it out, not stop it up with sedatives. We are scared of open emotion in H-wing, aren't we? I'm very, very sad. Engulfed by thoughts of her family, her children, her last hours. At first we thought Mr W. had died, he had his second very severe heart attack on Friday. However, he is off the critical list. Mr Hicks says it will be a long time before he's at work again. Then, at church, during prayers, it came out that 'she' had died. I just burst into tears, as did others. Some knew, some didn't. Awful rumours are flying around. It's terrible. We desperately need something *good* to happen to lift us.

Oh what deep sadness.

I've spent much of the day helping one of my favourite girls. Her trial was a farce. Would you believe (you know you would) that her solicitor (a woman) went off to Spain on holiday in the middle of the trial? Then her barrister left on holiday the day before she was sentenced. Constant requests for an Appeal to her solicitor, even a phone call from here, have been ignored. She was given Appeal forms, and we decided today to sack the solicitor and ask for (a) extended time to lodge the Appeal and (b) Appeal grounds ourselves. So I've been sitting on her bed with *Criminal Procedure* in one hand, pen in the other. We are going to send it directly to . . . yes, you've guessed it, Master McKenzie, soon to be H-wing's Personal Registrar. She's got life and nothing to lose. I cannot tell you any details.

I can tell you that she has been through hell and that fighting her own fight is the best tonic. She'll sleep tonight. Suggested I train to be a solicitor. I hate the fuckers. Who wants to be one of them?

What, as a matter of interest, were you doing at five o'clock this afternoon? I dozed and had a lovely dream.

I'm awfully anxious about you, please take care of yourself at least till I'm out and can take care of you. I don't know why I should feel you need anyone, you've done pretty well on your own. Just part of loving you so much! I want to wrap you in layers of love, care, protection, so nothing and no one can harm you.

I figured out how we could marry. We could 'pledge our troth' in front of our friends and have a wonderful reception outside.

Hells Angels do it! Broom Broom! I love you, *Sara* xxx

Darling,

What a luxury. I'm seeing you tomorrow and have till tonight to write to you.

It's been a hectic week since you've gone, I've been bubbling and happy tonight. Are you in London? Just before my last visit with you, Mr W. called me into his office. He asked about you. I said you were my legal adviser. He looked me up and down, very slowly, very insolently, then with a lifted eyebrow sneered, 'among other things'. I resolved to get rid of him and discussed it with Tracey, S., etc. His problem is that he only likes women if they are totally helpless. I felt he definitely didn't like me. Anyway the next morning we were told he had had a very severe heart attack and was not expected to live. I wasn't unduly concerned, I save my worry for those that matter – hard bitch, aren't I? I wouldn't sign the 'get-well' card either – this was Friday, I think. Sunday morning just before church we were told (whispered) that he had died. Nobody was too bothered.

Then as I told you in my last letter we heard that Mrs Williams had died. She was lovely and had been on duty the night before. It's since been revealed that she committed suicide.

They are saying the funeral will be on Christmas Eve. Awful. Miss C. is close to a breakdown. What can I write about Mrs W.? If she was on duty, the atmosphere was good; if there was a late post, she'd do it because she knew how important it was. The only officer to ever come to church. I had a long talk with her once – about domestic violence. Even though the courts awarded alimony, her husband never paid it, and nobody made him. To say I loved her would be too sweeping. I liked her very much. More importantly – as an officer she was a unique source of comfort and support.

Love you, *Sara* xx

Darling,

Lovely to see you, touch you, after what seemed like weeks away! So much has been happening – it's good that the graph of self-confidence in H-wing seems to be rising. Maybe people are afraid to feel important in case they are expected to do something important. So they behave like I did sometimes at school when I didn't want to be noticed, at the back of the class!

Mrs W.'s suicide is very sad. It's hard not to see it linked to other things there, such as the destructive/aggressive/negative bullying tactics of the 'Rottweilers'. For a person already suffering great inner stress and sorrow, such an environment will seem very demoralizing. We are on the brink of the collapse of this lousy system and the birth of a new one.

You need a solicitor to brief the barrister re problems arising from the trial, or does the Registrar think a barrister can get the info. from him?

I really love that photo of Luise – she's beautiful, and the story about offering to kill the Queen Mother to join you brought tears to my eyes, too.

You and I generate a lot of energy between us and it fascinates and disturbs a lot of people. 1 + 1 = 3! We have to be careful to use it well, don't we?

Does news of Russia penetrate the bleak stone walls? It's getting pretty bad. The whole USSR seems to be falling apart, which is very healthy, but all sorts of neo-fascists are waiting like hyenas to capitalize on the chaos. A rerun of the 1920s in eastern Europe, maybe, with hard-line bigots grabbing power? European civilization seems like a husk, without soul or purpose. Like your priests when asked about the system. All their energy goes on trivia and sentimentality – no substance.

I'm beginning to think that a powerful motivation for the official resistance to effective therapy may be an unconscious fear that happier, more stable, creative prisoners would show up less happy, less stable, less creative officials.

Please don't be too flattered by a 'nice' Registrar! I've seen judges at work and they can often flatter women to make the system work more smoothly. Believe in actions not promises.

I LOVE YOU, *George* xx

Darling Most Beloved Man,

This is your Christmas letter, I guess.

There isn't anything of a material nature that I could give you to show you how much I love you. One of my most treasured possessions is the photo – you have that already – along with my heart and all the loyalty and devotion that it signifies. I want to give you the rest of my life, when it's once again mine to give. Meanwhile, you know you have my constant thoughts, you figure in all my dreams, and I love you more than I've ever loved anyone, and with a joy I never thought possible.

One of my dreams these last few days has been to spend Christmas with you. Alas it seems it is not to be. I knew that was an extremely unlikely possibility, yet a part of me, the part that constantly yearns, and sometimes aches to be with you, would not always be stilled. Sometimes I'll think of what you are doing, trying to visualize you, and I am gripped by a terrible feeling of being apart from you – it's very hard to describe, I want to shout, 'let me go, I don't belong here.' It's not that being in prison is wrong, but being with you is *right*. I've started to block off my love for you, like I do for Luise, because the act of loving you hurts so much. It's no less, it's very strong, very deep – but it makes me long for you and I cannot function so full of longing. At lock-in I just think of you, sometimes for hours, and at weekends too. I imagine walking with you, eating a meal, lots of things. I carry on conversations with you. We have a secret life here in my cell. You are so much a part of me, that even on the days I didn't get a letter, I cared nothing, you are constant now, I have utter faith in you, your love, everything. I suppose that in a way is a gift, I trust you implicitly.

I wrote to Simon last night.

I lay on my bed, and stared at the card. I love it, because it's the first card with 'George and Sara' on it. That it should be from your eldest son makes it doubly precious. Suddenly even though I only had one sheet of paper left, I knew I had to write to him, so I did!

Our resident hypochondriac, S., has had everything.

At coffee break Tracey and P. were complaining of stiff necks. 'Probably bubonic plague – it starts with a stiff neck,' I said. 'Don't be silly, no one gets bubonic plague any more,' said H. 'Ask S.,' I retorted, 'bet she's had it.' Again a terrific silence – I expected an attack. She just blushed and laughed nervously.

Tomorrow, darling, you will see a visit with children involved. There may be tears as they are forced to leave. Such pain must be witnessed to be recognized.

I got your letter from Norwich today – I've just read it again – your letter really does caress my spirit, it's lovely. I'm glad you're proud of me, I'm proud of me (though sometimes I'm awfully ashamed too).

You should be proud of yourself now you have set new standards for me, I do and write and say things now that I would never have done before you.

You are a wonderful, nice, beautiful man and I love you dearly.

On Christmas Day, I shall think of you – at 7.30 a.m. I shall make tea or coffee and sit and silently wish you a Happy Christmas. I'll be in church at 10 a.m. – I told Mic the Vic to bring the wine – we need it!

A funny story. E. took all Father Algy's communion wine one Sunday and kept it in a Lucozade bottle. He *knew* it was her and waited a week for her to ask for forgiveness at confession! She never did. The situation became more and more tense as time went on, with Algy becoming angry and impatient, and she more stubborn.

Imagine me holding you, darling, I will one day, and I'll never want to let you go. *All* my love, dearest man – I love you.

I love you, *Sara* xxxxx

Darling Love,

All I want is to hold you and exchange love and warmth.

It's appropriate, somehow, that Christmas week will be the first week when we haven't seen each other. Appropriate because it shows up the barbarian nature of these prisons.

Your letter was *lovely*, very heart-warming and full of love and hope and commitment – I do adore you, you know. Deb Coles refers to us as 'two very strong individuals' – I hope she's right! I think so. There's hardly a person I talk to who isn't soon aware of you and me and the strength of my feelings for you. I have to smile at the way you responded to my burst of hurt anger yesterday – you said something like, 'well, piss off, then,' and I replied, 'I will in a minute,' – but both of us said it with so little conviction. I'd have been devastated if you had meant it. You're a fierce little vixen when you feel like it. When are you going to start behaving like a lady? I'll have to ask your father to send you to a finishing school!

The delay in the Appeal is a curse, because clearly there is a possibility of failure, which means a proper public campaign to free you will have been delayed for nothing. But this can't be helped.

I think we agree, basically, re: the religious issue. We don't know why we are alive, but we do know that we are alive, so being fully alive is a first commandment. That includes everyone. My horror of 'God' is basically that as an all-powerful, all-knowing concept, it allows a human being to claim infallibility when convenient, and also irresponsibility.

Do you realize, my best beloved, that our task is to help reform, from top to bottom, the whole damned 'justice' system? There are a lot of young people wanting to help. One of our problems is that almost all the people we are dealing with are functioning on about one-tenth of our energy! That's why it's so frustrating.

Later

Just watched *Elvira Madigan* – maybe you saw it too? Beautiful romantic young-love (doomed) story in Denmark, all summer sunshine and flowing blond hair and Mozart's music. They had a tiff and he wrote 'FORGIVE ME' on the back of an envelope and floated it down the river to her. Remind me. Awful if the ink smudged and she couldn't read it!

Your Christmas letter is lovely, the best present possible. Can you feel the kisses?

Funny that you wrote that I hadn't criticized you for nearly a month. You must have sensed you were stirring a whirlwind. Maybe you secretly like a good row occasionally? I have a new name for you, Mischief (Miss Chief) – it's true isn't it, you do like stirring things up sometimes? So do I, so watch it!

I walked across the courtyard just now. It's dark, with stars, and the castellated battlements were etched black against the sky. I felt I was in a filmset. Very strange place, but not at all spooky. Has a good atmosphere. I need you here – you are afloat in my love, darling, always. FORGIVE ME!

I love you. *George* xxxx

Darling,

I think there's one thing I've learned about you and me – we'll get nowhere by being 'normal'. We have to be different, new, disturbing, to get anywhere.

The more I think of it, the more strongly I feel you should try the unusual way of approaching Nicol direct, quoting the Registrar as your authority. If that works then you'll use the Reg. to get all the documents for Nicol. That way you'll make more impression on him – don't please be too inflated by his phone chat, but build on it, make him work!

Even that may not work. I think you should keep at the back of your mind the idea of conducting your own Appeal if these options are no good, don't you agree? Just in case. We could work out a very good Appeal 'speech' and if the Appeal is rejected it would be used as a major point of a campaign to release you. It would spell out the 'defence' blunder, the violence and stress you suffered, the rigidity and male bias of the court and law, etc., and relate it all to justice for you and others. Tell me what you feel, please.

Treat that place, not as 'home', but as a degree course in madness, injustice and human (and inhuman) relations. You've done brilliantly so far.

It's good being in a near-empty castle. I play music *fortissimo*.

Not the first, but the best, and the last, and the most adorable, you are lovely.

I love you. *George*

Christmas Day! Darling Beloved!

What can I say about today? Very low key – most of us tried to forget it was Christmas Day. The officers have coped well, especially when you consider that they only buried Mrs W. yesterday. Lunch was better than average – reincarnated turkey *à la* Bernard Matthews, which I donated, Brussels sprouts, which I hate, but the stuffing along with the roast potatoes was fine! This evening I ate five mince pies – love them. Watched *Top of the Pops* at 1.30 p.m., we went a little mad and danced around the TV room, whooping and clapping.

Carol service this morning. Mogg made it, gave all the girls a kiss. I couldn't refuse, but froze.

I know I said I would think of you at 7.30 a.m. – I did – and for most of the day too. I hope you were OK, darling – I wish you had spent the time with others at least one of us should be happy. I love you so much.

Sara xxx

Darling Powaqqatsi!

Powaqqatsi is the perfect word for us. It's a Hopi Indian word; POWA = sorcerer and QATSI = life. It means the consuming of life all around to produce more, new life.

Re the solicitor problem, I've just checked the Registrar's letter to you – he asks you to notify him of the new Counsel and 'upon receipt of that information I will forward all necessary papers in your case to that barrister'. No mention of any solicitors.

Walking a tightrope in a fog is tough for both of us, but if we concentrate we'll do it [the girl in *Elvira Madigan* was a tightrope walker].

Next Christmas? I want to have all the time Luise can spare in your arms. Luxury. I'll give you all my love and energy and brains till you're free, and then I'll do the same again, till I become a spirit and can live in you for ever.

Later

Simon delighted to get your letter. How many more are going to hang on Sara's every word? Said you sounded 'surprisingly upbeat' so I told him you really enjoyed your holiday in there. No, I didn't – I do love you!

We are trying to prove that fully qualified lawyers at your trial did not know what they were doing. I'm sure we are right, but the legal establishment is on their side, not ours. Their instinct must be to protect their own.

Take care – they can keep us apart for a while, physically, but we're together, gymnast!

I LOVE YOU. *George* xx

Darling,

Our Carol Service. Everything went great until 'Silent Night'. This was S.'s solo, with me just quietly strumming in the background. She completely dried up – so I took over the melody while the choir and congregation looked on, wondering when they could start singing. I kept playing and said loudly to Mic the Vic (master of ceremonies), 'you lot will have to come in second time round, OK?' I played a whole verse and started again. There was laughter, a little light relief – but I was haunted by the sorrow and pain on Miss G.'s face. I couldn't cry – everybody was watching me.

The girls left first for H-wing. Mr V. said, 'Sara – you did good!' I was the last inmate to leave, the congregation still in their seats.

Then outside the church, three guards and a panting Alsatian dog stood watching as the thirty most dangerous women in Britain went back to the security of H-wing. I felt quite overcome with it all.

Oh George – there is a fighting spirit in me now – how long has it taken me? Seven months? I can't leave now – they need me! Suddenly all these horror stories about solicitors and barristers are coming to light. And the girls are speaking out.

I want to just curl up and be loved and cuddled while you tell me everything you did in London.

LOVE YOU DARLING, *Sara*

Later – 3 a.m. in fact

Do you feel as I do, that we took an almighty step backwards in our relationship today? I'm bereft, I'm mourning the loss of you, for that's what I feel. It's all a sham, you don't trust me – you might as well have called me a liar today, you certainly insinuated this. You made me feel as worthless as all those hypocritical judges and lawyers out there. I don't feel angry, just deeply sad. I'm glad that there is no post the next few days, I don't want any letters from you. I'd be too scared to read them anyway. I'm not in the best frame of mind to make any decisions, let's just leave it for a while, I'm beginning to wonder if love is really worth all the hurt, I wish I could take a magic pill and never wake up.

It's not your anger that has upset me, it's your hurt. You looked terribly upset today, I don't want to hurt anyone, especially not you – I once wrote to you that if I saw all this really getting to you, I'd put a stop to everything. I've caused enough pain, I don't want to cause any more. Reassess the situation please, and tell me what you think.

Sunday evening

I have spent the afternoon falling in love with you all over again, or perhaps more accurately, returning to you.

I've got some smut to read – the blurb reads 'vampirism, necromancy, supernatural mayhem and shrieking bloody terror'! An average day on H-wing!

Love you, darling, *Sara* xxxxxxxxx

Boxing Day

Well, that's guitar play over, just bust the third string – I think it was my lucky rendition of 'Behind the Green Door' – I like that because all the cells have green doors. Just too much for the old guitar I guess!

Tearful phone call with Luise – I asked her to hug a tree for me.

Darling,

Snow beginning to settle on the battlements and turrets and cling to the upper walls and inlets – very pretty.

I only fully realized today just how identified I am with you – I find it hard, if not impossible, to enjoy anything which I know you are denied – food, fruit, drink etc. It's as if, unconsciously, I try to live and feel as you do so as to be closer. I think we are having to explore not only the nature of justice but the nature of love too. Love is so close to vulnerability and our culture is so wedded to security – no security without defence, locking things out, repelling threats.

Society pretends that crime and evil are trapped and isolated – whereas in reality crime and evil are the hallmarks of every living person, impossible to lock up. A prison is a social fantasy or delusion, cast in stone and barbed wire so that 'ordinary people' can walk 'free' and pretend they are healthy and moral without really trying. What do you think, darling Mischief?

If you really want to understand me just listen to Beethoven's music. His last piano sonata is being played on the radio – a breathtaking piece of music, as if someone is dying and floating away like a butterfly, delicate, light, fluttering to another world. Not sad, very profound, natural, full of feeling.

Can't stop smiling. Guess why? Yes, at last the drought is broken. Two letters from you – you're gorgeous, heart-warming, lovely. Consider yourself kissed and hugged.

You're right to accuse me of too little trust. I'm not perfect – very imperfect in fact. But I'm also pretty resilient (like you) and I hope you can see this from letters this week. As I wrote, I loved the way you and I responded to the initial shock of our 'brief encounter' last Sunday [George visited in the morning only]. Not with a flood of self-pity but just a half-hearted 'well, piss off, then . . .' Neither of us really wanted to fight, did we?

All my love, *George* xxx

Darling,

A strange day. A kind of gap in time. Not a black hole but a grey one. No letter from you.

When our love touches it either seems to inspire or disturb. K. is disturbed, as is D., to some extent (not to mention your minders) – younger people seem inspired, fascinated. I didn't tell you before because it sounds pretty silly, but V. wrote after my first visit to London that her group of friends thought of me almost as a 'demigod'! I was quite shocked at first, it's so absurd, but then I thought about it and I think I know why. They heard me talk about you, about the prison, they read your 'extracts'. What they responded to, I think, was not really me being so special in myself, but an adult (to adults) grappling with life and love in three dimensions. When a society loses its grip on reality, it (life) becomes rare and 'god-like' instead of normal and everyday. Like water in a desert.

Lawrence of Arabia on the box – are you watching, Mischief? Good shots of sand, awful bombastic music, nice camels, and some good quotes for you: senior officer to L. – 'I can't work out if you're bloody rude or just half-witted' – 'I have the same problem myself, sir!'; and, 'You're a clown, Lawrence' – 'Well, we can't all be lion-tamers.'

I love you more than ever. You're lovely, funny, brave, witty and too far away.

Here are some Shelley thoughts on love: 'Love withers under constraint; its very essence is liberty; it is compatible neither with obedience, jealousy nor fear; it is most pure, perfect and unlimited, where its voluntaries live in confidence, equality and unreserve.'

All my love, *George* xxx

Listen Darling Clever Clogs,

How did you know which piece of *Julius Caesar* I quoted to Hicks? I just carried on, 'Men at such times are masters of their fate – the fault, dear Brutus, lies not in the stars, but in ourselves that we are underlings!' It's the only bit I remember (apart from Friends, etc.). I could not believe it when I read that today!

Sunday

Church was a disaster. Mic the Vic is away, so Father H. took the service. He's a pixie-like eccentric, with a wispy grey beard and a strange odour. I felt nothing – except disruptive. We sang stale carols. At one point during the Father's brief sermon I asked, 'Why is God Father?' In a fit of pique, I gulped down all the communion wine, then choked on it when I saw Pauline's horrified expression. After the service I said to Father H., 'It was the same as the wine – went down the wrong way.'

I'm too angry to be placated by meaningless rituals. He grabbed my hands, gave me a kiss on the cheek. 'Darling girl,' he cried, 'you've been reading the right book.' I picked him a carnation from the spray of flowers, and stuck it in his robe. He said, 'I'll come and see you during this week and we can have a long talk – see what we can do!'

Lots of kisses, darling – you'll get this letter on 2 January – right? 1991 is in. I love you. Stop talking about funerals, please. We haven't started to live yet. Pray it's this year.

Had fruit salad at supper. I got a huge portion, it's keeping cool on the window-ledge (well, cell!).

I love you very much. Really. Happy New Year, etc., *Sara* xxxx

PS Loved your last three letters, I'm floating face up in love – yours!

Darling,

The end of a year, darling, what a year! So many strange threads, white, black, brilliant, brought us together, out of 'nowhere'. It's odd, isn't it? We have a lot to curse your defence duo about. Yet, but for them we wouldn't even have heard of each other. We'll have to send them a thank-you letter some day. Blessed are the incompetent for they shall bring love where there was desert. Happy New Year, love!

You asked what I feel about carols. I like them. They have a gaiety about them, a freshness, maybe because they were originally dances from southern Europe (many of them). They are child-like, not child-ish, aren't they? Innocent. Like snow that hasn't been trampled.

There's nothing you can't do, Mischief! I have oceans of confidence in you. The walls of Jericho are rocking.

I keep thinking of coming into the visitors' room and touching your curly head while you sat with your back to me – you have a special way of sitting and I love it. Very upright, alert.

As always, my thoughts and love are with you, in great quantities. You are very special.

George xxx

January

Darling,

As you are no doubt aware, we had a break-out on the men's side last night. At 6.50 p.m., we were hastily called to 'our rooms'; the only explanation I was given was: 'we have an emergency'. My first thought was the men rioting, but the grapevine soon told us – that and the spot-lights. We stayed locked up. At 12 midnight some of us called 'Happy New Year' through our tiny windows, a few fireworks lit up the sky and I sang 'Auld Lang Syne'. I drank a toast to you, our love, our future.

Reading through your last few letters again (and again and again), your comments about love. True, deep love does of course expose one to great vulnerability – I felt very vulnerable and afraid at the start of our relationship – even when you said you loved me, I wondered what sort of love – there are different ways, levels. True love can only stem from honesty – maybe that's why it's rare. People just aren't honest with themselves. I look back now and compare the 'love' I had for M. – and I'm appalled and saddened by the lack of honesty in our relationship. If, instead of trying to be the perfect, 'strong' housewife, if I had spoken to M. about my awful insecurities, my awful childhood, the hate I felt for myself, I might have made him accept and exorcize his own private demons. Instead, I probably magnified them. Poor M.

I feel good tonight – very good. I love you so much, as you say – hard (impossible) to put into words. Deeds – yes!

I've pinned your very first card (the cart-horses) to my desk, so I see it when I'm writing – to remind me always that we are a team.

I trust you – you have all of me willingly, joyfully given.

I love you. *Sara* xxxxx

Darling Demiurge,

Even half-gods have 'blue' days, don't they? You sent such waves of lost despondency – rambling on about love, marriage etc. Thank

God I finally achieved the impossible, and got a letter to you on a Monday.

Our absconders are still on the run – I've been singing the Queen hit, 'I Want to Break Free', all day.

'Let's make sure that neither of us has power over the other.' Oh, dear love, whether you like it or not, you have power over me. Loving you so much gives you the power to make me sad, to make me go weak at the knees, a loving letter or phrase brightens my whole day – it's endless, and surely it's natural. I know the power of a letter; why do you think I tried so hard to get a Monday letter to you? I know the power of my anger – because I love you, I am very, very careful – so how can you say we can live without power?

I can't help but see the irony in you being seen as a demigod by the inhabitants of the heart of English civilization – surely it should be the other way around. You really have no idea what a very beautiful, special person you are, have you? 'Beautiful' was the word Tracey used to describe you after meeting you. Believe it! Perhaps V.'s friends are a part of the dawning spiritual awareness! Also, darling, you 'touch' people. Remember what I wrote – 'you unlocked something in me . . .' The ripples of our love are spreading far and wide.

Had a strange dream last night. I dreamt I was being let out at 2 p.m. I went out with an officer, straight to . . . Sainsbury's. I found, in the fruit-juice sections, bags of pure sea water being sold! I thought, 'What a marvellous idea! Haven't things changed in the few months I've been locked away!' I've had quite a few dreams of being 'outside' lately, never used to unless it was 'past'.

I don't dream of you. Why? Maybe because I spend most of my waking hours doing so. Thoughts that are so tender, so poignant, so loving, one's insides momentarily tense in a totally helpless fashion. Oh, I love you!

Love you lots, *Sara* xx

Darling,

Your 'free spirit', Robin, is alive and well (and twice as fat as you) and living in Durham. I locked my bike this morning to the iron railings at the library as usual. I noticed a little fat robin sitting on the railing about three yards away. I stood still and talked to it quietly and it gradually came closer. It hopped down to the ground just ahead of the bike, then went between the wheel to the railing. Then it hopped on to the spokes of the back wheel, right next to me, then on to one of the pedals via the chain. As the pedal began to turn it hopped on to the front wheel, and then back to where it started! I've never had a wild bird come so close – must have been you, darling. I loved it, and you.

Please thank S. and Tracey for their good wishes. Tell them never to give up. Life's disasters teach more than the best universities – in fact H-wing is potentially the best learning source in England!

I'll enclose a copy of some Appeal thoughts for your critical comment.

Awful, the public cover-your-ass caution towards 'power' of a lawyer's mentality. It's a closed-shop mentality wrapped in feudal privilege – they are all tinged with it, though a handful try to soften the effects.

Yes, the break-out was on all the news programmes. One way of solving the overcrowding problems!

I'm glad you've found someone interested in 'therapy'. Keep trying. I'm a bit sceptical about the medical aspect of the word. The problems may be difficult and profound but they are entirely natural, aren't they? Would 'personal development' be a better description?

Christianity has pretended to sell this sort of 'redemption', but the medicine is just coloured water. Maybe our motto should be, 'WE PRACTISE WHAT THEY PREACH'?

You're gorgeous, lovely, adorable and I love you more than ever and wish you were here, entwined in me.

George xxx

Darling,

Before I forget, darling, if possible, please visit me on my birthday. It's a Saturday, and I know how much you hate coming in at the weekend, but I would like to see you on the day. Not too important though. I can't wait!

Spoke to an officer today. She agreed there is a very real need for therapy. There is 'stress counselling' at Frankland prison, Durham, for officers, but not here.

I was appalled to hear a 'psychologist' state that 'murderers are addicted to killing in much the same way that drug addicts are addicted to drugs'. This was on local radio. No distinction about what sort of murderers – psychologists are having a conference – and this is one theme they will discuss. I felt so angry. I don't want to have anything to do with a body of people who are so irresponsible. See if you can find an article about this conference – I'd like to write to them – and tell them what I think.

I'm used to being unpopular in here – as one inmate said the other day, 'Most of the officers would cheerfully cut your throat, Sara!' It's hardly an insult, is it? Gratifying!

I love you – *Sara* xx

Darling,

Our correspondence is a bit like one of those heart machines, with an electronic bleeper on the screen – when it misses a beat the line goes flat, and then it starts again . . . ! Hair-raising life we lead, don't we?

I had coffee in the cathedral cafeteria and visited the gift shop next door. On the way out was a notice on the door: 'Caution – a TV security camera is watching you.' I thought they believed in God?

You are not very relaxed about criticizing me, are you, love of my life? If I take criticism badly tell me so, calmly, with a smile. I'll survive, because I know you love me.

I'm about 400 yards from you – that hurts. I miss you, love you, want you with me, and long for us to be together to start *life*!

George xxx

My Dearest Love,

So much to tell you – uncensored – wonderful. My Appeal date has been set, 22 March. I have not had a bail-application reply.

My weekend will be topsy-turvy. I'm excited, too. Just think, in seventy-seven nights, I could be with you! In every sense, in you, around you, above you, below you, entwined, darling love, entwined!

Love you lots, *Sara* xx

Darling,

Hope you like this picture of my little grey house in the west!

By the way, the cutting I sent today about the anti-Nazi film made about Passau did not refer to my friend there, in case you thought she is the young blond author in the photo. Once, when I was walking with her in the town by the Danube, we met an elderly couple she knew. After we left them she told me they'd once been strong Nazis. I've never really understood why the most beautiful and super-ficially gentle part of Germany (and Austria) produced the worst Nazis.

Stop eating yourself up please, I need you whole! Be warned by this:

> Thus everything includes itself in power,
> Power into will, will into appetite,
> And appetite, a universal wolf,
> So doubly seconded with will and power,
> Must make perforce an universal prey,
> And last eat up himself.
>
> *Troilus & Cressida*, W.S.

Western civilization is addicted to power of every kind – technical, electrical, military, political, economic, cultural – and the tattered rem-nants of religious power. The effect of this power-lust is to wear out and destroy and degrade and pollute. Power fills the vacuum left by absent love, doesn't it? Love requires enormous energy to make it live – take away that energy and all that's left is a fake, a sermon, a 'lesson', a pious boast on the wall, a 'policy', a prison.

Tell me, love, what do you want to do when you're out, home free? (apart from dissolving into each other). Never let the 'outside' be a fantasy, please.

All my love, *George*

Darling,

One *very* important thing – I've been told that I can write a letter to the Appeal Court judges. If true, you could help me, and we could really sock it to them, couldn't we?

My chest is very bad; I think I'm coming down with bronchitis. I sound as if I have a bellows organ instead of lungs. How can we find out if the Appeal is being defended?

I feel like an army general suddenly seeing the enemy for the first time and mobilizing his troops. I guess you think I've been pretty complacent till now – if you could feel my heart (which I wish you could), you'd realize that I'll just survive eleven weeks of this adrenalin. Inspiration is coming.

I felt sick at the sight of Escott-Cox QC [Prosecution Counsel]. He really was horrible – not nice-looking, and he was snide, condescending and sarcastic to me. I must admit, I would not have got life, I feel, if he had been defending me.

Don't for one minute believe that because there is no signature on the letter, they aren't being censored. Every one of our letters is avidly read. Your letter to Mogg was seen by every officer on duty, and then some.

When Mogg wrote to you, cancelling your status as legal adviser, I could see them all smirking when I was given the copy. When I was locked in, I cried, ranted and raved, but as far as they were concerned I was pretty FATALISTIC. No big deal. They were furious when Hicks gave you an extra VO.

For my birthday, I want a lovely uncensored letter, please – something I can hold on to after you have gone.

I adore you – with all of me – see you in one week. *Sara* xxxxxxxxx

My Darling Man!

We've been locked in instead of going to the workroom – I don't know why, maybe a staff meeting. Still, it gives me time to be with you, doesn't it?

Have you ever heard the word 'nonce'? It's a prison slang term, and I only discovered last night that it means a child killer, child abuser, and someone who either kills or wounds an old person. Murder is acceptable if you kill a man or woman who is able to defend themselves. What a weird set of standards.

How can they ever accept their culpability with no love, support, forgiveness or understanding to strengthen them? I feel very strongly that none of us has the moral right to accuse, judge or condemn anyone else. The anger at the 'nonces' is really anger that arises from being housed with these girls, the stigma that rubs off on all of us. I'm caught halfway between – I do understand both sides. It's a very tricky, touchy, explosive situation.

I'm writing a funny song about H-wing – I'll play it on guitar to 'Hello Mother, Hello Father'. Lovely line: 'It seems at last the food's improving; the black bits are no longer moving.'

I love the idea of you carving something for me. No one has ever carved anything for me.

Yes, we do have a patch of grass and shrubs in the exercise yard. The major problem with it is that the men from the Rule 43 [mainly sex offenders] landing use it before us – and they spit everywhere! We can't even sit on the benches, because they have deliberately spat on them! Yuk!

Are my letters still being censored? Voyeurs, aren't they?

Like lawyers, prison officers are parasites on the body of crime – I once read that many firemen are latent pyromaniacs, so what attracts officers? Answers, please, on a postcard to – the Home Office, London. Thank you!

So, just because Shelley decided to marry Mary, you think you might too. No way, José, I want better reasons than that – follow my leader, indeed! I love you so, I just want whatever you feel happy with. OK? I'm still growing and changing – quite fast – the only thing that is constant is my love for you (and Luise).

LITL is *Living in the Light*. Turn it on, idiot! You started all these abbreviations, didn't you? I'm going to have to compile a personal dictionary, and one for the censors, or they'll think we're plotting an escape in code.

Take care!

All my love, darling, *Sara* xxx

Darling,

Beautiful dreamer . . . why don't you try to interpret all these interesting dreams? I like looking at dreams as elusive metaphors, with layers of meaning. Thus, 'going to Sainsbury's' has an obvious meaning (good food) but others, too. Sain – sane; bury. Maybe you're looking for a sane way of burying the past (?). 'Sea water for sale.' Didn't you say you were allergic to swimming pools? Maybe sea water has special value as your favourite element? The sea, in Jungian terms, symbolizes the unconscious – maybe it's a 'change' for you to explore and value your unconscious? A source of creative energy?

Sorry about my despondency blues – I'm suffering from withdrawal symptoms, not seeing you.

Re 'power'; it's a word with many shades of meaning, isn't it? You are using it more as an energy/influence – I was using it more as 'authority over', as in the Shakespeare quote I sent.

Walking around Durham Cathedral the other day just emphasized how Christ's personal inspiration turned to stone. Huge buildings and tiny minds. I feel that personal inspiration should stand or fall on its own personal merits. When you say you feel a 'universal spirit' I'm sure you're right. It's your insights tuning in to life.

Glad you liked the 'Mask of Anarchy'. Shelley was anti-monarchy, pro-republican and against the wealthy's exploitation of the poor, and wanted to write something for 'ordinary' English people. When he heard of the 'Peterloo Massacre' in Manchester he was outraged.

Andrew Nicol just phoned (he really is the only non-pompous lawyer I've met) – he's very apologetic re his other trial commitment BUT suggests another barrister in the same Chambers, who is none other than Edward Fitzgerald, who won a recent case at the European Court re: life prisoners and access to reasons for time to be served, etc. I told you about it. A.N. has already mentioned your case to E.F. and the latter is interested, potentially, to take it on. Good news, I think and hope. Hope you agree? I told A.N. I'd tell you. E.F. will phone me soon (he's recovering from flu) and either he will come up to see you and me, or I will go to London first to see him.

Take care and only eat food please!

Snow all around.

I LOVE YOU, *George* xxxx

Darling Love,

I've just written to the Registrar, asking why Buchanan's name is on the Appeal notification form, why I haven't heard about bail, and about the 2 per cent success rate. I also pointed out that I didn't have the time to instruct a barrister, due to distance and postal restrictions, but that you could, and would he have any objections?

I saw Mic the Vic today. He would be willing and able to join a discussion on therapy, as would Sister A. and two teachers. He cannot contact you (none of them can), as you are close to me – security breach. I'll get them together on the inside, and you get them together on the outside. I've been advised to contact the prison psychologist, who could be very interested. I'll let you know.

Saw Hicks today, I told him I still hadn't been able to instruct a barrister, and that I needed you for my case. He understands, but his hands are tied.

The dock in the Appeal Court does not have bars, but it is high up. I want you near me.

Love you. *Sara* xxx

Darling almost-thirty-something . . . get that hug ready, please, I need it and maybe you do too.

A.N. says Ed is a tough character who will stand up to the wolves in sheep's clothing.

I've so many things to show you . . . and oceans of pure sea-water love to give you, every day your birthday. By the way, all that solicitor bullshit was a con. A.N. never mentioned them once. Mogg was part of the con, with his 'bona fide solicitor' waffle. 'Experts' are never as expert as they make out.

Don't, whatever you do, imagine that you deserve imprisonment – you don't, and it's an insult to Luise and to me! We deserve you out, free, with us, fully alive and in love – please.

All my love and a million hugs. *George* xxx

Hello Darling Lover-in-Waiting,

I've just written to the Home Office, quoting a few recent cases of provocation and probationary sentences, told them I will never accept their judgement of murderers.

Thank you for your invitation to live with you. I have a couple of minor problems to overcome but, as soon as I've done that, I'll hotfoot it to the castle or wherever you're at. It isn't something we have discussed, is it? It seems like an impossible dream, doesn't it? At least it does to me.

My head is too full to interpret dreams and I love the way you do it. I'm just delighted to be having such positive dreams.

I love you, and I can hardly wait till Saturday.

Sara xx

Darling,

I miss you – it's terrible. I feel lost and lonely. A bit like a constant pain, one gets used to it, but it's always there. I slept with all your letters in my arms this afternoon. Cried! Sometimes I just wander around, unable to actually sit down and concentrate on anything. The only release is sleep – and then I don't dream of you!

I have been thinking about Edward Fitzgerald – yes, that is a good change. I feel very comfortable with the thought that he has been to the European Court and I like the idea of him being in the same chamber as K.J. and A.N. I will feel much better when I've talked with him, and he has told me exactly what we can use, and how we will present it.

You are right in what you say about Christ. He sets an impossible standard, doesn't he? I never thought about it – that and the fact that every time one goes to church, you have to think about your 'sins'. I'll bet half these women aren't even aware that their greatest sin is not being 'alive'! Certainly Mic the Vic would never point it out.

We've suddenly got many more male officers on the wing. It seems to work; there is less bitchiness between officers and inmates, but you can imagine the problems, can't you? Thank God I no longer need to measure my value as a human being in terms of my sexuality. Intelligence can be very sexy – I think you are!

Do you know what I want from you for my birthday? A big, long, beautiful birthday kiss, filled with all your love! Think you can manage that?

The Rottweiler is to have a heart transplant. Can't think of a better irony – makes me smile!

When I went to see Hicks yesterday I pointed out a piece by Jean

Paul Sartre – about mankind – and said very firmly, 'Homework'. I haven't had the book back yet.

I love you – see you Saturday. xxxx *Sara*

Darling penfriend,

Ed FitzG. has just phoned (thirty mins) – he sounds OK, friendly, interested, etc. – asks if you can write to the Reg. pronto and ask him to allow Edward Fitzgerald of Doughty Chambers, etc., to represent you at Appeal – then when Reg. gives E.F. the go-ahead he will come up to see you, and me, maybe next week. I gave him a snapshot view of the case and he said, 'It's fiendishly difficult but very interesting.' He doesn't want your hopes to be raised too high – he mentioned a case reported today (I'll give you a copy) of a woman who killed her husband because of his love affair with her twin sister living in the same house. Her plea of provocation was accepted and she's got two years! Yet the provocation was cumulative. He asked if you want a QC as well, and I said you'd had more than your fill of the other one and didn't want someone snooty who would give you a twenty-minute interview and disappear. He understands. You can discuss it with him. I told him it's very important for you to discuss it all fully. He may be very good. Let's see. He did say that he didn't think the judges would like the implication that the B.&B. defence was useless, but he thought he could get past that problem. Neither of us mentioned K.J. – I forgot.

Of course you're crazy if you make bread at midnight! Better bed than bread! I'll only let you do it if you let me listen to cricket reports from Australia in the middle of the night!

Please stay healthy! Going from bronchitis to volleyball sounds a bit daft. Isn't it? Your soul mate needs you in one piece!

It's important that E.F. works out a bridging argument to supplant the plea of diminished responsibility. He must show the Court of Appeal not that your Defence were fools, but that they narrowed down the evidence too drastically and thus lost sight of the larger reality. I think you and I should work out a statement reflecting all this to give to E.F.

Keep sparkling, darling! Make good use of all that adrenalin and inspiration.

See you soon. I love you always. *George* xxxx

Darling Atlas! (the girl who held up the world – the world's biggest hold-up).

The Gulf Crisis is a marvellous example of fascination with surface events and superficial 'solutions'. Almost no effort at all is going into causes. It's amazing, isn't it, how reluctant human beings are to acknowledge how soft and fragile we are? For ever acting tough and hiding behind steel and bullets and bombs and missiles and helmets and slogans and war cries. Most sickening of all is the way the old and safe propel the young and stupid into the front line. Young people should have a trade union to protect them against senile exploitation.

If love doesn't spark creative action it's not really love anyway, is it? Creative action disrupts the duck-pond and generates new experience, which revitalizes love, and so on.

All my love, *George*

Darling,

So tomorrow I'll be thirty-six years old – middle age if I make it to seventy-two – what do you think? If you are not around when I'm seventy-two – then I don't want to be seventy-two.

All day I've been bubbling with only one thought: 'Tomorrow I'll see him – just a few more hours!' Oh, do you know, really know, just how much I love you? Someone said I should have kept our love secret, so Mogg wouldn't stop the legal visits. Tracey laughed. 'Secret?' she said. 'Just look at her!' There is uproar in the wing over Mogg's reply to you – the last paragraph. How dare he? They are getting a petition together. What has made them so cross is that Mogg wouldn't know what their attitude is towards me – he's never here. Marilyn stood on the landing and shouted, 'Mr Mogg is a liar!' They really are upset. Also he called us 'dangerous'! He's put himself in the shit by calling H-wing a 'top-security wing'. He keeps telling us that it is just a 'dispersal prison'!

Everybody was locked up – another escape – only this time they didn't get over the wall. They used the same escape route as the previous four! The officers were aware of it. Apparently it came over the radio tonight that the Prison Officers' Association states that it can no longer guarantee public safety as far as Durham Prison is concerned.

I will, this weekend, write to Ed FitzG. How can he tell me not to get my hopes too high?

I am very curious as to why I haven't received notification of bail.

How it will be when I'm out I don't know. I'll be a different person to the woman sentenced – I've grown so much I hardly know myself. I'm sure we'll have some almighty clashes – but the air will be sweeter and purer afterwards and it's so good to make up. My mother was an ace stirrer – she could start a full-scale family war with one look, and frequently did! But our disagreements so far have stemmed not from a complete difference of opinion, but from misunderstanding. I'm sure that I will, to a degree, test you, as you will test me.

My behaviour may well be very strange if I'm suddenly released on 22 March, and you'll have to be prepared for that, and not condemn me too much. I'm not sure how secure I'll feel with your love, or how secure I'll feel about me – you'll just have to keep telling me that you love me – and showing me! I sometimes find it hard to believe myself. I do love you. Believe it!

I remembered something strange the other day – I don't know how you feel about fortune-tellers, etc. About five months before I met M., I went to a fortune-teller. Actually, she had a 'psychic shop', and I went in to look. I ended up paying for a reading. She told me I would have much heartache – but I would find happiness. She told me that to meet the love of my life, who would never break my heart, I would have to move away. He was an older man, with two sons (at first she said one son, then said, no, two). She also said (and this is the bit I remembered) that I would be living in a very built-up area, possibly high-rise flats or something, as she could see a lot of brick walls. She stressed the moving right away before I could meet him, and the built-up area! I, of course, thought it was M. He was older, he did have two sons, I did move (though back, not away). I often wondered about the wall bit but figured she'd got it wrong! You can't get more walls than a prison, can you? I take these things with a pinch of salt.

I have the most ENORMOUS spot on the side of my mouth. I'm so, *so* embarrassed. I *never* get spots. Why now? I went up to see Sister A. 'Have you got anything for the boil on my face, Sister A.?' 'Like what?' she asked.

'Like a brown paper bag!' I replied. 'I've got a visit tomorrow.' She laughed and said, 'It's hardly noticeable.' Like hell! She's a liar. It's one of those spots that screams at people, 'Look at me – I'm a pus-head!' She said that up north they call spots 'plukes'. So, if it's still bad tomorrow I shan't kiss you, and don't you dare say you didn't notice my pluke!

The other night I heard one of my favourite pieces – very emotive and used, I think, for *This Week*. I wasn't too surprised to hear it was . . . Sibelius. Yes, I *do* like him. More, more!

Yesterday afternoon, after the little escape that wasn't, I looked over the balcony (OK, landing) and saw two strange workmen, with hard hats, carrying a long wooden plank with bits on it. I shouted, 'Hey! Mr Hicks – that's my glider!' 'You should have hidden it better, Sara.' The two workmen were horrified – I don't think we are supposed to joke about these things. Everyone laughed, and the probation officer said, 'I *told* you to hide it in my office, didn't I?' Later I saw Hicks downstairs. 'So – you've lost two more?' I asked. 'I don't know what you're talking about!' he countered. 'See, girls?' I said. 'I've told you, the problem in H-wing is a total lack of communication.'

Love you for ever! *Sara* (aged thirty-six years!)

Happy birthday, darling,

Gita phoned to say they've set 30 January, Channel 4 *Dispatches*, for your programme.

It's getting late and I wish you were here to come to bed with me, warm, all entwined, glad to be relaxed and in love and without prying eyes, and official self-righteousness, and locks.

George

Darling birthday woman,

You've still got lots of spirit, never lose it. If it can survive that place it can survive anything. And, honestly, your pluke was entirely irrelevant – I didn't even notice it, if it was there.

Your trial report is excellent and very useful. It should help 'educate' E.F. E.F. has to convince the Court of Appeal that justice was not done, because far too little of the real events and motives was presented to the jury. He has to present the flaws of your 'defence' case as if they were those of the Prosecution, which, in a sense, they were. What do you think? My line would be to imply that you were a woman (and mother) under mounting stress and in great danger, who showed remarkable self-control for a long time but finally could endure it no more. Then he could point to the very limited nature of your attack on M., with mutual 'goading' and a medium-force wound, etc. In other words, even at the lowest point of your self-control you still showed evidence of a considerable amount of restraint. But of course that argument requires a good, short, accurate picture of what you had to put up with.

One of the Appeal Court judges, Sir Alec MacCowen, has the same birthday as you – a lot older, of course!

I went out of the prison with B.'s visitor, and he told me, 'I've been in some awful jails, but this is the worst of them all.' 'The Unfriendly' took me in, and out. 'Is that really your address, just Brancepeth Castle?' 'Yes.' 'Isn't there a unit number or something?' 'No.' 'Do you live there alone, then?' 'No, several people live there. Do you live alone in your house?' I asked her!

'Almighty clashes', hey? Why? I don't want to clash with you. Both of us probably react too quickly for our own good, sometimes. We need to slow down. No more cracks about your 'strong-arm' exploits, I promise. I do accept what you said, and I'm glad you can defend yourself.

I love you, *George* xxxxx

Darling,

What a great visit! What an idiot I was to respond to your lovely, wonderful proposal in such an awkward fashion. Yes, I will agree to us marrying.

I came back on the wing after the visit, and could have kicked myself. Do you know why I was so hesitant? I should have been honest, instead of being so flippant, garbling on about you capitulating or me playing hard to get. It's not a game and I have never treated it as if it were! It's that bloody nine-year tariff. I just couldn't bear the thought of you being saddled with a woman in prison. My martyr streak interfering again. Forgive me please?

Have also written to E.F.; just a brief letter confirming his appointment as my barrister.

The phone call with Luise was great. She and Billi sang 'Happy Birthday'. Luise told me, very solemnly, that she had hugged a Redwood for me – 'it was too big to get my arms all the way round, but I gave it a kiss and said, "Mummy loves you."'

Your flying pigs are flying – I have put them directly opposite the warm-air vent, above the shelf at the foot of my bed. I think they're crazy, great! As for your proposal card, well, the girls are very impressed (me too!).

In church today, we repeated the usual dogma, 'Christ has died, Christ is risen, Christ will come again!' I said afterwards to Mic, 'He'd better make his coming pretty soon, or there'll be nothing to come back to!' No response. Wouldn't it be funny if he returned as a Jew? Ooops! I sometimes feel a sense of panic: Is my life sentence longer than the life sentence of the world? Dear God, I truly hope not! I sit in my cell and meditate.

Our future hopes for peace lie with our children, we must wean them away from a diet of violence where guns (Rambo) and brutality can solve every problem.

I love you – it's getting desperate! I could have done with double the time on Saturday.

I feel beloved. Do you?

All my love, *Sara* x

Hello, darling, hope you are in good heart.

The bit of *This Week* Sibelius you like is from his *Karelia Suite*. Karelia is an area of Finland, near Russia, I believe. We'll explore it, right?

I hope to enclose the news item about Holloway and children. Why not write a letter to *The Times* (Appeal judges read it) and mention your case very briefly and explain what emotional stress is caused by your separation from Luise, and the need for continuous contact, not token days? I think this mother/child issue is very important in itself but *also* for swinging public sympathy (and judges).

The world was coated in freezing icing sugar this morning – everything tinged white. Beautiful, and the only time I've ever slowed down on my bike because of the cold air penetrating gloves, ears, everything.

It really does seem a long, long time since we first met. You're right, you have grown and changed a lot – I hope I've changed and grown a bit, too.

Woodcutting in this weather is more like the Middle Ages than ever. Poor man bowed down under pile of wood struggling over frost and snow to the castle walls!

All my love, all around you, darling, *George* xxx

Hello Sweetheart,

Whilst in search of washing-up liquid this evening, one of the officers, commenting on the size of my jumper, said, 'You should tell George that we put you on the rack and you've stretched; if you told him shit was chocolate he'd eat it.' Isn't that amazing? Typical that without knowing you, she feels she can make such a sweeping statement.

Yes, you're quite correct on my attitude to receiving gifts. I sometimes have to pinch myself, and tell myself that others get as much pleasure from giving. To a degree, I am at war with myself – if I am out in March – a small nagging part of me says I haven't been punished enough. Don't give me logical arguments, just don't let me sabotage the Appeal. It's something I have to work out for myself. After all, I spent ten days at that trial being convicted, and condemned by *all* the experts. I need to hear the experts say I'm not guilty before I believe it.

All my love, *Sara* xx

Hello, pardner!

Major calls Hussein's action in invading Kuwait aggressive and destructive, yet says nothing about our actions. I can't help but see striking similarities between the war in the Gulf – i.e. provocation and proportionate retaliation – and domestic murder. Is it just me – or am I right?

I've checked, and a VO was sent out today – I do hope you use it, and not play safe – be impulsive – come and see me!

I sat and ate a full meal tonight. First time in ages – I feel so free – so relaxed.

I do know that if I follow my gut feelings I feel strong, better. Maybe to you it's all just natural; I think it's marvellous to have a book where someone confirms you can be yourself! Myself is thought of as *nutty*, yet I can be (and am!) undeniably happy – not at all appropriate for prison life! Solutions don't come from books – they come from within us. Let's discuss – soon!

I wish I had known it was Jason's birthday – I would have sent him one of my personal cards.

Apparently *The Times* has a photo of Saddam Hussein praying. To whom I wonder?

The night-lady just told me that it's Moses's fault – he should have turned right instead of left! I like that.

Here's a weird dream – I dreamt (night before last) that I had been freed. We went to a VIP house and I disgraced myself by taking off my clothes and lying down in the most enormous fish tank. I could feel the fish nibbling my toes – can still see the fronds of weed. I didn't see you in the dream – but I know you were there – you tried to apologize for me, explaining that I had just come out of prison etc. I merely lay with the fish, tropical of course, so the water was warm. I love you, my darling man, everywhere – always – even in 'wet dreams'!

Sara xxxxx

Darling,

You should note the names, etc., of any other officers using insulting language about you, me, the others, and I'll make sure their names are listed to the Governor, Home Sec. and local media. It's time that sort of foul-mouthed abuse was stopped. Typical of the disgusting hypocrisy of the place. Make sure they know I'll do it, please. Yes, I know that one or two of them are human, but the rest should be fired.

Please don't say you 'need to hear the experts say' you're 'not guilty' before you believe it. Judges are not experts on you or me or anyone – they are very limited elderly men with their heads full of legal quibbles. Justice, real justice, is surely a delicate combination of many unique ingredients, special to each person. You are 'guilty' of killing a man who drove you to the edge of sanity, at a time when he was in a suicidal, aggressive state, and you were in despair and confusion with a young child to protect.

You don't need judges or me or anyone except you to say you're OK. But I'll say it anyway – YOU ARE LOVELY. Full of universal spirit.

You have all my love, darling.

I love you, sweetheart, *George* xxx

Hello Darling Woodcutter,

Can you imagine Judge French chuckling as he wrote that bail refusal? I can!

My personal officer, Mrs A., has been on all week. She really is a cheerful, lovely woman. She's on a diet – I caught her eating a chocolate Club biscuit, so I took it off her, and having given her an orange instead, ate it myself. She complained of hunger at lunch-time, so I gave her a slice of orange till she could eat her lunch. I enjoy her – wouldn't it be marvellous if we could all have that sort of relationship with all the officers?

Funny, when your letters arrive there are eager, expectant faces, waiting to see what cuttings you've sent. Keep it up – we love you. (I adore you!)

When I got your letter today, there was no mark on it, but the pages were in the wrong order. Yesterday's eight-page letter was so well read it didn't even fit neatly into the envelope!

Keep warm, my love, keep chopping, you'll *need* strong arms to hug me enough!

Sara xxx

Darling,

They had a TV report from HMS *Atherstone* in the Gulf. You're entirely right to link 'provocation' and 'murder' with that 'legalized' war. A young gunner in the Gulf (Brit.): 'You're killing people for a stupid reason. Just because the man at the top is not all there.' Tornado pilot: 'If we can get away without killing people, that's fine. We're into taking out real estate.'

I like your dream. Lazy as ever, you offer no interpretation. Please do it. You're throwing it all away if you don't use your imagination on it. My ideas are just mine. Here are some: Taking off your clothes in VIP house – laying yourself bare to experts? Telling the whole truth? 'Disgraced' yourself, and my apology for you – you associate me with the 'experts', judgemental, apologetic? Huge, warm fish tank – swimming in your own unconscious energy, warm, happy (very positive). Christ is the sign of the fish, a symbol of truth latent in the unconscious – the fish 'nibble' at you – trying to wake you up? Draw you up into life? Warm water – your childhood – Pacific? Seems a very positive dream, drawing on your own deeper energies – BUT there's a gap between your inner exploration/revelation and the VIP world. Close the gap by learning how to *relate* your inner truth to their outside power.

Story of Beethoven in Vienna – visitor asked if he'd been sick – he said, no, but one of his shoes was and he only had one pair, so he was under 'house arrest'! Very poor. Very deaf. Very lonely. One of the most brilliant sparks in millions of years.

E.F. knows a lot about law and nothing about you. You are his teacher. I think it's going to be important to present a new official psycho-assessment of you to the Court. Let's ask him. Maybe Dr H. Bullard? If we could get her to reverse her knocking evidence and admit she was wrong, that would be marvellous, wouldn't it?

It's another of those odd moments when I'm writing to you before seeing you, knowing you'll read it afterwards! A kind of love sandwich.

See you soon, hug you soon, kiss you soon.

All my love, sweetheart. *George* xxxx

Darling Sara,

Isn't it a marvellous symbol of this country that when the *Antiques Roadshow* was postponed to show Nelson Mandela's release from prison, millions complained? UK 1991 – The Antique Roadshow!

Well, they've started their war. One of the RAF Tornado pilots: 'Absolutely terrified. Terrified of failure. Terrified of dying. But happy now.' Honest guy. The language is so false: 'denying' airfields – 'taking out' – 'degrading' military capacity – and there's a Wing Commander Brinkman!

Saddam Hussein: 'God is great, God is great, God is great' . . . Ho hum. God is a piece of chewing gum pushed into the weirdest of shapes.

I love you so much, always. *George* xx

Darling Love,

I wonder what you're doing? Lying on your bed watching pigs fly?

What I really object to in that kind of picture of God-becoming-baby is that it refers to one single event, long ago, thousands of miles away, which makes it remote in time and place, and supernatural. Instead of making every human birth a key event in evolution (which it is, in my view), the Christ 'magic' actually devalues everyday birth. Just as having a king or queen devalues the ordinary citizen and puts all the glamour and importance in one family. Doesn't it strike you as absurd that God would put his 'only son' into a town in the Middle East to demonstrate the power of love, and do it in such a way that for the next 2,000 years human behaviour (Christian and non-Christian) remains as violent and cruel and greedy and unloving as ever?

I think our love is as important as anything anyone else has, and far more important than historical stories and myths and legends. You are the only human being you will ever know from the inside. So am I, for me. We are at the centre of our lives, aren't we? Not kids with noses pressed to the window of some mythical toy shop full of saints and gods and whatnot! What you and I are struggling with is the essence of life, not its surface. That's why our love is such a threat to those whose identity and security cling to fixed institutional power and status. What do you think, love of my life? It's time we all grew up – life shouldn't be kind to us, we should be kind to life!

I do love that photo of Luise – she is lovely, with a sweet, innocent expression.

All my love, *George* xx

My Darling Love,

Written from the cell of a condemned woman – lucky you, today you get two letters.

I've been placed on report – I figured it out last night. I went into

182

the wing office – and the officer folded a slip of paper so I couldn't see it. I figured I would be told I was on report this morning – didn't bother to dress and hey presto! – at 8 a.m., my door was unlocked, and I, standing barefoot in pyjamas, was formally told that 'at approximately 15.55 hrs, I called Mrs C. a liar' – this comes under 'using threatening, insulting or abusive words or behaviour'. Now, the problem is that Mrs C. *is* a liar – so if she finds the truth insulting – that's her look-out, isn't it? I plead not guilty to insulting behaviour – I do plead guilty to calling her a liar – if there is any guilt intended. I'm now awaiting adjudication – I'll let you know what happens.

The doctors in here are truly marvellous. He's just looked at me – to see if I am fit for punishment. Not my physical well-being – but my mental health. *I* do believe he has deemed me mentally fit – after a ten-second consultation. Aren't they clever? Maybe I should call him to my Appeal!

I was all prepared for martyrdom, but it was not to be – £3 fine suspended for two months.

I *need* to see you darling.

All my love, *Sara* xxxxx

Darling Love (and all our other lovely readers!),

You naughty girl, getting on report! Go back three places. I'm afraid you are about as (un)diplomatic as I am.

I've been 'driving' (flying?) the washing machine! Makes me feel I'm flying a jet liner. It howls and screams and does everything but take off. But more or less works.

How's this for awful God-speak? US pilot interviewed after attacking Iraq: 'When you shot down that Iraqi plane (it blew up in bits) did you think of the pilot? Maybe he had a family like yours?' Reply: 'Hmmm. I guess the difference is that I'm from a God-fearing, God-loving people.' A multi-purpose God, a God for all seasons.

This war is getting close to being an electronic board-game – a 'good, clean, desert war'.

The point of a letter to *The Times* is not to directly influence judges but as public education – changing the social climate in which judges exist. People should know and feel guilty about the punishment of innocent children, shouldn't they? Judges follow social trends, they don't make them.

All my love, *George* xxxx

Darling,

Sorry about the rushed scribble.

> LIE-IN
> Was Sara lying on her bed,
> Or was she lying in it?
> Big Sister stamped her foot and said,
> 'The blame, on you I'll pin it!'
> 'No doubt at all, I saw you lying,'
> Big Sister did repeat,
> But it's fate she herself was tempting,
> By lying on her feet.

This Gulf War is very strange. So far it seems almost bloodless, and highly electronic. They keep showing video pictures of bombs disappearing into buildings via air ventilators and describing Cruise missiles flying along a street at 100 feet. Very like a pub game. In a way it's appropriate. The whole thing is like a war between insects in a desert. A Tornado pilot described how, after he returned to base, he cried for a long time over the crew shot down. Battle of Britain Spitfire pilots didn't do that (or nobody told us about it). The whole thing seems a large step towards 'fighting' wars from underground (or undersea) studios. Love is a poor waif in this bleak landscape, isn't it?

Keep fighting, keep winning, keep loving, and get some rest in between please.

Here's a bit from Jeremiah: 'For they have healed the hurt of the daughter of my people slightly, saying "Peace, Peace", when there is no peace' (Jeremiah 8–11). Rather typical that the motto of the US Air Force is: 'Peace is our profession.'

When I appeared as expert witness at a case at Huntingdon Crown Court (re nuclear protesters), I gave the court a statement citing a whole list of law extracts, etc., and the judge dismissed it as 'political', without referring to a single point of law. But at least everyone in court read it (while I was shut out). 'Political' means it challenges his prejudices.

I like it when you say 'bless you' – do it to yourself sometime you lovely, wonderful woman. Much more valuable than candyfloss from a judge.

See you *soon*.

All my love, *George* xxx

Hello Darling!

OK. I plead guilty to my not very 'constructive' response to *Living in the Light*. First, I haven't read all of it so my response, such as it's been, is more or less valueless. I really will read it, because it's important to me to understand why something makes a lot of sense to you. I don't like being left out. There are a mass of things we don't know about each other's interests – a lot to explore and to learn. Books can be strange things, sometimes very important at a particular moment in one's life. After leaving university, very disappointed with the 'learning' aspect, I sold all my text books and bought one which made more sense to me than all the compulsory books. It was *Sane Society*, by Erich Fromm, a German/American psychologist/psychiatrist. I still have it. He also wrote a good book called *Fear of Freedom*, which analysed why people (most) are far more scared of real freedom than authoritarian rule.

See you soon. All my love, G. xxxx

Hello Darling Man,

I've just written to Edward Fitzgerald, asking him to contact Henrietta Bullard [psychiatrist]. I explained about her evidence, and said I would like an honest, updated report. He can rephrase it tactfully to her.

I talk to some of the girls in here, they know I have 'something' – they also know it's not religion in the strict sense of the word. I talk to them about spirit, energy – and they are understanding and accepting it. Perhaps they too are ready for a rebirth. They ask me questions and I don't have answers, because I've such a long way to go myself.

You asked about the scar on my arm – I told you a little, but not all. As I said, I had the BCG – standard serum in the Pacific. However, at age fourteen, Mummy, for some reason, decided the serum used had been faulty – so she insisted I had another. They just scratch the skin. I had a very painful arm for weeks – I told my mother. 'Stop being a baby – none of the other children are complaining.' One night, I was in such pain, I got out of bed – a very brave thing to do. Mummy, in examining my arm, gently squeezed it with her two thumbs, the top of it blew off, and pus hit her full in the face. The relief was immense. For quite a while, pieces of spongy white matter came out; a tuberculosis ulcer had formed all down my arm. Needless to say I wasn't taken to a doctor, but since then, X-rays of my chest have puzzled doctors. I have TB scars on my lungs, so at some stage I had TB, yet my mother refused to listen to my complaints of feeling unwell. Is it any wonder I have a strange relationship with pain?

All my love. *Sara* xx

Hello, Love.

Sorry I smelled of grease! – you smelled fine. It was wonderful seeing you, as always. I am concerned about your health, despite your idiot jokes! It's not funny, but I know you use it as a way of releasing stress. I'm glad you explained what you had written to the Registrar – it took me only about one minute to understand what you had done and why. Keep explaining please.

One thing you said yesterday made me think – that you feel you need and deserve quite a long period of punishment. I want to try to express some ideas on this 'punishment' feeling of yours. As you said, you've been deluged with negative comment by psychos, judges, lawyers etc. Society has officially branded you. But it has also given you a right of Appeal. I don't think that's nearly as important as how you view yourself. Your Appeal (and campaign) could be sabotaged if your heart really isn't in it. Let's focus on this for a while, shall we? If we don't get this right we won't get anything right.

The first point is that it is a basic psycho-truth that children take on themselves the weight of their parents' failure. Parents are always right, thinks the child, so the child must be wrong. You have obviously assumed a major responsibility for your parents' failure – not so much outwardly (joking and anger) but inwardly. Then, because in your heart you feel you're 'bad' you tend to act 'bad' to prove you are right. Thus feeling bad becomes a perverted feeling good, the best feeling you have. It's an upside-down value – i.e. 'If I'll never feel good I'll enjoy feeling bad.' It's a short step from there to wanting to be punished – it would feel 'wrong' not to be. It's the same sort of thing, morally, as putting a heavy weight on a child and making it live day and night carrying it. After a while the weight will seem natural. Life without it will seem 'wrong'. How did you feel, deep down, before M.'s death? I bet you felt just about as deserving of 'punishment' as you did afterwards. If so, it means that whatever the Appeal judges decide, you will still feel 'guilty', needing to be punished. Luise doesn't deserve to feel guilty because of you, any more than you and your parents, me and mine, anybody . . . Please, darling self-flagellator, try to feel yourself as a young child, helpless, lost, at the mercy of authority (parents) – you needed help, love, comfort, security and you didn't get it and blamed yourself. IT WASN'T YOUR FAULT AND IT ISN'T YOUR FAULT! You must forgive yourself before you can do anything of any value.

You and M. were waifs in a storm, totally incapable of giving each other real security because you didn't believe you deserved it. The simple, basic truth of your killing M. is that it was a matter of crude survival – it was you and Luise, or him. All the pretence (and reality) of a loving relationship had gone. There was nothing left but fear, violence, life and death. It was a primitive act like millions of others in history (the Gulf), neither bad nor good but survival. The law allows the right to life under threat of death. He might well have killed you and Luise. You tried very hard to save him from suicidal (homicidal) alcoholism – you failed, partly because you were at war with yourself. He was a growing threat to you and L. Defending both of you was lawful homicide. You deserve to be free, and so does Luise. The judges have the power to set you free, physically, but only you can free yourself inwardly. Please do it. Soon. Now! If you don't you'll sabotage this Appeal by treating it half-heartedly. Give yourself the best chance, darling love, not a mediocre chance. Let's go all out to reverse the Court's verdict – prove that you tried very hard for a long time to endure the unendurable, that you were and are a good mother and need to show it now. Let's get Hen. B. to make the statement re alcoholism, and give evidence of your strength in appalling circumstances. The Defence misled first themselves, then you, then the Court and the jury. The Prosecution merely poured petrol on the fire. They hardly had to do anything. Stand up and demand your freedom! I wasn't being clever with my comment about 'deserving life'. You do. You have one life, you deserve it, you need a chance to show what you can do with it. Yes? Don't waste precious energy fighting idiots.

It's sunny, brilliant, like Sara Eliz . . .

I love you, sweetheart. *George* xxxx

My Darling,

I forgot to say in my last letter how well you looked – on my birthday visit you seemed tired and a little drawn, but yesterday you looked and felt great! Scruffy as ever, tramp. I wouldn't have you any other way!

P. said tonight, 'Sara, if you are going to be freed, you only have eight weeks of prison left.' I hated her saying it, made me feel very scared. I really do want to hope, but cannot imagine it. E. said, 'If you come back from your Appeal, Sara, I'll cry!' They feel that if I don't succeed, they have no chance. Thinking tonight, I'm scared of the DPP. They were so horrible at the trial, Escott-Cox QC [Prosecutor] will probably make me feel physically sick when I see him. And that policeman, H., he has a horrible, bland, cold face with dead eyes. You'll see! As Tracey has said, many girls just don't go for their Appeals because it is so frightening. I can understand why!

I heard a song on the radio this afternoon, I thought of M. with a rush of love and understanding. A good feeling, no anger, no blame, no bitterness. I'm so happy to feel that way. It's taken a long time to let him go – there's a beautiful song from *A Star is Born*, with Barbra Streisand: 'With one more look at you, I might overcome the anger that I've learnt to know, find a peace of mind I lost so long ago.'

I can hear your voice in my head, you know! All I need is a smear of engine grease, and I'd think you were beside me.

LOVE YOU. *Sara* xxxxxxx

Darling Sara,

Marriage is not a necessity, it's an option. If it begins to confuse and disrupt our love I don't want it. It's only good and sensible if it makes both of us, and Luise, more relaxed, happy. Yes? I suppose there must be a level in both of us which identifies marriage with failure, for obvious reasons. And for you, tragedy and horror.

You said I just 'skim through' your letters. Not so. When you see them one day you'll see all the marks I put on them to remind me which bits to reply to, etc. I read them several times.

Re Dr Bullard, I feel the important thing is to try to get her to (a) introduce the 'alcoholic' statement, and (b) reverse the implication of her original approach to you, by describing how she was misled by the Defence.

My poem was just a joke! Not a profound revelation of the meaning of the universe. A play on the words 'lie' and 'lying'.

I hope you are close to your 'wise spirit' because if so you will know that your 'guilt' and 'deserving punishment' are leftovers from a highly disturbing childhood. (The vaccination problem and the pus in the eye of your mother are marvellous symbols of this, aren't they?) You're very brave struggling through and out of that chaos.

Saying of the week, by a war correspondent accused of having a death-wish: 'The last thing I want to do is die.' (And it was the last thing he did.)

Later

'Battle-shock' is in the Gulf. Army medical officer: 'It's not an illness. It's a normal reaction to a highly abnormal situation, and usually short-lived.' Remind you of anything?

Wherever your spirit comes from, keep it coming! I need your love.

You have all my love. *George* xxx

Darling,

You sounded a bit forlorn in your letter today and I just want to hug you and try to cheer you up. You say you sometimes walk around 'talking' to me. I do it too! I often have an almost desperate need to talk to you and say things and ask questions and just listen to you.

Love is the biggest threat to every form of brute power, and always has been. I think we've both been under a lot of pressure recently and our letters have become a bit scratchy and tired.

I'm still surprised and delighted that our paths crossed. It makes me smile to re-run in my mind that first encounter – we were probably as nervous as each other. I loved your quickness of response and openness and I was amused too by your humour in the midst of horror. You don't fit into the usual English class categories, thank God. Your vaguely 'North American' personality attracted me – a combination of energy and hope, and the courage to trust and take risks. Your lovely, eager, impulsive face and smile stayed with me then and still do.

My article is an attempt to look at the underlying human implications of H-wing, the veneer of minor concessions and the destructive effect of imposing militaristic constraints on basic human needs. The system is hostile to love and subservient to force and power. Its claims to be humane are a sham, a fig-leaf to hide the irresponsible behaviour of society. The death of a few, in exceptional circumstances, is punished by vindictive self-righteousness. The death of thousands is organized and justified to protect oil supplies. Love is a waif in the desert of self-deception. Mogg is just a pawn in this game. Not a 'Nowhere Man' but a nobody man, a weather-cock.

Give me a vegetarian recipe please. I hope you are feeding that lovely, athletic, sexy body of yours – please do.

Headline in the *Sun* of several days ago, 'GO GET 'EM, BOYS!' above photo of Tornado fighter's backside, flying off. Like setting a dog on a rabbit. The Rottweiler culture in action. Two thousand years of Christianity and that's the end product. I imagine the bigoted oafs *en route* to the Crusades a thousand years ago had similar impulses.

Mozart's *Magic Flute* opera starts soon. My favourite. It's a kind of fairy story of love and the triumph of love and good over evil, with parallel pairs of lovers, Pamina and Tamino and Papagena and Papcaeno. Tamino has to go through various ordeals and trials to 'win' Pamina, who is in the grip of the wicked Queen of the Night. You can be Pamina if you like, with your mother as Queen of the Night out to sabotage your love and life.

I need you safe and sound and warm and loving.

All my love, *George* xxx

Hello my darling fellow scribbler!

I didn't write yesterday, so you won't get a letter tomorrow, which is now yesterday for you. (Figure that out, Einstein!) I felt like the weather, cold and damp.

Spent some time with Mogg this evening – he was in his bashful mood. S., M. and myself played him 'his' song, 'Nowhere Man'. He said it was cruel. Also said the Registrar did stop your legal visits (well he said he was a liar – *no*, he said very pointedly, 'some people do lie!') So, here is my token poem:

> I was wrong by far,
> About the Registrar.
> He's a slimy son of a bitch.
> He should be impaled,
> With a sign, firmly nailed,
> Saying liar, cheat and snitch!

Many girls told him they objected to his letter to you. He said legal facilities like mine are granted only for a short period of time.

Finally finished my soft toy this morning. I've told them to price them ridiculously high, so no one wants to order any more!

A vegetarian dish? Why don't you make yourself some French Onion Soup? Chop a couple of onions up fine, fry in marge till soft, using a saucepan. Add some flour and some stock (veg. Oxos are good), black pepper, a little sea salt, then leave to simmer for about half an hour – when cooked, put a piece of bread on top, cover it with cheese. Should be Gruyère, ah well! And put it under the grill. Great meal. If you like soups, I can give you lots.

Must go darling – I'm buzzing and full of energy. I love you – so much. See you *soon*.

All my love, hugs, kisses, *Sara* xxx

Darling,

Many thanks for your brave, weary letter today. I love you.

This morning is a beautiful January freeze, all life like a frozen, glittering ornament. My ears likewise.

Funny how our life together moves in somersaults. (Why did I fall

191

in love with an acrobat?) The legal profession and judiciary have an overriding loyalty to themselves. There's nothing they hate more than a member of the public infiltrating their defensive mystique. They are an intellectual, desiccated priesthood, not a public service. One of Shakespeare's characters says at one point, 'Let's kill all the lawyers.' The final solution!

Awful picture from a dreadful war, last night on TV news – a cormorant wading, dying, in black oily sea water off Kuwait. A ghastly symbol of greed and violence. Cormorants are known as 'greedy' by humans, though all they do is eat fish to live. We dig up oil to gratify childish whims, hates, fears, greed, and kill them, too.

Always remember, I'm not an expert at loving, just an apprentice. Yes, let's teach each other as we go along. You've taught me a lot already.

I'm seeing Mic the Vic at Ruth's on Tuesday, I hope. Should be interesting. I'll have to put an armed guard on my tongue.

Your poem on the Registrar is great. Send it to him (better wait till after the Appeal). Had a thought; the strength of the prison officers versus Governor is like the tail wagging the Mogg?

You have all my energy and a lot else.

Hugs by the million, *George* xxxx

Hello darling,

I think you seem to fall for women who are very academic – am I right? You always put their Ph.D., doctor, whatever title, before you write anything else. Also made me wonder what you are doing loving a country bumpkin like me? I'm *not* fishing, that was/is the feeling I had. Sometimes our culture/age/generation gap disturbs me – you must wonder about it too? You seem so wise much of the time, I feel as if I'm lagging. However, that's only on a bad day. Today is a *good* day.

Your question about M., and my saying he was 'healed and happy'. Well, it's quite obvious we have a slight difference of opinion on what happens to a soul after death. Am I right? You seem to think that the soul becomes a part of a collective consciousness. What about the old theory of reincarnation – believed by Thoreau and Goethe – to name two. I believe it (I know it) to be true. It makes such sense.

Reincarnation means that a man's life (present and future) lies in his own hands, *as you have been telling me!*

During an Ecumenical Council, of Catholics, in Constantinople, AD 553, it was decided to omit from the Bible any reference to reincarnation. Why? Because Christ preached that God is within us, the Council wanted God within the Church. Power, control. Bye bye, truth. Hello, oppression, corruption, hypocrisy. They also invented heaven and hell to even the status quo, and give themselves a little more leverage. It's true! Anyway, for me, it's one of the final pieces of the puzzle slotted into place. I've been a nasty, gossipy, bitchy woman for a month or so, subconsciously 'testing' God, declaring that Jesus was out of date and waiting for the thunderbolt to strike. All that happened is that I made myself thoroughly miserable and unhappy. I'm not a bitchy person naturally. It was all part of the growing I have to do. I've learnt, experienced *so* much in such a short space of time.

One thing I have learnt is that everybody's awareness changes and grows at their own pace. I love you, darling.

Anyway, went to church for the last time today. I was due to read the lesson from the New Testament. I stood up, shaking (after all I had thirty-six years of religious conditioning to overcome), and told a very startled congregation what I have just written for you. I turned at the end and told Mic I felt I could no longer go to church, said thank you and walked out. I think it has upset them a bit. Mic said the bit about the Council of Nicea (AD 553) was *not* true. The theological students want proof! That's a joke. I'm supposed to accept their dogma and theories with faith. But they want proof. P. told me this – I'd gone.

As it stands, Mic was sad I walked out, he would have liked me to stay for a discussion. I left because I didn't want to disrupt the service – silly, really – I did anyway. I didn't think they would take it so seriously, I felt they'd think, 'Oh, it's just Sara and her imagination again!' They want a discussion a week on Wednesday. Twenty against me! Hah! If they think I'm giving them the truth on a plate they can think again.

The girls are a bit rattled. After all, the thought that you can sin, cause pain, and hurt people all week, then go to church on Sunday, confess your sins, have a sip of wine, a piece of wafer, and be forgiven is very attractive, isn't it? But, as I asked them today, 'How many of you really benefit, really find something, in church?' I regret none of it. Once more my name is MUD – who cares? Do you? Far better to be honest about these things than talk in whispers. Too many whispers in here. 'Sara is only marrying George to get out!' A little whisper. It hurt me. I felt our love tarnished.

I love you dearly, honestly, always, *Sara*

Darling Love,

Brrr, it's cold! I wish you were with me to wrap up with. Hello, my beloved!

I jogged twenty-five laps of the yard. Peeled off to my gym suit, briefly. I felt snowflakes on my arms. Wonderful how something like that feels when you are in prison. Wonderful, anyway!

Saw the specialist – the lumps (I have several though I only felt one) are benign fibroids – of hormonal origin, which is why they get bigger and sore just before my period. See – I told you not to worry.

I don't think you realize how much thought, energy and pain has gone into my search for God, truth etc. I just had to work it out for myself.

This whole issue is so intensely private and so important that I think it's something to discuss on winter nights, in each other's arms in front of a fire! But please, ask questions. As many as you want, especially on reincarnation!

Do you know what I love about you (us)? I love the way I can be so completely honest, and know you'll still love me! It gives us a great freedom. Don't you think?

Must post this – the sun is shining and so am I – love you very much, darling.

All my love, *Sara* xxx

Hello Engaging Man,

I wonder what sort of a day you've had? Interesting I should imagine. I *loved* your letter this lunch-time. I've read it over and over. Thank you, just what I needed! Let's have more, please. You still haven't told me when you started loving me – or when you realized it. I too love to look back on our first visit. I thought you were wonderful, so warm, clever, articulate, intuitive. Scruffy, endearing and totally original. Nowhere in the world could I have met a man who matches me so perfectly. You'll see. But then you know my original thoughts. You read them – remember?

Saw Sister A. tonight. Apparently the rumour is that I have denounced God! They didn't even listen to me, or perhaps they have associated God and the Church as indivisible – silly people.

Keep your ears warm – till I'm there to do it for you. And *many* other things.

Sara xxx

Darling,

I was glad to hear of your benign bumps. Treat them gently. Two will do, thanks!

It's not true to say I 'condemned' *Living in the Light* out of hand. If you read what I wrote you'll see that I said both times that I hadn't read the whole book, so my response was just a first opinion. I can only say again that beliefs are cheap and actions are expensive, so I tend to pay far more attention to what people do than what they say or write.

We are so insane and immature that we could turn this world into a spinning crematorium in the name of God!

Tell me, please, why you think it matters whether Christ got to India or Tibet. I spent nine months visiting lots of places in India and I didn't find anyone who had any interest in Christ (apart from a handful of Christians). I'm sure they'd be polite about him, because most Indians respect other people's religious leaders.

All my love, *George* xxxxx

Darling,

Who are these 'very academic' women? The truth is I'm very sceptical about very academic anyone. I haven't mentioned a single Ph.D. to you, have I? The German friend, Uta, is a medical doctor. In fact, if I think back about all the women I've known the only 'category' appears to be artists of one kind or another. I like people who make something out of nothing, who create new life out of old. You and I are trying.

You say you are disturbed by our 'culture/age/generation gap'. Wasn't it you who, many months ago, told me to shut up about our age gap? I did. But if it really bothers you, please say why. I'm not saying it's wrong for you to feel this, but I can't do anything about it, so if it really is a problem, let's look at it. You once wrote to me that if I ever want to break off our relationship I should tell you, kindly and honestly. The same applies to you, please. I am surprised and delighted each day that you love me. I won't be very surprised if you stop. Sad, yes.

You a country bumpkin? You may be a bumpkin but I don't know if you know anything about the country! In fact I wanted to write a book once about English rural life, called *Village Idiot*. That makes two of us, doesn't it?

Where did you get the idea that Goethe and Thoreau believed in reincarnation? Thoreau once said, when asked if he believed in an 'afterlife', 'One life at a time.' Goethe, incidentally, believed that the creation spirit is essentially feminine, the *ewig weibliche* [eternal feminine] as at the end of *Faust*. I agree that around AD 400/500 most of the original insight of Jesus Christ evaporated and became a pawn of Church and imperial power and authority.

I love you darling, *George* xxxxx

Darling man,

Stop loving you! Is that what you are thinking? Oh, love – of course I've not stopped loving you – in fact, whilst sewing I thought of you this morning with such a yearning it brought tears to my eyes! It's hell here at the moment – and I miss you! Hurry and see me – I'll show you how much I love you!

As far as the age/generation/culture gap is concerned, I'm only worried in how it affects *me*! You are all too aware of what little sense of worth I have, a result of Mummy and Daddy's constant demoralizing. I'm getting better, H-wing is now the worst place for me as far as this problem is concerned. This sense of worthlessness does make me behave in what are at times hurtful ways towards you. For example, your proposal. Whatever you may think, you are wise, worldly-wise, though your age has nothing to do with it. I think you must have been born wise. I'm not concerned about the age difference in any other way, believe me.

As it happens I do know a lot about country life and living rurally. I love it, and spent much of my childhood in Cumberland and the West Midlands alone with the birds and animals. OK, so they are not academics, but all qualified. Well, I still feel like a country bumpkin. You've replied in hurt instead of really thinking and trying to understand what I said!

Come and see me – don't spend days brooding. *I love you* dearly. *Sara* xxxx

Darling man,

I am a very spiritual person, and my belief is a way of life as an everyday practice, not a theory that's kept on the shelf and dusted down when the occasion demands it. What you don't fully grasp yet, is that only through realizing my full potential as a highly evolved creature being fully in touch with God (or the Divine Will, or the Universe, or whatever phrase is compatible) can I fully love and appreciate *you*. The more I love God – the more I can love and reach you. You are not in competition, you *are*! Please, listen with your heart or spirit, not that logical brain of yours, and you'll start to understand. It was important to me about the Church and Christ, it does matter. I feel the Church has lied to me, it's not enough that they just did, I need to know *why*!

I'm not asking you to believe what I believe, I'm asking you to have an open mind – and be open to me! I was told today that Mic has organized a religious discussion resulting from my talking in church.

Friday lunch-time

Well, darling, it seems we are both in the doldrums. Let's lift each other out! I'm feeling sad and under the weather. Physically, I'm run down. I have a stye on my eye to prove it.

I'm awfully tired – don't know what's the matter with me. This weekend I'm going to eat and sleep, think of you, write to you. Problem with writing is that I 'talk' to you much of the day, and I forget to put things down. Quite often I feel that I have already told you –

and I haven't. As far as marriage is concerned, I feel we have just decided that we'll marry one day, but at the moment there are more pressing issues to face. OK?

The punishment bit is something I've had to work at – I think that's tired me. Much of it comes from the women in here – I have to keep remembering that they are not, in every sense, normal women. I take their criticism and their condemnation very much to heart, and I pretend or think they are the same views as the outside world. Of course they are not. In fact much of what they say stems from resentment and jealousy. Not sound viewpoints.

Please, my darling man, cheer up – I need you happy, strong and fighting. I love you very, very much.

Please try and understand that there are many things that I cannot write about, even though Mr Mogg assures me that my letters have stopped being so thoroughly censored. To write of prison politics involving girls is not allowed. To do so now would be a betrayal of trust. There's precious little trust here, and we, as inmates, are largely to blame.

I hope I see you this weekend. I love and need you darling.
Sara xxxx

February

Darling, lovely woman!

One of the many good things about us is that we're getting quite expert at picking each other up, aren't we? Like struggling through deep snow together, hand in hand, and pulling each other out of snowdrifts.

When did I start loving you? I'm not sure – it stole over me silently and slowly – maybe after our second meeting. I just found myself focused on you, morning, noon and night.

My favourite recent saying, on local TV news: 'A warning has been issued about dangerous teddy bears!'

I saw a bit of a *Kilroy* programme this morning on alcoholics and living with them – several couples discussed it. One woman described the Jekyll and Hyde aspect. 'I had very low self-esteem and thought it was my fault. I thought I was losing my mind . . . it was a kind of madness.'

A woman from a clinic said there are at least one *million* alcoholics here, with two million relatives directly affected. Another woman: The alcoholic becomes an obsession – I babied him – I stayed because I loved him, there were good times. Another woman who had been alcoholic said she went into pubs and 'provoked men'.

Please accuse me of the things I do wrong (plenty to choose from!) not the things I do right. You accuse me of insisting on writing to the Registrar, but that is exactly what I did not do. I might well have done, because I am impatient, but I decided to ask for your agreement first, so I wrote and asked if you minded me writing to him. Please read what I wrote! I haven't yet written to him and you haven't yet replied to the question. Grrrrh!

Sorry about my competition with your God. Darling, I do know how important your spiritual quest is – it's important for me too. And I love the way you work out and protect what you believe. You say that your beliefs are not theory but practice. OK, fine, but why then do you spend so much time describing belief? My concern is about your actions, our actions.

Isn't it possible that there's something wrong, immature, crazy, about the vast majority of human perceptions of 'God'? Why should an evidently ignorant, half-awake human being (all of us) claim special access to a God Almighty? It's ridiculous, isn't it? Like a child dressing up as Napoleon or Joan of Arc! It's worse than absurd, it's dangerous, because it arms ignorance with infallibility, as in the Gulf War. Millions of half-wits killing each other to service their delusions of Godliness.

I love you so much and the last thing I want is to knock down your confidence.

My logical brain is a Mickey Mouse toy compared to kissing you. I LOVE AND ADORE YOU.

My response to your *Times* letter was 'great, brilliant'. Lovely idea putting in the children's names.

Darling, I'm not hung up on 'qualified' women! Please believe me. I'm hung up on you and you have all sorts of qualifications I love. You're a qualified mischief-maker, a very qualified life partner, and a highly qualified soul mate. We can award each other honorary doctorates in Questology, can't we?

Back to our early meetings – I was first enchanted by the life in you (bionic, hey?) and then by your love. What more can I say, gorgeous? You are just filled to bursting with life, creative energy.

I love your 'freed to', not 'tied to'. I'm well and truly freed to you, darling 'disgruntled' of Durham.

See you soon – pulse rate increasing, hopes rising.

With all my love, *George* xxx

My Dearest Love,

If I don't post one Monday you'll have a black Tuesday – I can't have that! Want you still starry-eyed and misty from all the love and caring I'll show you Monday afternoon. I'm so looking forward to it.

Went on exercise this morning. Two officers took us for volleyball. Only four women played and it was as slippery as if we were wearing kimonos. My side won, game, set and match.

I feel a tremendous sense of peace and well-being tonight.

I saw Mic the Vic, and two of his trainees this morning. I told Mic I didn't think too many would be at this religious discussion on Wednesday. 'Never mind,' they said. 'We'll be there.' Each man chooses his own path to God – I have made my choice; they have made theirs. Sean said, 'One of our sheep has strayed.' I replied 'BAA!' He was not too impressed. I'm looking forward to it immensely.

I've done a lot of work for E.F. this weekend. Please don't worry that my attention is wandering from my Appeal. I wrote and asked Lord Gifford QC to be my leader. I love you, my darling, can you still feel the kisses?

All my love – *Sara* xxx

My Darling Man,

Isn't it cold? I've been locked up for hours – yet it seems like minutes.

I had to laugh at P. today. She went to hospital yesterday. She said, 'I was in the shower when I heard you being marched to your adjudication – singing. I thought, that must be Sara.' I was singing 'The Bare Necessities of Life' from *Jungle Book*. Do you know it? And doing my little dance like the bear does in the film. When she heard I'd got seven days 'behind the door' she thought, God help us! What will she read this time? What's she going to be like when she comes out? I do love it, no more queuing for supper, I lie in bed and the officers bring it up!

Went to see the doctor this morning. When I walked in, he said, 'Sara, there are two lady doctors who have come to look at H-wing.' 'Lady doctors?' I asked. 'Why not just say "doctor", I can see they are ladies?' 'Just tell them, if you don't mind, Sara, what the problem is. Why have you come?' Looking earnest, I said, 'Well I'm deeply in love with Dr Flood so I find an excuse and see him every week!' He blushed red. The lady doctors looked stumped. Sister A. and I laughed. Anyway I told them we had no salt on the wing for a week, no ketchup, no sauce, no salad cream. 'Why no salt? It's cheap enough!' asked one of the visitors. 'Because we are being punished for daring to complain about the food in the first place!' I retorted. It's quite true, I'm sure of it. The lady doctors got a bigger taste of prison than they expected!

I want to see you again, it's a terrible yearning. I've thought about you all day – oh love, will this torment end?

I felt E.F. was very earnest, and I really don't want to start doubting him till he's at least had a chance to see all the papers. Stop feeling miffed and left out. You are not. I needed to let him see that I can be a forceful, articulate entity alone. Anyway, if you had been there, I would have been all gooey and starry-eyed, unable to concentrate on anything except your dear face. I love you very much, darling.

I sent Lord Gifford a copy of my letter to *The Times* with the research.

I'm going to sleep and dream – I love you. *Sara* xxx

Darling,

Regarding Henrietta Bullard, I feel the best and most credible thing is for her to say/write that her evidence was not fully presented and should have included a full statement of the pressure you endured – and that in her opinion a full presentation would have conveyed a very different picture of you – e.g. a picture of someone valiantly struggling to stabilize a fast deteriorating and high-risk situation.

E.F. would know, I hope. I didn't criticize him. Not yet. I just think that it would be a big mistake to follow the existing appeal too slavishly.

You won't take seriously my question about God and the Gulf! Of course I know that oil is a prime motive but that isn't the point. Why is it that all of them use God as the Great Excuser, not oil?

Childish simplicity leads to bloody complications. Hundreds of millions of 'believers' support this orgy of self-righteous killing.

There's something very wrong with the idea of God, unless it leads to creative uncertainty – the very uncertainty people run away from. It is 'not knowing' which allows the mind to stay open, free, fresh, alive, isn't it? You told me to be open-minded. How can I be open-minded if I go around telling people I'm in touch with God, act for 'him', know what he wants, who he hates, who he likes?

Do you know what a US pilot said after a raid? 'I saw them scattering, like cockroaches in the kitchen when you switch on the light.' Killing cockroaches for Bush, who's fighting for 'good against evil'!

More tomorrow, lovely irritant! I do love you, *George* xxxx

Darling,

I had a tough dream the other night. It was night-time and dark, and a woman was running amok with a knife (or similar weapon) – I could see bloodstained clothes – then suddenly she appeared, dancing about and waving a large knife around and laughing in a crazy way. I was frightened but went up to her and grabbed her by the wrist so she dropped the knife. She was dark-haired but not obviously recognizable.

Maybe this dream touches on half-hidden fears in me – could be related to you, or to my own unresolved 'feminine' side (what Jung calls the anima)? Violence, which is untamed, unresolved, is in each of us (all of us).

It's perhaps good that in my dream I was scared yet came to terms with the violence?

One reason I love getting your recipes, because they are you-attached-to-the-earth, not floating sky-high in 'other lives' at other times. Don't be cross with me, darling, I know this is over-simplified and a bit mischievous.

Later

Your letter – lovely – I love the universal energy flowing through you. Let it flow on.

I laughed at your 'lady doctors' – you ought to refer to him in future as the 'gentleman doctor'.

And I was not 'angry' at any point of our visit re E.F., you 'forceful, articulate entity', so shut up! xx

I'm not sure what scares me about you most – when you regress into a 'bad' schoolgirl? Or when you are at your most coherent, mature, creative (because then you challenge me most)? You *are* a challenge, all the time (I love you for it).

I love you, *George* xxx

Darling,

The troughs of deep depression aren't confined to the weather! I had a letter from Billi at lunch-time – four pages of fulminating against the war, and as an afterthought a couple of lines saying Luise had just been asked out on her first date! They are going to the movies.

The 'religious discussion' was a farce – held in the workroom at the coffee-tables, the only 'girl' to join in was not there when I spoke two Sundays ago, and I have to say I dislike her intensely. It's a mutual dislike and I felt she was present merely to put the boot in.

When she said, 'Since becoming a Christian and living by Christ's teachings, I have felt a great inner peace,' I thought of her bullying first one girl last week, then another this week, and I wanted to pass the sick-bucket! More of this saccharin hypocrisy and I could keep quiet no longer. 'Some Christian you are! When I think of your behaviour these last couple of weeks, I have to say that if you are an example of living by Christ's teachings then I want no part of it!' I was accused of being 'personal', to which I responded by saying religion and belief are personal. Mic spoke for twenty minutes, all I said (in four) was rubbish. He really wouldn't let me speak at all. G., one of the theology students, asked me how Christ got to India. 'Well, if you believe his miracles he could have walked on water!' That finished his input.

They wanted me to bare my soul, so they could attack me yet remain behind their armour of belief and power! R. said, 'If you don't like the Church, Sara, don't come.' Smirk!

The whole episode left a very bad taste in my mouth, because whether they realize it or not, they (Church) came with the sole intention of putting this little upstart in her place.

I'm heartily sick of the women in here, I can really understand how apathy sets in. I blithely demand you do this, photocopy that! I'm unfair and selfish. I'm sorry. I LOVE YOU, DARLING.

Love, *Sara* xxx

Darling,

I want to scribble this quickly and post it in Brandon – I'm going to walk through the snow – (2 *miles*) – and will send something longer this afternoon. Just got your sad, grumpy letter and want to hug you.

Don't give up on dreams, my love! My comment on your comment on my dream was because I didn't want you to assume that anything 'wrong' must be your fault. I was trying to protect you from your pessimism.

Be a bit kinder, gentler with dreams and treat them like a handi-capped child, trying to tell you something, not an ogre out to punish you.

Smile please, I need you and love you. *George* xxx

Dastardly Raver!

You do go on, don't you? All right, let's settle this business about God. First, let me answer a few other points. I had a good gut feeling about Gifford when you first mentioned him some months ago – we need someone who is willing to stand and tell the Appeal judges that the first trial was a farce. I feel Gifford is a man who would do that. Don't fight the system, use it!

So, let us get back to God. Even at my lowest ebb, I have never lost my faith – although my perception of God has altered. But people seem to have little faith in themselves as divine creations of God, so they look to others as a source of their faith. I too (and you) have to fight apathy – it's everywhere, especially in H-wing. By being open to the higher consciousness I can be a creative channel. Sometimes it's not always apparent when I'm being very creative. I just trust my intuition. It does not make me better than anyone else, or more power-ful, but gives me happiness and a love of life. Work hard, don't lie, don't hurt people. That is all it's about. Enough for now, darling man. Some of the things you write, the real beauty in it comes from God. So there! Billi sent me two gym suits – one in black, a one-piece – I look like an exclamation mark!

It's getting worse, the weather I mean, I've got layers and layers on, but I wish we could be allowed outside in the snow, I'd love to jog in it.

Darling, keep warm and cosy – I wish I was with you – I love you very, very much, maybe next winter we'll be together. We can just stay by a fire drinking mulled wine – I love mulled wine – do you? Make it in the slow cooker.

I love you. *Sara*

Darling infidel,

I walked into Brandon this morning, except a van driver stopped and gave me a lift from halfway. I wasn't hitching. Just kindness.

I enjoyed walking back, with a blizzard at my back and thick snow falling.

The drivers passing must have watched me with guilt and pity – the only person walking. I was hoping nobody would stop and wished I had a sign on my back saying, 'I'm enjoying myself, thanks!' A girl was riding a black horse in a field by the road – they looked great in a sea of white. I thought of you doing it. I passed a farm called Little-White – well named. The trees are plastered with snow and it's sticking to walls.

Why not challenge the Holy Rollers to a snowball fight in the name of Our Lord? A just war! Winner gets first go at the communion wine.

When J. said, 'Unless we are perfect we can never feel God,' you should have said, 'Well, that solves the God question, then.'

It does matter to me that people walk around with their heads stuffed with religious polyfilla.

Garbage in, garbage out, as they say about computers.

Take care, sweetheart. Smile, please. I love you, *George* xxx

Darling

Do you feel beloved? I can still feel your strong body, your kisses, your touch. I felt very close to you today. C. said to her husband, 'Squeeze my hand every time they kiss.' She was remembering my earlier frustrations. 'Did you kiss him?' 'Nooo!!' 'For God's sake kiss her, George, and put us out of her misery!' Remember? Anyway, she told me her hand hurt, so I must have had a good visit!

Why were you so reticent about London? E.F. and Co. are working for me – I am granted the legal aid, so if I decide that I want you involved, then involved you will be. Damn it, I've fought hard enough for my rights, let's use them!

E.F. also told me that my nine-year tariff is equivalent to a fourteen-year sentence. The injustice of that takes my breath away.

Until I read what you had heard on the *Kilroy* programme I had forgotten once again how terribly important the facts of living with an alcoholic are. E.F. had seen some TV programme on it, so he too is aware. It all goes back to Henrietta B., doesn't it? Why, oh why didn't Henrietta speak of it? I know you worry and despair. At times I think my 'faith' and an almost complacent attitude drive you to distraction. But please, darling, have a little patience.

I will be having a wing review on 21 February – exactly a year to the day that I first spent in prison! It should be very interesting, all sorts of people will make assessments of me, including Mic the Vic, though quite why he feels qualified, God only knows! He's never once helped me, nor knows any of my problems either spiritually or emotionally.

This has been a chatty letter, please note how I have so far studiously avoided any reference to religion. I'm waiting for your reply to my last epistle!

Did I tell you M.D.'s thoughts on my crime? She's the only Indian in H-wing, a grandmother. Anyway, last week she said to me, apropros my sentence, 'Men here so stupid to put women in prison. You kill husband, husband very bad. No woman kill good husband!' I thought that summed it up very neatly.

No woman in her right mind would kill a husband that is good to her. I love it!

On that note, darling man, I shall go to sleep. I dreamt about you all afternoon.

I love and miss you, all the time, keep warm, and take care. Hope you've chopped lots of wood.

All my love, darling, *Sara*

Darling,

This weather is made for hibernation. How good to be a bear and wake up after six months to the sound of streams melting.

I misunderstood your comment, 'I'm glad I'm being punished . . .' I thought you meant in relation to being in prison, but I realized this morning you were referring to your cell punishment. Sorry!

I want a tape of you singing 'The Bare Necessities of Life'. Sounds exactly right for your theme tune, in every way!

Keep warm, darling, I love you, *George* xxx

Darling,

The thought of you going to Brandon on foot just to post me a letter made me feel dearly loved. Thank you. You're a real romantic at heart, aren't you? I love you.

Finally got to go outside Friday afternoon, briefly for five minutes. It was snowing, but they had cleared a little track in the exercise yard. I felt like a prisoner in Siberia.

Went out again this morning, the snow very deep. I made a snowman (of sorts). At least I made the base, rolled it till I could not move it – and so I started on the top. One of the officers said that if I was making a snowman I'd have to knock it down before we came in. Security reasons. I was told they made one last year and Control thought that there was a man in the yard!

Something wonderful happened in here on Friday afternoon. One of the girls won her Appeal. She had been in prison four years (sentenced to twelve) and was not taken to London for the hearing. She was just called to Mr Hicks's office, and told that all convictions against her were quashed and she was to be released immediately! I went to congratulate her, she was numb and white-faced with shock! The tears only came when she realized she'd have to leave her budgie behind! She'll collect it later. She left with a carrier bag of stuff, and was driven to the station to get a train to Liverpool. Can you imagine the sensory overload? After four years? Unbelievable. I hear she's getting married. I think it's great. I'd love to have heard her grounds for Appeal, though I doubt even she knows them.

I'm over the sadness I felt at missing Luise's first date – in a funny way, she probably understands now how you and I feel! She's a great person, my daughter. I've spent much of this weekend just thinking of her, she was more like a mother figure to me sometimes. At the school dance, 'Mummy, if you don't put your shoes on, I'm not going to dance with you.' 'Mummy, come back, the Star Trek dance is for the infants.' 'Mummy, if you keep singing I'll cross the road and pretend I don't know you.' Last Christmas at home a young boy, totally smitten with her, bought her an outrageously expensive Christmas card. Before he had time to draw breath, I had him and his friend in, drinking Coca Cola out of crystal, and quizzing him, 'What does your father do? What are your favourite subjects at school?' Ridiculous of me. Luise is probably quite relieved that I'm not there to overlook this supreme event. Billi will be outwardly casual and laid-back, but I want to know *every* detail. I shall write to Luise and say if she gets up to what you and I get up to – how does she rate it?

God, I love that kid!

All my love, *Sara* xx

Hello Darling,

So you are keeping me at arm's length till I 'simmer down', hey? Cheek! But you're right to challenge my anger. It's more frustration and exasperation than anger – I love you as much as ever. In fact, if I didn't love you so much I wouldn't have the energy to be frustrated.

The discussion about 'God' is getting pretty silly, isn't it? You say I'm 'terribly wrong' to refer to the 'creative uncertainty' of my sense of life and meaning. All I can say is that there is no *space* for creativity in a mind which is solid with its own certainties. Uncertainty is part of responding to a big problem.

Let's be more specific and practical – your Appeal is a challenge to our creativity, isn't it?

My view (I'm only asking that it should be seriously assessed) is that the key missing discussion is nothing to do with your childhood and everything to do with what happened during the months preceding M.'s death.

You're driving me crazy! I suspect that you don't like my approach to the Appeal because it shows you in 'too good' a light? You prefer to explain (via childhood) why you were 'awful'?

M. could have killed you and, or, Luise. He was the one who deserved diminished responsibility, not you.

Mulled wine? Lovely. With you, too? Heaven!

See you soon (if you give me permission, Your Excellency . . .). I love you, *George* xxx

Darling,

I once wrote and told you that I 'get on better with men than women'. A funny thing has happened, the situation is now reversed. I find that I'm very distrustful of men, all of them. I actually open up much more to women. Did I always distrust men, but not realize it? Or have I, because of Daddy, only just come to distrust men? You don't count, darling. I trust you implicitly. I think I trust E.F., maybe it's just that men who are dominant figures in my life, have quite suddenly, all at once, shown me what shallow hypocrites they are! Your thoughts on this please, my love.

I feel good though, the contact from E.F. has helped lift me.

Good night, my darling love, I adore you. *Sara* x

Darling 'exclamation mark',

Stick to basic and recent facts. Simple, straightforward, lawful. Please believe me, my 'anger' is only frustration that you are underselling yourself. Focus on the good, use all this faith and make it count.

I went into Brandon for food as well as posting a love letter! The food of love . . . and the love of food.

There's a sign by the golf-course saying, 'Private. No sledging', so I took it off and buried it in the snow and was happy to see lots of kids sledging there just now.

I'm smiling, and love you. *George* xxx

Dear One,

I am rankled (hence the endearment).

We must be very careful about blaming the original defence team.

The Appeal judges are angry and sensitive to the criticism they are getting, therefore we have to gently tell them why I changed. Not ram it down their throats. I think we are both extreme, you think too much of me, i.e. 'lawful homicide', and I think too little of me, i.e. guilt. Let's find a happy medium – then we'll be a great team. I have so much to tell you.

Funny, I used to feel part of the 'girls', now I feel like an outsider looking in. I just don't think like these people any more. Oh God, these girls just love to hate. In this low state my belief in the judicial system of this country just flies out of the window, along with my hope.

I said it before, and I'll say it again, don't let me sabotage this

Appeal. A year of living in an environment where we are considered one step up from shit, does after a while have a cumulative effect. Strip-searches, cell searches, body rub-downs at least twice a day, constant surveillance, cameras, gossip, venom, apathy, are all very, very demoralizing. I don't think I'll fully realize how destructive it is till I'm out. Can you imagine me leaving a pub with you, and holding up my arms for a search at the door? It's getting to me, but I'm learning all the time.

I am beginning to see the victim/rescuer syndrome in me. Now when the girls come moaning I listen, then say, 'Don't moan to me. If you feel you have been treated unjustly, then simply make an official complaint!'

I love you very much, *Sara* xxx

My Darling Love,

It's nearly 10 o'clock, I have lain on my bed since lock-in at 8 p.m., just thinking of how much I love you, and trying to conjure the delicious feelings I had when you held me! I loved our embrace at the end, our first good stand-up cuddle. There are endless possibilities. I hated letting you go, I just have to pull a shutter down over my emotions. I'm getting very good at it. You must be, too. I just wanted to come upstairs and lie with your lingering presence, but the girls, ever curious, ever eagerly awaiting the newspaper articles and other offerings they know you bring.

S. wants to know if we can sue the Home Office for sex discrimination. I feel it must either be because we are Cat. B inmates held in maximum security or we are denied the many privileges that exist for men in Cat. A situations.

As soon as I had put the tea tray away, I was called to census. There was a letter from E.F. He writes: 'Tony Gifford (QC) has contacted me and tells me you want him to be my leader. You should have consulted me first. But Tony is excellent, and if available, will do a great job. I take it you want me to send him the papers. He says he will be back in June, so we may have to adjourn the case till then – but could probably spend the time usefully.'

What do you feel, darling?

With Gifford on my side, I feel strong, he must be working for the

Birmingham Six Appeal. That will be 4 March, I hear. God, I *hope* they are freed.

Why don't you ask me something simple like, 'Do you want more children?'

Mrs C. said last week that people are nervous about talking with me. She said I have a very athletic mind, and quoted the last meeting with F. She counted ten separate topics I mentioned, from the Gulf War to humanity and respect – all in twenty minutes. Can't she see they are related? I sometimes get lonely, you are the only one who stretches me! I wish it was physical as well as mental!

I've been writing for over an hour! It's very warm in my cell. My little piggies are fairly flying around in the warm air! Nothing aches tonight, except my heart. I miss you! Realized on last visit, how *solid* you are. Do I really want to wrestle? Yes, yes, yes, *Sara* xxx

Darling,

Stop punishing that lovely exclamation mark, please, or there will be nothing left but exclamation!

I *love* your Valentine card – the best I've ever had.

As for the 'kneading', I do need you, always, and will knead you, always, but if you ever knead me I'd stop needing you!

It was a good visit, wasn't it?

One of my many favourite things with you is looking you straight in the face – I love your face, all of it.

I don't think you're an expert on Appeals, Trampoline – why don't we just say what should be used and let E.F. say what can be used? How can the judges be strict if these QCs are allowed to ramble on and on?

Please be very careful about your accident trend (I saw a lovely road sign in India, 'Beware of Accidents' – put it over your bed).

I love you always, *George* xxx

Darling,

I really want Gifford. He has the guts and integrity to attack the judicial system, a rare quality.

He feels I shouldn't be in prison, he made that quite clear before he even knew I had an Appeal or any interest in him. Having someone as well thought of as Gifford interested in defending me does a lot for my self-esteem. I need that, as you know. I don't want to fail and say, well, I wish I had asked for Gifford. He's the one I want. *And* he doesn't need to seek fame and glory! He's got it already; but he does have a reputation to defend! I like the way he's written this gutsy, honest book. Please tell me if you have any objections, apart from the fact that he's a lord!

I was talking to my trusted councillor tonight (Sister A.). I asked if she would be present at the wing review; she said, 'No,' with a rather wry smile.

I think that is disgusting, so tomorrow I am going to see Mr Hicks, and ask that she be allowed to submit a report and speak at the review. She, more than anyone, understands me, my guilt, my fears, my struggle for the truth. If she's not allowed to speak I will publicly condemn the whole farce, and write to Judge Tumim.

I haven't sent you E.F.'s letter because I'm sending it to Luise. It's so badly written that she'll be tickled pink to see that her writing is better than a leading barrister's!

I can't begin to tell you how good it was to see you today, darling, I love you so much, you're so dear to me. I'd rather have you for two hours a month than any other man with freedom. Believe that! Yes, six months on 17 February, isn't it marvellous? I feel as if I have known you for ever, in a way my life really did start with you. I look back and wonder, how did I ever survive without this love, this feeling of belonging? Are there couples out there who have felt this way all their lives? If so, they must be very, very lucky. I feel lucky, and privileged and I've loved you for just under six months. Let's never take it for granted. I want to be grateful *every* time I open my eyes and see you beside me.

My 'soppy nonsense' was written yesterday whilst we were locked in awaiting searches. I'm somewhat surprised at myself – I've never written a Valentine poem for anyone, and certainly not such an unashamedly sentimental one. Please, don't let people see it, it'll spoil my comic reputation. P. and M. read it, thought it 'beautiful'. I could have sold it ten times over! They asked, 'What are you going to do if George brings you a red rose?' I thought a minute. 'Naaa – I can trust him to be far more original than that!' Of course you were – I had a visit, no one else did. That is original, and gratifying and lovely. Thank you, darling. Keep an eye on me. I suspect I could be awfully soppy given the chance.

Loving, therapy key? Like yours, my darling. *Sara* xxx

Darling,

The trouble with you, if you'd been a man you'd have won a VC for some lunatic act of suicidal bravery! But you're getting a bit better at admitting pain. Perhaps that's related to feeling more at home with women? Maybe you're more at ease with being a woman?

Yes, go ahead with Lord Gifford.

I still don't like the idea of an adjournment.

But it may have to happen. Never assume that more time means more work – it can mean more time wasted!

Yes, ditch A. The Asian solicitor is R.S.

I think you'd like him – very quick, enthusiastic.

Lord Gifford won't be any use if he doesn't transform the trial verdict into its opposite. Expect it from him.

Yes, I loved our long hug.

It's good to feel each other, silent, warm, alive.

Snow going, Spring coming, love growing, I love you, *George* xxx

Hello Love of my Life!

Where are you? Do I too have to suffer 'Black Mondays'? The thought of a letter from you kept a happy smile on my face all morning, then *bam*! – no letter. God, I was disappointed. I'm just spoilt!

Love you, *Sara* xx

Darling,

I've had a quiet weekend, how about you? Warm, I hope. Spent all this afternoon indulging in my favourite pastime, lying in bed thinking of you! You just don't know how much I love you really, do you? Well, I do.

You think gut feelings come from tummy ache – wrong! Gut feelings are instincts. You recognize it in animals, why not in humans? Because your logical mind overrides!

I want to know as much as I can about (a) violence and (b) fluorescent light. Just how dangerous is the constant fluorescent light? Of course the frequency is very fast. I'm just interested.

I believe as you do that my spate of accidents was caused by ... confusion. I think I know what. I have become very aggressive, very male, blocking all my feminine, womanly feelings, and it just hasn't felt right.

I have meditated all weekend. As a result I feel calmer, softer and the sexual fantasies are the most vivid and beautiful I've ever had. Comment please! (not on the SFs).

Last night one of the officers told me we wouldn't be allowed to have plugs in our cells, in case someone decided to electrocute themselves. What a stupid reason, what a stupid woman to think we believe it. There are plugs everywhere, even in the washroom.

I've loved you so much today, fairly bursting with love – always, darling, *Sara* xxx

Darling,

I'm still basking in the glow of your lovely letter.

Your comment on men seems very sensible (provided you keep on not counting me in the hit list). Men are in a lot of trouble these days. They are clinging to the wreckage of worn-out traditions, institutions and power play. They don't know how to express the worldwide value of true feeling so they don't create or really love.

Women are in a different kind of mess! They are like people who have inherited a once grand hotel only to discover that it is bankrupt. If they step into male shoes they will make equally big fools of themselves (e.g. Thatcher) – they have to learn new 'rules' for a new game.

We're in the same leaking boat, darling love.

How's this for an interesting insight? Child abuse in Scotland. The incidence of child sexual abuse is especially high in religious households (father a minister). Why? Because, they say, the ministers don't commit adultery outside – they keep up a holy front.

By preaching cosmetic 'good' they act out hidden 'bad'.

I have a fantasy of lying by the fire listening to you play the guitar – or you can play while I struggle with your recipes.

Brilliant Russian documentary on remote villages – one woman said of the authorities, 'The whole system is a morgue. They treat us like shit. It's as if they stamp on us with their right foot, while the left foot is scared.' Remind you of anything?

Take care – treat that lovely exclamation mark with love, until I can.

I love you, *George* xxx

My Beloved,

Two letters from you today, manna from heaven. Civilized overseer said, 'You've got two from George, Sara, I know he likes his bike, but recycled envelopes?'

Great, you've accepted the Appeal postponement so gracefully, darling. I thought you might have congratulated me on acquiring Lord Gifford. Perhaps you don't want to admit the strength of my gut feelings? I'm stirring – I *love* you.

A funny-ha-ha day today. I'm sewing a satin nightdress case for Ella, and inside she wanted 'Failte' embroidered. It means 'Welcome' in Gaelic. Mrs H. asked me what it meant this afternoon. I replied, 'The bomb is in the left-luggage locker!' Naughty of me really but we all broke up. Set the tone for the rest of the afternoon. Mrs H. said that in my report for the wing review – she said, 'Sara is very entertaining!'

M.L., one of the girls who lost her Appeal last year, was handed a twelve-year tariff date. We were all stunned. I passed her last week, she was sitting alone at the table downstairs, one look at her face and I started crying, so she did too. She has two young children and I could feel her pain and despair. There has been a special investigation ordered by the judge at her trial into the police's behaviour during her interrogation, yet she still lost her Appeal. I begged her to fight, but she refused, I guess she thought she'd get a low tariff. Anyway, she sidled up to me tonight, and asked rather shyly, 'Sara, can I write to the Home Secretary?' 'M.L., darling, you can write to whoever you want,' I replied, 'I've probably got the address.' 'I'm going to fight, Sara!' she said.

Funny thing is, the minute she decided, 'That's it, they are not doing this to me!' she felt great. She's lost that drawn, haunted look and is ready to go. Hallelujah! I shall help her as much as I can.

I've written to E.F. I said I don't want to be 'fitted in' by Gifford, either he accepts or refuses!

One thing E.F. told me, which surprised me greatly, was that we could have used both provocation and diminished responsibility as a defence. That was the first I heard of it. Makes sense to me.

Be careful on your bike.

I love you, *Sara* x

Darling,

I looked up some stuff on Appeals. The Appeal Court can order a new trial. However, this power can only be used in cases where there is fresh or credible evidence and the Court considers that it is in the interests of justice to receive it even tho' it was available and admissible at the trial. Surely H.B.'s evidence on living with an alcoholic comes into this category, doesn't it?

The *Dispatches* thing is on tomorrow, according to a card from Faction Films.

Hope your cold has gone and you're well and warm.

I love you, *George* xxx

Dearest Groucho,

I'm very hurt that you won't visit with Marnie. My first instinct was to sulk, but that wouldn't get us anywhere.

I'm trying to understand you, though I think your logic is wrong.

I agreed to diminished responsibility as my trial plea. Barker said, 'You've no chance with self-defence, we have to go on dim. res.' I said, 'OK.' End of discussion. Why so brief? Because I was very scared. He was the expert, and everybody was saying, 'For once in your life, Sara, shut up and do what you are told!'

I think that in some ways I was emotionally traumatized.

One of the teachers from the male prison saw the *Dispatches* report.

This teacher said that they got the message across, the law must change. That, as far as I'm concerned, is *all* that matters.

Sara x

217

Darling,

The Gifford letter is quite friendly.

They expect the barrister to do all the work, and the QC gets the centre stage. Prima donna act. Maybe QC stands for Quite Conceited?

You, darling, are the only real expert on you.

I'm worried by that last sentence of yours for the *Dispatches* report: 'I accept my culpability.' I know what that really means, that you must accept that you did it, but it sounds much more like you are to blame for it.

It's crazy referring prison officers to GPs for stress if the GPs don't know what goes on inside.

Feel my love, on you, inside you, around you, all over you, part of you, please. Sexy, spiritual, purring.

In the Middle Ages destructive power was often in the hands of wicked individuals. (Saddam Hussein is a kind of throw back). Today we are trapped like flies in bureaucratic cobwebs, webs of rules, regulations – just like prison. Eichmann was called a 'desk-murderer' because he just organized and signed papers. He spoke only 'Amtsprache' (officialese). Today we have 'desk-torturers', faceless Home Office civil servants who snare people in rules and statistics. Nobody accepts responsibility (unlike Genghis Khan) because nobody is responsible.

Take care, my heart and spirit are with you – *George* xxx

My Dearest George,

I've had a pretty good day, apart from your letter this lunch-time.

I feel betrayed by your latest letter. Have you not yet realized that I don't fit into your social boxes?

I thought if you met Marnie you could help me see why I care for her so much. But, first you refuse to meet her, at least with me, then you label my feelings.

Don't *ever* compare me with any of your ex-girlfriends. That makes me very angry!

Love, *Sara*

Darling star of stage, screen and H-wing!

I've just watched *Dispatches* and it was very well done – you will have seen it by now?

I'll write to Gita – she done good, as the footballers say. It was well put together and moving – the woman who spoke your lines (they stuck to the agreement) was a bit actressy but clear, precise with a straight BBC accent – just like you!

The filming of the Crawley public meeting in support of Kiranjit was excellent – colourful, sensitive, emotional, genuine.

As usual, forceful, articulate lover-in-waiting, you wrote an excellent piece for them. You can be glad, proud of yourself.

Keep warm, well, loving. I adore you, *George* xxx

Darling,

I wish I was with you. I'm well aware that my last letter will have hurt and unsettled you, perhaps even ended our relationship. But it's terribly important for us to be honest.

I'm not angry now, just very sad. Under normal circumstances I'd be euphoric over *Dispatches*, but I just feel that it's nice. That's all.

Had my first 'fan' letter today, from a woman in Sussex, a psychiatric nurse. She says it's bad enough that men's violence forces women into psychiatric hospitals, but when it forces them into prison it is unthinkable.

Whatever you feel, whatever the outcome, please try to remember that I love you very much. Adore you, as you said in your letter. Makes me feel awful.

All my love, *Sara* xxx

PS Lovely letter from A. You must have told her about your Valentine card. She wrote that you were 'delighted'. I'm glad to hear it, you never told me how you felt about it. You just gave me a credit rating – wonderful. I need to know how you *feel*!

Darling aggrieved,

I hope you're feeling better.

I laughed (yes!) at your 'left-luggage locker' joke! Keep joking, Groucho.

Please smile, feel our hug. Don't give up.

I love you, *George* xxx

Darling Fury!

I was reading your letter with a depressed frown, but when I got to 'I'm so bloody angry ... Damn you!' I had to laugh! I do respect your fighting qualities.

I'm sorry if I didn't express enough feeling about the Valentine card. I thought I had. Anyway, it was lovely and made me feel very loved and loving. I did tell you it was the best I'd ever had, didn't I?

Please don't get angry with me if I decide whether I want to see you with someone else [Marnie]. That's my right, too, isn't it, love?

Must tell you about the 'support group' meeting last night.

It was a disaster, but illuminating, absurd, a little bit hopeful too. First disaster, R. and her friend had a car crash on the way there – nothing very serious but she was quite shaken and white. I have to be a bit careful describing some of the participants – one of them was unbelievable, absurdly uptight and pompous, saying she had signed the Official Secrets Act and couldn't stay, say anything, and didn't want to be in the group, anyway. A real prison person.

It was soon very clear that the insiders were there for sabotage – not a glimmer of a positive thought or suggestion. Not a glimmer of acknowledgement that anything could be wrong. A desperate, flat, lifeless position. Talk about being institutionalized. Any suggestion of reform, change, is regarded as a personal threat.

I read out a list of what I felt (from my experiences and yours) were/are real and immediate problems in H-wing – visits, children, food, power, emotional health, information, law, rules, etc. I asked if they'd seen *Dispatches* – most had. I mentioned you – most of them are terrified of mentioning a prisoner by name.

They were (most of them) shocked by what I said. It was soon apparent that the wreckers would prevent any sensible planning of a group. So it ended without any real agreement or plan. Sabotaged by *fear*.

BUT, the good news. After the insiders had gone the rest of us (six) had a much better discussion and then it got even better.

A lot of laughter, mostly about one of the main wreckers – J. gave a very sharp description of the latter putting on her scarf and stalking out!

M.M. was great. I think you'd like her humour – she tells me to shut up, like you do!

So the meeting was a disaster, on one level, but hopeful on another.

I'm dying to hear what you (and the others) thought of the *Dispatches* film. It was much better than 'nice', darling. It was very good.

You can be as rude as you feel – just tell me you love me, later, and I'll survive!

Hope you are smiling again, darling. I love you – *George* xxx

Darling,

I've had a truly miserable weekend. Mooned about, tried to watch TV but ended up in my cell, just thinking of you. I haven't done any of the things I'd planned to do, didn't even go out on exercise. I feel lonely, lost and sad. The only thing I am certain of is how much I love you, and how much I want you in my life. Please believe that. Hurry up and tell me you still love me.

I finally got to see the *Dispatches* programme. Not a single officer commented on it.

General consensus was that it was good.

There were tears. I felt very tense, and I *didn't* recognize myself. The first photo was taken when I was sitting in the kitchen. I looked like a zombie! I can still remember the beating I had when we came back from the 'do'.

Kiranjit's story is very sad. I agree the meeting was very moving. I'm glad they balanced it with shots of English women supporters. I'm glad you are pleased with it. The girls that saw it are pleased for me, and proud of me. Saturday, I listened to a girl's account of her first violent marriage. She shook and cried, even acted out her running away and the gate being locked, but I think she felt better afterwards.

I really need to see and hold you, darling. Marnie wrote that as soon as she's got the money together, she'll be up. She's going to phone us this coming week.

I awoke sobbing this morning – dreamt I went to visit and man a woman. They were in a big house, a huge, unhappy house. The woman didn't speak at all, she was a grey, blurred figure. The man kept making me fancy cocktails which I didn't want to drink. When I cracked the ornate glass he was serving them in, I was too scared to tell him. He saw anyway, and kept poking me with a gold swizzle-stick. It hurt, and each poke was accompanied by 'stupid girl' over and over again . . .

I can't make head nor tail of it. Of all the feelings I have for this shadow-man in my dreams, from intense loving and forgiveness to deep sadness, the one overriding feeling is fear. I am terrified. Why? I don't know why and I want to know why.

I feel blocked.

I imagined this weekend never seeing you again, not getting letters from you, and it hurt. Just a bleak, lonely future. Bear with me, sweetheart, please, me and my angry pen. I want to be with you, to hold you, and tell you, and show you how much I love you. Damn this bloody prison! Just when you write that you need my support I pull it out from under you. What is wrong with me?

I adore you, no matter what. I *hope* you still feel the same as you did. If not, I'll try to understand. Just tell me.

Love, *Sara* xxx

Darling,

It's the best, sunniest, most spring-like day of the year, and all the birds seem to agree.

Reading some more of Fromm's *Sane Society* again I suddenly realized what the medical definition of H-wing must be – sado-masochistic. Sadism he defines as the seeking of security through power over others – masochism is seeking security through submission to outside power.

It is a system which has to dehumanize to survive. Agree? Which is why all the 'reforms' are cosmetic efforts to present an ideal face.

I've meditated on our latest tiff. I think the real problem is that I'm starved of you, you are starved of me (?), but you are also starved of other people you want to see. So you are more starved than I am!

If you want to ask me if I want to share a visit, please do. But you have no more 'right' to be angry at my refusal than I have any right to stop you seeing (or loving) someone. OK?

I love you, *George* xxx

PS Judge, when he sentenced the B'ham Six seventeen years ago: 'They stand convicted on the clearest and most convincing evidence.' All that evidence is now acknowledged as rubbish! – just like yours.

Hello Love,

I feel low, can't seem to snap out of it.

We get body rub-downs at least twice a day, strip-searches before and after leaving the wing, like going to hospital. Strip-searches when we have a room spin. You know the indignity I've suffered during those. A complete lack of privacy, all the time. Even our phone calls are listened to.

'Seeking security in power over others.' A perfect description. I'm very pleased you wrote that, so are many of the girls – they agree.

Being told to conform to the most stupid archaic rules, e.g., we have to hand in our tweezers every evening. We can't keep them in our rooms, yet we have razors, glass, china. For me the most exhausting thing has to be the censoring of mail and the way we are treated as children.

At my wing review I was asked about having male officers on the wing. I replied that as I no longer measured my own worth in terms of a man's opinion of me I didn't care one way or another. I'm holding my breath for the Birmingham Six. They *must* be freed! The judiciary is certainly taking a knock.

I wonder if this will make the Appeal judges more lenient or more harsh in their verdicts? They are human after all.

Take care. Spring is here, isn't it? *Sara* x

Darling Love,

Smile and joke please. Your wing needs you. Not half as much as I do.

Looks like the Gulf War is almost over.

One pitiful sight, four Iraqis surrendering to US marines. A young marine held a revolver in one hand and gave them orders to lie down. They thought he was going to shoot them and kept imploring him not to. He kept repeating (in English which they couldn't understand), 'It's all right – it's all right,' in a soothing tone. Rather typical of the whole thing, no mutual understanding.

We can organize a war brilliantly.

We can't organize peace at all.

The girl who remembered her violent marriage shows how 'remedial', therapeutic, it can be for someone to know about somebody else's trauma, doesn't she?

Some thoughts on your dream. You are exploring a source of your unhappiness (the house) – the woman is ghostly (irrelevant) – all the colour (energy) is around the man. 'Fancy cocktails' which you didn't want. *Cock tales*? You 'cracked' the ornate glass he was serving them in. 'Cracked' (as in code?). Ornate glass. Glass can symbolize the intellect, rationality – something you can see through. 'Ornate' – elaborate. Elaborate 'reasons' which you reject – they don't convince you. You were scared of telling him that. 'He saw it and kept poking me with a gold swizzle-stick.' He knew you knew. 'Poking – *sex*? Gold – expensive, bribing (?) you with cash (using clothes, etc.). 'Stupid girl!' He was offloading his guilt on to you by putting you down?

You say, 'I can't make head nor tail of it.' Tail? Cock tale? What do you think? 'Swizzle-stick' – swindle prick? When are you going to play your part in the dream exchange, darling?

I need your imagination just as much as you need mine.

All my love, *George* xxx

Hello My Dearest Love,

Apathy over!

I felt yesterday that you hadn't given full consideration to our life. All I had was one short paragraph. I felt you didn't really care. I know better now. I love you too. How? Well, differently from anyone I've ever loved or ever will. My love for you is unique, that's why it's so special.

My love for Marnie is like that I feel for Billi. I guess a lot of it is based on genuine concern for her situation, a lovely young girl slowly and helplessly destroying herself with drugs.

There's an aura of tragedy over Marnie, maybe some instinct tells me I have a short time to show my love for her. She wrote today, she has no breasts, her periods have stopped, she's slowly dying. Maybe she needs a lot of love. Like a baby suckling, the more milk it takes, the more the mother produces.

My love for you is different. Love isn't really the word I want to describe it. It's so near yet I look back and wonder how I ever thought I was complete without you? It's as if I was a 1,000-piece jigsaw puzzle and you are the one piece I couldn't find.

Your Iraqi soldier story brought tears to my eyes. Couldn't the US have at least taught their soldiers the Arab words for 'peace' or 'you are safe now'? Too much to expect.

As far as my dream is concerned I did have a vague nasty feeling about it.

I had my tutorial. Nice man. Said he's really earned his money. The problem with society – I said it was spiritually bankrupt – everybody was too selfish. Eventually he had to concede. I enjoyed it immensely. A real battle of wits.

Yes, I'm smiling again and tap-dancing.

My Love, always. *Sara* xxx

PS   Simon says he's not sure if he can like someone who doesn't love Liverpool FC!

Darling,

My heart always misses a beat when I don't hear from you.

I just love hearing from you, even when you're hopping about in fury.

Re my thoughts on your dream, please realize that my response is always filtered through my experience, bias, values, etc. Your own response is far more important.

If your dream was about the things I suggested then it's important that you take good care of the 'child Sara'.

An experience like that would very likely have 'frozen' your emotional growth to some extent. A legacy of shock, trauma, hurt. So any future 'immaturity' would probably be rooted in that frozen response. A part of you, then, would be a frozen child.

She needs your forgiveness too, because kids always seem to blame themselves. You did nothing wrong.

By the way, one of Mic the Vic's observations at the meeting before he left was that he had his own ways of making his views known on prison. He didn't explain but I presume he means via his union. But it was yet another excuse for not developing a support group specifically for H-wing. Typical!

Hugs galore. *George* xxx

Darling Distant-beloved,

I'm not at all sure you want this letter but you can have it anyway. I find your anger much easier to deal with than indifference.

H-wing may be a good (accurate) mirror, externally and institutionally, of what you experienced internally as a child. The same sort of surface gloss and 'care' – the same sort of underlying cold indifference and power?

You keep asking me what I feel, yet your feelings seem to be in what London taxi drivers call a 'kipper state' – flat. Why not tell me what you feel too?

I feel sad, upset, angry, confused, resentful, thoughtful, anxious, fed up, and I wouldn't have this jumble of feelings if I didn't *love* you so much and care so much when things go wrong. Is that enough to go on with?

All you had to do re Marnie was tell me she was a friend you wanted to see. Neither of us has to explain or justify our love for others but we do owe it to each other, don't we, to take a lot of care with our love and the great tension which surrounds it?

I can't send this without letting you know how much I love you (and want your love). There are parts of you and of me which will destroy our love if we let them. Let's be careful. Please.

I love you more than ever and feel dreadful while we are so distant.

Please, darling dragon, can we kiss and make up? Stop staring moodily into space and look at me! I'm smiling – wish I could kiss you for hours.

Take care, smile, massage your heart, love me! *All* my love, *George* xxx

March

Darling Beloved,

Just got your letter, written in the sun, but with shades of insecurity. I am *not* fed up with you, I adore you, so please don't think that. It's you and your letters that give *me* sunshine despite my surroundings. The thought of you and our love is my armour against everything bad.

You are right. I'm still angry and at times disappointed in myself when I think back to how easily Tigger and Co. manipulated me. I guess it comes out when I write about it. 'Bullet-proof' says, 'She's on her soap-box again.' I'll be thrilled when all this is behind me (us).

I try to remind myself that the pain will be worthwhile when I can see us using these lessons to help others and change the law, OK?

Life. What shall we do? Well, to start with, get married, then I think write a book, have a baby and work to release a few more women 'lifers'. Also a TV film, and a support group. Plus learning about each other, and our love and life – is that enough to contend with?

Please feel *all* my love for you. Yours! *Sara* xxx

Darling Sara,

I'm glad you described your love for Marnie. I wish you had done it when you first wrote about her. She certainly needs love – I hope you can help her.

My comments on the celebration were a bit humourless – I suppose I've always hated fake celebrations which are based on nothing but a desire to get drunk.

You didn't say much about the dream ideas. Hit or miss? Or a near miss, or a near hit, or a hiss, or what?

If Saddam Hussein thinks he's won a 'great victory', your father probably thinks he was a 'father of all fathers'!

Judge Tumim was interviewed in the same series as Gifford. Best comment: 'Feeling sad is not a medical problem.'

He's a good Dickensian favourite bachelor uncle – *kind*, unoriginal, sensible, practical. Pity there aren't more of him, but not too many!

Glad you're smiling – wish I could see it/you. I *miss you*.

All my love, *George* xxx

Darling,

Just got your irate letter.

Yes, you are right, though I didn't see it, this place is just like my childhood! I'm making life terribly difficult because I'm fighting like mad against the lies and hypocrisy. I couldn't understand why my failure makes me so angry, mad and upset. My rage has at times been almost unbearable. But, looking at it like you do, I guess that I understand better.

I'm sorry if I'm hurting you, but I've got to travel this path, till I've freed myself from my parents. If you feel you can't support me, let me know. I'll still love you anyway.

Sara

Darling,

Just want to tell you how much I love you. My grouches and depressions are real but my love is a thousand times stronger. So be patient please.

Can you believe how sentimental Americans are – report on the radio about people stopping on freeways when the national anthem is played, to get out and stand to attention! They've just killed and crippled 100,000-plus people and fed another dose of high-tech violence into the world's bloodstream, via the Gulf War.

Our love is the most precious thing of all because it's our key to life – I think you were describing that in your last letter. We have a long way to go. Stay with me, please, darling.

I love you so much, *George* xxx

My Dearest Man,

Finally I can pour my heart out! This is part of the problem, with the really enforced security.

The officers are losing their power, first within the wing, and the Woolf Report has scared them. The sense of power they enjoy is the only way they can compensate for the awful job they have to do. Add to this the fact that the courts themselves are now seen as fallible, and my TV programme, you can imagine the way they are. I put your clippings about jails on the board downstairs (first had to ask Mogg to tell officers not to remove them). With the inhumanity bit underlined it has given them a fright. Suddenly judges are saying what you and I have been saying. I get furious when they use (abuse) their power. They decided two nights ago to stop giving out second post (contract does not stipulate they should). When the girls asked why, they at first lied and said there was none. Then they were told we'd seen it come in, so they blamed their behaviour on me!

Your letter posted Sunday – I am sure it was withheld. The envelope was not 'fresh'. It looked like they do when I've carried a letter around for a couple of days. But I can't prove it! What I do know is that they are still reading all my letters and yours; you are my weak spot and together we are strong. The H-wing support group is merely another threat.

For 'our' sake, I have to pretend that you are doing it alone. They could, in the name of security, stop our visits. They are omnipotent, they loathe us now and would do anything to hurt us. This of course doesn't apply to all the officers, but a good few. Even without me, they have problems. I won't go into detail about the tactics, suffice to say I sent you an example this lunch-time. The thing is, I think like a prisoner, you think like a free man.

I think that you are asking too much of your support group! Don't force them to run before they can walk. Why not go for one thing? Therapy, for example? When they have achieved that, they will have the confidence to do more. A lot feel that nothing can be changed, I can understand why they feel that. Change means fear.

All my love, *Sara* xx

Darling,

The ultimate idiocy of a maximum-security prison, when the fire regulations are secret!

Saw R. this morning and had a good argument with her – she is a gradualist.

As I suspected, she ticked me off for being too 'angry' at our meeting last Friday. So I said that at least we exposed all the contradictions and problems very quickly, and that if she knew you as I know you she'd be angry, too! (Smile, please, love.)

It's raining, sleeting, grey, miserable, but I feel warm inside about you and hope you do, too.

I'll enclose some cuttings.

All my love, *George* xxx

Hello My Love,

Funnily enough, all those who supported me before and during the trial have dropped by the wayside, as if in doing that they used their last reserves.

I feel that the ones who can offer the least constructive help are the ones that are most imprisoned. Just feel sorry for them, they are entitled to their own destiny. I feel so lucky that I'm sad for anyone who doesn't have you as a prospective lover/husband. So there, stop moaning. You'd better come and see me, sounds to me as if you need a big dose of loving.

I love Judge Tumim's comment, 'Feeling sad is not a medical problem.' I feel like having it printed on a card and distributed to all those awful psychiatrists I have to see!

I've bollocked E.F. He had approached a QC in his Chambers, called Geoffrey Robertson, to act for me. A man I've never heard of. So I told E.F. that, as he points out, the choice of leader is mine! If Gifford can't give a firm commitment we'll look elsewhere.

I also told E.F. that I am no longer prepared to speak out at the Appeal Court with a diminished responsibility label. I am not nuts and never was. It's provocation. I also told him to use first-class stamps. This last letter was posted 27 February. A week wasted. A week worrying. I told him to contact you. This is all shorthand, darling, so don't go mad at me! I said he is to ask Henrietta Bullard why alcoholism was not discussed, why they framed me – that's how I see it. I want E.F. to tell the Appeal Court that the wrong defence was used.

Do you want to visit this Friday afternoon? I can't think of a better way to start the weekend!

Thank you for your lovely letter today, I know you love me, darling.

Finally I'm beginning to realize maybe I'm not so crazy.

I love you. *Sara* x

Darling,

Your comment about H-wing being like my childhood was great. You clever perceptive man, *that's* why I feel such anger at my helplessness. I sometimes look back on my childhood and wonder why I was so spineless as to let Mummy and Daddy treat me the way they did. Maybe the constant fighting in here is the little girl who is finally saying, 'You are wrong, unfair, and I no longer accept your condemnation!' I know I'm feeling even more confident now.

You complain that I treat you like a father. Darling, you are all to me, father, brother, uncle. At the moment I seem to see my father in a lot of men, but not in you. Probably because the men I come in contact with here are pretty weak and pathetic. And scared of me. You are at present the only man who treats me for what I really am!

Please try to think like a prisoner so you can see my angles. Read between the lines of my open letters if you can. I love you so much but if you feel you can't cope, if I'm hurting you, we'll stop. I don't want to hurt you. I liked your letter today. Whew – like the top off a volcano. I knew you were feeling bad, it's good to release it. Marvellous that you realize I can take a letter like that. Six months, no three months ago I would have been devastated, now I see the love too. See mine, darling man. I do adore and need you. I'll save the rest for tomorrow a.m. xxxxxxx

Before I forget, I told Martina that if her breast pills work, I'll order a T-shirt for her with 'Boobs not Bombs' on it! Tracey says she's going to get a notebook and write down my sayings. Now that's fame!

Wow! I now realize why they didn't want to give out the post. It's one thing to read my condemnation in a letter but seeing it formally typed out in your report is different. Powerful! It's a good report, darling. I'll read it through thoroughly this weekend, but yes, you've got the problem spot on!

I'm walking round with a hot-water bottle on my shoulder – when asked why, I reply, 'I'm not allowed a parrot!' Now the girls walk past and say 'pretty boy'.

In your arms is where I want to be. I love you.

I adore you. *Sara* xxxx

Darling ace letter-writer,

I felt the blood warming in my veins as I read your lovely letter – thank you.

You make me smile, urging me to be sensible, patient, etc., with the 'supporters', while you are fighting lies and hypocrisy. We both are.

I think we both need to remember sometimes that you are a prisoner but free, and I'm free but a prisoner. We are equal and opposite points of a whole. Aren't we?

I am not a therapist for others in the group – I am fighting for my own ideas and needs (and hopefully yours) and I expect others to do the same.

Hope your shoulder's OK again. You and your 'parrot', you ought to call yourself Long John Sara! The pirate of H-wing.

I'm sorry if you feel I 'deride' your spiritual quest. I don't, honest! I respect and admire it.

Please, if you think I'm being derisive, accuse me of it, ask questions, criticize, suggest remedies. Will you? It matters a lot to me, and to you.

I saw a girl yesterday afternoon as I was posting your letter who reminded me of what you'd said of Marnie. She was standing near the main crossroad of this village in pouring rain, with only a light-weight jacket on. Her face was pretty, white, and she just stood there, slightly huddled. Black hair, short skirt, about nineteen, twenty. There was something odd about the way she just stood there, in the middle of the pavement. Maybe she was waiting for a lift. On the way back from the postbox I said to her, 'Are you all right?' and she just turned and smiled slightly. Very strange. Maybe on drugs? I've never seen her here before. It's horribly sad when young people want to escape out of life rather than into it. I can admire your love and concern for Marnie.

When adults fail to make life exciting and challenging they condemn young people to premature old age (like the photo of the young Jewish boy in the Warsaw Ghetto with his hands up and a look of hopeless old age in his eyes). First the adults give up, then the children crack up.

You're the glow in my heart.

I love you, *George* xxx

My Darling,

It's 11 o'clock, I've been meditating since nine. I feel very good!

You're still feeling wretched, yet I've passed through that, and now, if anything, love you even more.

The coordinator from the Open University came to see me this morning. She saw S. and me together as we are both doing social sciences. When she asked me what I thought of it so far I replied, 'Boring!' I told her it strikes me that too many people spend their time and other people's money writing essays and theses on the problem of society, but none actually *does* anything practical. I said that the course makes me angry – especially as I'm constantly reminded of the gender differences that have always applied in our society. Far from being dismayed by my frank answers she said, 'I'm glad you feel like this – it means you've got the makings of a brilliant academic future!' Stunned by this, I then attacked the judiciary, the penal system. She was thrilled!

'Bullet-proof' asked me about my Appeal this morning. I told him it was adjourned. 'Eh, you'd better check on that, Sara, 'cause I've not been told.' 'No, you haven't,' I said, 'I've only just written and told the Registrar myself. He'll inform you when he's ready!'

Lovely letter from you today – glad you are glowing again. I take your comments about God – and agree – so I've decided that I'll refrain from using the term 'God' and will refer instead to 'Spirit of the Universe'.

I hadn't bothered to explain my feelings for Marnie, because I didn't really understand them myself. You bullied me into exploring. Do it again, it's good for me. I'm sorry I hurt you. I love you so much.

I think this is a wonderful time to be alive – we are emerging from a Dark Age – our whole identity is changing, becoming more aware. Feel it, hear it, and experience it. I love you *always, Sara* xxx

Darling Love,

I've been thinking about the B'ham Six and its relation to your case. It's clearer to me than ever what is the real difference between a 'male' and a 'female' case. The former is all about facts, forensic tests, scientific evidence, lies, power (forced confessions, etc.). It's all objectified. Did they do it, or didn't they? With your case it's entirely different. The essence of your case is behaviour and its meaning. Were you behaving like a subnormal, irresponsible woman going for money and revenge, or something much more interesting, complex, normal? So there has to be a massive effort of interpretation.

This is why, in my view, the dim. res. plea was such a disaster. It perverted the true nature of the problem by twisting it towards the usual 'male' case, e.g. using pseudo-scientific psychobabble about 'disorders' and 'abnormalities'. Fake facts! If your Appeal team doesn't expose this distortion of the truth they will just perpetuate the lie. What do you think?

I must tell you about an interesting programme last night on immune systems, mostly filmed in California. You'd have loved it. It was about the human immune system as a personal 'pharmacy', creating a variety of chemicals, etc., to ward off disease. The key to it was the mind, the attitude and feelings of the individual.

Particularly relevant was the description of the related effect of death, trauma, etc., e.g. the effect on a close relative/friend of someone dying, being hurt in an accident. They found that the immune system of the relative/friend deteriorated sharply as if in 'sympathy'. Made me think (a) of your mother dying and your suicide attempt, and (b) of your own depressed behaviour in relation to Malcolm's alcoholism/ violence – i.e. you 'catching' his suicidal/depressed behaviour (and of course it's possible he too was to some extent negatively affected by your underlying pain).

I wonder if A.B. saw it and I wonder how she really relates to her life and illness. I get a strong feeling from her letters that she has quite a powerful resentment against the everyday pressures and demands on her. I'm glad you've written to her. So did I. She asked if I wanted to stay there, so I said she would be better off coming to the castle here for a couple of days and if so I'd wait on her. She'd get my bed (comfortable) and I'd have a good sleeping bag and eiderdown etc. on the floor! I hope she does come, but her treatment may prevent it. (Guess what's just started on the radio? Prisoners' chorus from *Fidelio* – it's called 'O Welche Lust', which doesn't sound quite right! Isn't it typical that the English converted '*Lust*', *joy*, into *lust*?)

My mother may have told you about her admiration for Lord Gifford? Just had a letter from her. She heard of him many years ago when he took on some unusual case – she wrote to congratulate him and got 'a charming reply'. She's been a 'devoted admirer ever since'. She also saw the TV programme I noted for you.

Darling, please don't think of the child Sara as 'spineless'. Children are not spineless. They are children, possessed by parents. You would never think of Luise as spineless, would you? It's a miracle you survived with so much lovely spirit, energy, intelligence, life! Be glad.

I hope you know how much I love you. *George* xxx

Darling,

I'm not sure I like the 'in spite of' theory of love. It is the difficult parts of you which make me re-evaluate my attitudes and ideas, and thus strengthen my love for you. So it's all 'because of' with you! Because you are *you*, all of you, puzzling, funny, maddening, witty, impossible, careless, careful, loving, warm, rude, impulsive, sexy, unpredictable, energetic, daring, brave, blind, perceptive, opinionated, fresh, *alive*! I love you because of all of that, not in spite of anything.

H-wing destroys (or tries to) the feminine inside with its impersonal rules and bars and power. Don't let it! Perhaps it's love which turns 'in spite of' into 'because of'? Like turning grapes into wine, and caterpillars into butterflies?

An interesting thing about butterflies (maybe you know it?), did you know that 'psyche' is from Greek for breath, spirit, soul? And that Psyche, the mythological figure, was the beloved of Eros (union of physical and spiritual love)? Our mechanical civilization has degraded psyche into something objective, almost impersonal, to be measured and analysed. What a difference if psychology meant the 'study' of soul/spirit/breath! And the term 'psychopath' is another degraded term, 'path' is suffering – so psychopath is suffering soul, very different from a cold-blooded individual.

Yes, I think we're made for each other, too. The world's best sparring partners. Never give in. Always love in!

I love you, *George* xxx

My Dearest Man,

Just because we are having a visit tomorrow, it's no reason for you to be deprived of your Saturday letter is it?

Maybe I accepted, perhaps even attracted, Malcolm's physical and mental abuse of my spirit and physical body because it measured my own feelings about myself?

I know I wrote that I felt that hitting me was the worst thing you could do, but I don't think it is. Deliberate dishonesty would hurt me more, because it would reveal dishonesty in our relationship. That I couldn't take easily. If you hit me, or for that matter I hit you (I've got a great right hook), we'd have to sit down and find out *why*.

Of course I would still love you – I really can't imagine you doing anything that would destroy my love for you. Gosh, that's a very sobering thought but I mean every word! In loving you, I'm also loving me, my love for you is nurtured by your love for me, and vice versa. So, my loving you, in many ways, reflects my loving me. I've put that clumsily, do you understand what I mean?

One of the questions I asked a Visitor was, how much does it cost to keep an inmate in H-wing? To date (three months) I have had no answer.

I love, love you! *Sara* xxxx

Darling Love,

Your Sunday Snail post was 'Super Snail post'. Lovely to get your letter – talking of snails, I realized tonight that I had eaten only a little fruit salad in twenty-four hours. I felt quite sick, and had an awful headache. Sister A. asked me what I would most like to eat. I thought for just a second and said, 'Six escargots, followed by a fillet steak stuffed with Stilton cheese in a port-wine sauce. Served with French beans, jacket potatoes and a side salad – a Chablis to drink.' 'Oh no, a claret,' said Sister A. which led us to a discussion on wine.

I had a long letter from Marnie today. She has been on bail. She is going to Hope Street Clinic for treatment, she has a drugs counsellor.

All my love, *Sara*

Darling,

It felt very good to see/touch you yesterday.

You have no need to be defensive about your body, I love it. When I said your leg was dainty you immediately referred to your muscles. As if I was insulting you! It was a compliment, believe it. You have an amazing and unusual body, very delicate yet very strong – what better combination do you want?

I'm very proud of your self-restraint re M.C., though I suppose you incited her verbally. I realize how much stress there is in such an encounter. M.C. must have had a lot of violence in her past, I presume.

All my love, *George* xxx

My Darling Love,

I put your prison officer advert on the board. It was ripped off about five minutes later by one of the nicest officers we have. I was a bit surprised so I asked her about it. She said she felt it was sarcastic, and we agreed after some discussion that it is a propaganda job by the Home Office, following the Strangeways riot. We can put anything we like on the board, so it was returned to me when I asked for it. I put it up again. It lasted till lunch-time today. They just can't take it. I'm not too bothered, made my point!

I love your 'true' meaning of psyche. I read it out to some of the girls – they were thoughtful. I have to see a woman psychiatrist some time and quite frankly I'm nervous. I just don't like them. I came face to face with her a couple of weeks ago, outside Sister A.'s office. I was my usual exuberant self and I think she was a bit taken aback. She didn't smile or anything. Doesn't like the idea of a happy prisoner?

Of course you are right about a person being important in psychology, religion etc. The trouble is that we don't give that person time and attention because we are too busy.

We've made the world a temporal domain and forgotten our spiritual life.

How many people actually do or live the way they really want to? You do – and I love you for it! I was looking at the weather on Friday and I remarked to Tracey and S. that I feared you'd be soaked. 'Does he have mudguards on his bike?' asked Tracey. 'I'm not certain if he's that technologically advanced,' I replied. We laughed, but not in a nasty fashion – you are just so unique – and admired. The girls have a cherished vision of us both visiting, both with matching bicycle clips, because they know we are very alike in that respect. When we had our misunderstanding last week I was moaning to Tracey. 'Oh shut up,' she said, 'you won't finish it. I just can't imagine you ever being without George!' We might as well be married, darling.

All my love – for aeons, *Sara* xxx

Darling patron saint of worms!

Do you think they love you as much as I do?

Don't be a brilliant academic, please, be a brilliant, critical, adventurous, creative action-woman. You do learn, very quickly.

I've been thinking about your comment about being 'framed' and I think you are right – framed by prejudice and fears and a lousy, antiquated system of 'justice'. I'm not sure how much of this can be presented at your Appeal – depends on whether E.F. and G. understand – but *if* the Appeal fails we must expose the whole rotten case as publicly – loudly, as possible.

I adore you. *George* xxx

Darling,

Your Sunday letter came this evening.

When I opened it Tracey looked over my shoulder and said, 'That's not a letter, that's a fucking exam paper!'

Your comments on the Dark Ages. You're right – it seems particularly bad now. Yet I feel one cannot achieve spiritual awareness without first feeling totally helpless. It's certainly how it happened with me.

Your anger and stubborn refusal (like mine) to play the defeated genius causes others to be terribly uncomfortable. It happens with me in here all the time. I think we'll find that we'll intuitively attract those who are spiritually free.

You had an example of the 'new awareness' when you went to London. 'Demigod' they called you! You didn't threaten them because (a) you are of a different generation and (b) they are achievers in their own right. Independent young people who are doing what they want to do because they enjoy it. The prison service is full of people who are doing their jobs either for money, ego satisfaction, or simply because no one else will employ them. I don't feel that anyone who is enlightened could work within the penal service.

'Growing religious bigotry' – yes, that is in fact becoming very apparent. Our churches are emptying.

Since I left the church here, Tracey, S., P., L., and A. have left, too. From a full chapel, we've gone down to four. They aren't copying us – it's just that they too were brutally subjected to the hypocrisy – my little speech, and Mic in pathetic attempts to rectify it. Our only 'true' Christian, R., has turned out to be both a bully and a thief. She of the 'inner light'. As I've said before – actions speak louder than words!

As far as justice is concerned, we've reached an all-time low. Birmingham Six case is opening eyes everywhere. I heard today that the police who handled the original investigation have not answered a single question satisfactorily. So, in one fell swoop, the Home Office (forensic scientists), judiciary and the police have been laid bare and bleeding to the public. Add to this the Strangeways riot and the Woolf Report – netted the lot in one go!

The darkest hour is truly before the dawn! AIDS is probably the worst affliction we could have, drug and alcohol addiction are epidemic – yes, we are a very rich world. *But* coming up behind us are new people, a generation that are *not* willing to accept our mistakes, souls who are being reborn, maybe right now, who will start to heal our world. Have faith, darling, in you, in us, in the children, and most of all in the creative power of the Universe.

I guess we can help heal or start the healing. I don't really know.

Tonight I said to S. (apropos of one of my ongoing battles), 'What am I going to be like if I'm freed on Appeal? Who am I going to fight?' 'You'll be fighting for us, Sara,' she replied, with the utmost quiet conviction. What started as a joke with me, finished as a deep, almost frightening statement of faith. I hope I don't let them down.

As far as my Appeal is concerned, of course I want your help. In a strategic way, it's your future, so therefore as much your Appeal. I still don't feel a big part of it. E.F. is frightened of you, you know more about domestic violence, etc., than he does and he's not about to let you teach him. Once he's caught up he'll be in touch. You are too radical, his main consideration is to free me, and I don't think he's too bothered how he does it.

I need your brains, your brilliant ideas, and your faith in me as an intelligent woman, so don't lecture me, darling, 'suggest'. You catch more flies with honey than vinegar!

Enough! Hasn't the weather been glorious? I awoke to a sun-filled sky – it shone in me too.

Yes – I am more with you – you're quite right. Spend most of my time alone (by choice) – I felt it today as I marched round the exercise yard (going to catch the No. 17 bus!). I always walk as if I'm going somewhere, never just stroll around the yard.

I'm not alone mentally, tuned to you always. Be patient with E.F. I finally came round to your view on my defence – but look how long it took me. I think E.F. will contact you – I don't want to push him. You are a threat – perhaps he realizes that both of us together will challenge his entire views on the judiciary, and life itself!

I love you. *Sara* xx

Darling,

Your comments on my body – the problem is twofold. First, I know your comment was a compliment. I can't take compliments, I have a very different image of my body. To me it's a big, ungainly, squat, chunky blob! I don't look in the mirror. When I catch sight of myself I'm always shocked. Logically I know I'm slim, but my mental image has nothing to do with 'daintiness'. It's very common in here, at least, the mental picture is a far cry from the reality.

We did a good workout in gym, and then the trampoline. Suddenly

I've started doing really good back-somersaults, as if in giving up, I have relaxed.

In a way, I've had to form a whole new relationship with my body. Instead of punishing it and pushing it I've got to enjoy it and be proud of it.

I just want to shower now, and meditate. I love you and will answer your letter tonight.

Sara xxx

Darling,

Isn't it hot? My first summer in Germany (gosh, seems like light years ago) was a very hot one. Speaking only fragments of German I'd say *'Ich bin heiss'* and Helmut would say, *'Nein, nein, Sara, du bist warm!'* It wasn't till I'd learnt more German that I understood that to be 'hot' in German meant that one was sexually aroused!

The German for nuts is *Nüsse* – whereas the slang for prostitute is *Nutte*. My first Christmas I went into a local store in tiny Kuchenheim and asked for 'prostitutes'. 'What for?' the shop assistant enquired. 'In England at Christmas we put them all over the place so that guests can help themselves,' I replied!

You mentioned the past in your letter today. In this respect, we are uneven. I've had to tell you so much more, in order for you to help, understand and love me. We'll balance the scales soon, darling.

Guess what? *Shelley, the Pursuit* has arrived. I'm taking it out of the library this weekend.

Luise thinks it's funny you talk as much as me.

I LOVE YOU. *Sara* xxx

Hello Dear Man,

I've cried twice today, first time when I saw the release of the Birmingham Six at the start of the ITV news, and the second time when I saw it at the start of the BBC news! Words can't begin to describe how they must be feeling. I loved what one of them said, 'There are others . . .' Yes, we are others!

They said on TV that people will confess if pushed hard enough. I remembered my second interview, with that policeman trying to force me to say I deliberately set out to kill Malcolm. Thank God that I'm stubborn, eh?

I'm very angry tonight for two reasons. First, I had a hypocritical, patronizing letter from G. saying in effect that my continuing poor relationship with Daddy caused him distress, and that having read your book he feels that 'We cannot replace war with legality and that if we are to countenance indiscriminate killing, we might as well do it with nuclear arms.' I wrote and told him that with the hysterectomy of his best bitch being the major problem in his placid, comfortable existence, he has no experience and therefore no right to say any form of violence is acceptable. I said that if he could agree to the slaughter of women and children in Iraq because it isn't his problem, then he's the same as everybody else in this country who feels that punch-drunk husbands can beat their wives. It's 'legal' because it's not his problem.

I'm heartily sick of being a target in here. Just because I won't retaliate does not mean I'm a bloody punch-bag. I'm sorry if people's jealousy and insecurity means they need to reduce me to improve their own egos.

I shall go and see 'Bullet-proof' tomorrow and tell him quite bluntly that if I am attacked again by any inmate I shall bring criminal charges of assault not only on the person responsible, but also on the Wing governor and the Home Office.

Please don't worry, I'll be fine, I promise, it just shows the urgent need for therapy, doesn't it? It also, I think, gives you an indication of the type of stress I live under – so be patient with me.

Just try to imagine what I am going through on a daily basis. OK, darling?

I love you so much, dear man – *Sara* xxxxx

My Love,

I saw a consultant psychiatrist, Dr Whitfield. Quite out of the blue, even Sister A. didn't know she was coming. She's a good lady, from Glasgow. We talked (I did anyway) for over an hour. At the end I asked, 'Well, do you think there is anything wrong with me?' 'No,' she replied, 'I think you've had a very unhappy life.' She asked if Mummy and Daddy received any therapy. She asked why I didn't when Mummy died. Later, Sister A. told me that she said I was an 'interesting woman' and privately thought I should have been acquitted. I've asked if a copy of her report can be sent to E.F.

I've written to E.F. and told him I want 'severe personality disorder' struck clear from my records.

Played volleyball outside yesterday and today. Glorious lovely spring weather. My cell is so warm, I'm sitting topless. I loved your line, 'Summer is coming and so are you.' You are so right!! My feelings of confidence increase daily, how about yours?

The problem for me with the social sciences is that I find it hard to remain dispassionate about, say, famine and its causes. We aren't supposed to go into it too deeply, but of course I do, and a one-week assignment has become a two-week assignment and I'm asking about famine-related diseases, etc.

I need to get deeper. It's all too superficial. As such, I wonder what good it is ever going to do me.

Women have been subordinate for *too long*! Get off the soap box, Sara!

P. says I must tell you my Baader Meinhof story. She was in stitches.

I'd been living with Helmut for about eight months (maybe less). Usually I went off around Europe with him, but on this occasion he was only going to Wannstein in Germany for four days, so I stayed at home. Weather very cold. The night he was due back, I'd run out of cigarettes. We lived in a block of four flats, on the ground floor. I spent much time in bed with my electric blanket on, reading. This night I dressed warmly, put on sun-glasses (to protect my sinuses from the wind) and a hat, wrapped a scarf round my throat. I knew there was a cigarette machine on the outside wall over the road. I didn't have three Mark pieces, so I ventured into the pub, and feeling too rude to just change money, I ordered a Pils and slowly drank it. I chatted with a couple of old bods.

I finished my beer, got my cigarettes and went across the street back home. I threw off my clothes, and dived naked back into bed. Some time later, about half an hour, perhaps, the door bell went. It's Helmut, he can't find his key, I thought, so I went and opened the door. '*Halte!*' said a stern voice. I turned. Two German policemen advanced into the kitchen, one with a sub-machine gun! They sat me, still naked, on a stool and searched the flat. I'd left my passport in the glove compartment of Helmut's car! One of them spoke some English. I told him I was British and showed him letters from Gran and Grandpa, photos. Eventually they left, first telling me I must report to the police station with my passport the next morning. Shaken, I went back to bed. I couldn't forget the sight of the machine-gun pointed at me. Poor Helmut came home to, 'Oh you won't believe what happened to me!' We later found out that one of the men in the pub swore that I was a Baader Meinhof Gang member and phoned the police. They started their search at the top of the block of flats, hence the delay.

I love you very much, darling, you don't know how much. *Sara*

Hello Darling Man,

Studying yesterday afternoon, I was told I have a visit on Friday afternoon. 'Thank you,' I replied, 'George Delf and how many officers?' 'Pass,' came a muted response. Of course all the girls are saying, 'Wear the dress, Sara!' I don't know, darling, I'll see how I feel on the day. I haven't worn a dress since 23 February 1990.

Loved the Lord Lane cartoon! I asked the PO if I could put it on the board. 'No,' he said, 'Mr Hicks wouldn't like it, though I do!' So Martina pinned it to my back and I paraded for an hour amid laughter and 'For Christ's sake, Sara, stand still!'

Your plea views are interesting. I think what struck me most forcibly was the difference between them, i.e., diminished responsibility being a plea from an abnormal person, provocation being from a normal person. In all this time, I never thought of it like that. I agree with what you say – but it's not only Luise who is agreeing to my normality – plenty of people in TNT and Atherstone would have been willing but the Defence never bothered to take their statements. The ones the police used are all biased against me. I think I told you that lots of people in Coventry wrote letters to the judge asking that I be treated kindly. A. never used them.

Quick break to get dressed. Only three things to put on, so I'm happy. I dress very fast. Another coffee, and I'm ready to face the day. I warn you I'm a bomb in the mornings.

Read an article in a women's magazine yesterday that said, 'The older woman has more orgasms'! When do I start being 'the older woman'?

By now, you'll have read my Whitfield report – you know, darling, it has done wonders for my morale. I think that part of the problem is that the people in here who can't tolerate me (inmates) say Sara's sick!

The psychiatrists planted that evil seed. It is, for me anyway, up to them to kill it.

The sun might not be shining but I am, darling, and *full* of love for you.

Sara xxx

Darling Love,

I sometimes get the feeling you want to put the whole world to rights – you can't and neither can I. Please accept our limitations, my first priority is winning my Appeal, if you want to start something in the meantime go ahead. But you saw what it was like with the support group. I suggest and believe that you and I have a lot of personal growth to go through before we can change the world! Don't push me all the time.

As far as famine goes, we create famine partly to prove there isn't enough food to go around; as a race we are terrified of scarcity.

Oh boy, have we got some talking to do! One day – though I wonder if we'll find the time to shut up and enjoy ourselves?

On a completely different note – I had my hair done tonight. It's not how I wanted it, but I like it.

All the girls who've seen it love it.

The sun is shining – what a beautiful morning. I'm definitely a child of the sun, it makes such a difference, doesn't it? The news says that in China they have sentenced a man to death for killing a giant panda and selling its skin. I'm speechless – China puts a low price on human life anyway – but a death penalty?

The sun has gone in – and it's getting colder. Dashes my dreams of seeing you in a T-shirt tomorrow.

I Love You. *Sara* xxx

(handed over)
Darling,

Some people meditate and chant for years and years and still don't get where I am.

Let me tell you something really intimate that I've never told another person. I've always felt a sense of 'destiny' about my life; I've always known that something very important was going to happen to me. Of course I never believed it would turn out like this! Gran sensed it too. She loved me most of all her grandchildren, she knew I was special, I think.

I think it is this attitude that really gets up people's noses. You remember Ella saying, 'I get the feeling you are just passing through.' In Risley I prayed, 'God, please don't let me out till I am irrevocably committed to you!' I thought that meant years of incarceration, patience, and saint-like acceptance. No wonder I got into such a muddle. How could things ever be changed if I accepted them? I still marvel at the journey God (Universe) has guided me on, and the most rewarding part, you, my love. I don't kid myself that I could have done this without you, don't you either. Your love (*so* precious, *so* healing), your suggestion, you were the one who suggested the successful threat of an Appeal strike! [re: permission to change defence lawyers.] *You* make me feel worthy enough to fight for freedom, I wonder if perhaps without you I would have been quite content to be the martyr and change things from within. We'll never know.

The sun is flooding my cell and me, in less than eight hours I'll see you – it's going to be a beautiful day.

All my love, *Sara*

Darling,

After the visit, Hicks called me to his office and told me that I would be going to Bullwood Hall (Essex) on Thursday 28 March. I immediately asked for an extra VO so that I could see you and hand out some papers. He granted this, so darling that's the long and short of it.

I've cried. But I feel it's a very important step for me to take, part of my learning programme. I haven't heard a good word about Bullwood.

L. says lesbianism is rife. 'Don't dress like that, Sara – you'll be raped!' It's 'run' by Miss P., a big bully of a woman, who's been in the prison service for nineteen years! Who does she remind you of? When Marilyn wrote a letter to a friend, telling of the awful conditions, it wasn't sent out, but returned to her four days later by the Parson's Nose!

Of course things could have changed a lot.

Great seeing you Friday – I felt in a 'silly' mood, you are *so* serious and yes, you *do* lecture me! I'm smiling (honestly).

I'm not going to let you mention the Appeal this time. If you do I'll just kiss you!

What, my darling man, are you going to do? My first thought, one that also occurred to others. 'But what about George?' greeted my news. 'He's *not* transferable,' I replied. 'He'll move to Essex.' Will you? Whatever you decide darling, is fine with me. I'll love you anyway!

Had a letter from G. He says he is sorry. Silly man! I judge men by you and your standards now – impossibly high – only you! I'm looking forward to seeing you, darling. I'll try not to be so fidgety this time. I feel calmer.

Remember, I adore you – this is the second stage!

Sara xxx

Darling,

I'm shocked, of course, by news of your move to Bullwood Hall. Sad and apprehensive, too. The ground is shifting under us, isn't it? But I know you're right. It really is 'a very important step' for you. It marks a change of gear as well as a change of place.

Even before you go I can feel the sense of loss. We have gone so far in such a short time here, haven't we? At present it is hard for me to see much gain in the loss but I trust our love and where it will take us. I promise to smile again soon!

It's Simon's birthday today, too, so I don't have an excuse to sulk for long.

At least Bullwood Hall has more space, I assume. Maybe even green grass? Perhaps the horrors have been exaggerated. You will soon change things!

A goodbye kiss, please, full of hellos.

All my love, *George* xxx

The main entrance to Durham Prison, which contains H-wing
(© North News and Pictures, Newcastle)

Brancepeth Castle, to which George moved when Sara was in Durham Prison
(Photo by George Delf)

Sara's case aroused enormous public interest,
which was reflected in the coverage given to it by the media
(*Top*: © the *Guardian*/Graham Turner; *bottom*: Headlines courtesy of
the *Guardian*, the *People* and the *Independent*, August 1991)

Friday August 16 1991

George Delf, who is leading the
campaign to free Sara Thornton,
argues that her plight exposes the
sterility of Britain's legal system

Hungry
for
real
justice

Friday 23 August 1991

Protests on the question of provocation

Hunger strike put
murder case law
under scrutiny

SARA THORNTON yesterday
ended her 20-day prison hunger
strike in protest at the life sentence imposed for killing her vio-

Patricia Wynn Davies, Legal Affairs Editor, argues
that the Sara Thornton case adds weight to demands
for ending the mandatory life sentence for murder

Let's see
justice
for Sara

HOME Secretary Kenneth Baker
should have murder on his mind this
holiday weekend.

Sara Thornton: the rejected evidence

LAST month Sara Thornton, jailed for
life for murdering her husband, lost her
appeal to have the conviction changed

While she protests about her murder verdict by hunger strike,
Dr M... 't protests by interview; his expert evidence on

nor of addiction behaviour at the Insti-
tute of Psychiatry.
"He is a ...

Sara leaving the court after her unsuccessful Appeal in 1991
(© the *Independent*/Peter Macdiarmid)

Outside Holloway after receiving news of her release on bail in 1995
(© the *Guardian*/Martin Argles)

George Delf and Sara Thornton
(© Christa Stadtler)

Three Letters

Three letters conclude this part of Sara's story: from her daughter Luise (aged 12) to the Court of Appeal (July 1991); from George to Sara during the first Appeal (22 July 1991); and from Sara to George during her fast for justice (16 August 1991).

Letter from Sara's daughter Luise, from California, addressed to the Court of Appeal, July 1991:

My mum is a very loving person, not like any person I have ever been with, and a loving person would not mean to kill a person for whatever he did.

Malcolm was very mean to my mum and me, but not all of the time, just most of the time. My mum has been very nice to me and Malcolm too. My mum did not tell people when Malcolm hurt her, so that means she loved him very much and so did I when he was not drunk. Me and my mum did not like it at all. We tried to get out of our house. Sometimes we did get out of our house.

I don't think she should be in prison, because she didn't want to kill him because she loved him. I miss her very much and I would like to do fun things with her because she is a fun person to be with and I love her very much and I think I should be with her.

Luise June (twelve years)

Victoria Bus Station, London, 22 July 1991:

Darling Sara,

I love you more than ever. It's 12.12 a.m. and I've missed the last coach to Durham by three minutes. So I've made myself a 'nest' of chairs, packing crates and detachable fencing! I will wait for the 9 a.m.

coach. It's a warm night, luckily – just right for tramps (there are plenty of us!). I will write this and then read the rest of *The Idiot* and go to sleep. While you are snug in your cell.

What an amazing day, for you, for me, for a lot of people – I wish I knew what you thought of it all. You're very brave, very strong. I'm full of admiration and love you so much. I couldn't take my eyes off you up in the dock. Was very glad to have a few words with you.

It was like a dream, wasn't it? You, your father, M.'s sons, and your life story dribbling out of the legal machine like processed peas. Even the end of the world would sound boring in the mouths of lawyers. On Friday I thought the three judges were not too bad. Beldam seemed fairly human, Buckley looked like Robespierre to me (thin, handsome, pale, pedantic), Rougier was at least appropriately red-blooded.

The organization was dreadful and no apology (except to you) for the wasted time and money of dozens and dozens of people, QCs, solicitors, journalists, TV men and supporters. Pathetic. Rougier's absence when the Appeal restarted this morning seemed bad, but his replacement, Saville, turned out to be a trump card, don't you think? Sharp, interested, quite friendly, trying to help Gifford express his points.

This morning I was quite despondent. Beldam came across as nervous, negative, irritable. So did Buckley. Only Saville seemed all there and positive. Gifford was fairly feeble, I felt. He failed to clear away the diminished responsibility fog before moving on to provocation. Beldam kept returning to the former. Saville encouraged Gifford to have a go at your trial defence ('Are you saying they were negligent?' etc.), but Gifford only partly responded. He seemed on the defensive. At lunch we were all dismayed.

I stared at you for hours, trying to send my love. After lunch things seemed to improve. Beldam came alive, Gifford improved. Escott-Cox QC [Prosecution] was awful and made no impression. But I still feel Gifford didn't make the most of (a) bad defence decisions (b) the cumulative emotional stress you suffered (c) the urgent need to update and clarify existing law relating to domestic violence and female behaviour. Luise was not given enough attention. You may not agree?

It was sickening you couldn't say anything. It's a tired, bloodless system. I just hope and pray they have enough insight and heart to release you. Gifford and Ed. Fitz. think it will be a close decision.

Darling, you must get out. They will issue their verdict on Friday, probably.

I feel really starved of you. You're a lovely, brave, intelligent and wonderful woman. I'm very proud of you. It's 1.30 a.m. and I'll start on *The Idiot*!

I love you, darling. See you soon. *George* xxx

Two weeks into her hunger strike, Sara wrote to George from HM Prison, Holloway, London (16 August 1991):

Hello Double Agent,

You sneak! I sensed an urgency in your manner and I instinctively reacted accordingly. I thought that someone was there, that's all. Now I could kick myself because I simply can't remember what I said. [BBC Radio recorded their phone conversation as a news item.]

The high point of my day. I was sitting in a half-lotus position on the grass when I felt a light touch on my arm. A tiny, perfect cricket sat there. We looked at each other. I spoke to him silently, telling him he was beautiful, that I was his friend and very glad of his company. I asked him to sing for me. I could see his singing legs up behind his back, with two miniature cymbals.

He started to sing. It was so beautiful, so perfect it brought tears to my eyes. I felt he was singing just for me. I felt humble and honoured.

When they called us in I said goodbye and blew him gently on to the grass. Does lack of food heighten perception of the world? Is that why Jesus and Buddha fasted? I only know that afterwards I felt a great sense of compassion for the world. How complicated we make life when there is true joy in simply watching a tiny cricket sing his heart out.

You'd better be on TVam tomorrow. All the nurses are watching.

I adore you, darling. *Sara* xxx

Life After H-wing

by George Delf

Sara's move to HM Prison Bullwood Hall, set in suburban Essex, initiated many changes in her life. Separated by 250 miles, she and I met once a month at most. In contrast to H-wing, the visiting area was large, noisy, full of people, with loudspeaker announcements. 'Like life in a railway station,' as Sara told me.

On 9 April 1991, she wrote: 'When we were leaving Durham Miss C., one of the officers who accompanied me, said to Mr V., "What do we do if George is outside on his bike?" "If he's riding a tandem you've got problems," replied Mr V. They half expected you to follow us down. Mrs H. suggested a rope – "we could tow you."'

A few days earlier Sara expressed a growing sense that 'at the end of the day I have me'. Without inner faith nothing could succeed: 'If you were locked up in a tiny cell you might understand.' Her mood was bleak but determined. As so often, her spirits soon rose again. 'Like the Appeal notes you send me,' she writes (9 April), 'the letters act for me like cattle prods. When I feel dispirited or down, I read them and once again I'm clear on the way ahead . . . Now I find I have no need to be convinced. The mood is catching, the girls say "that's the right attitude".' She felt our love was as strong as ever but it had lost the element of 'father love'. Sara knew she had been searching for a loving father 'all my life'.

Sara's first Appeal, presented at the Appeal Court, London, by her new Defence Counsel, Lord Gifford QC, and Edward Fitzgerald, was heard at the end of July 1991. Lord Gifford explained to the three Appeal judges in great detail during four hours why her case should be treated in the light of provocation rather than diminished responsibility. Public interest in the Appeal was intense. Women's groups had begun to adopt Sara's case as a litmus test of the way English courts treat women.

On 29 July, Sara's Appeal was rejected. Lord Justice Beldam, giving the judgement of the Court, rejected the suggestion that in using the phrase '*sudden* and *temporary* loss of control' there was any misdirection of the jury. He maintained that 'there was no suggestion that she had reacted suddenly and on the spur of the moment, deprived of her self-control, to the provocative statements of the deceased. On the contrary, she always insisted that she had gone to the kitchen to cool down and had cooled down. She insisted that she had no intention of stabbing the deceased or doing him any harm.' (Law Report, *Independent*, 30 July 1991) Lord Justice Beldam asserted that 'most advocates' would have used the defence of diminished responsibility, contrary to Lord Gifford QC's argument.

Sara was driven back to Bullwood Hall prison to continue her life sentence, having sat in silence through two days of hearings. Her Defence Counsel, myself and a growing army of supporters were appalled by the Court's verdict. The Appeal Court had not recognized the fact that stress can be cumulative and eventually destructive, particularly in the case of women such as Sara who suffer for months or years before snapping.

At the heart of this decision lies the uneasy relation of statute law (made by the highest authority, Parliament) to case law (based on judicial interpretation). In 1957 Parliament passed a Homicide Act. A single paragraph deals with provocation as a defence to a charge of murder. It reads as follows:

> Where on a charge of murder there is evidence on which the jury can find that the person charged was provoked (whether by things done or by things said or by both together) to lose his self-control, the question whether the provocation was enough to make a reasonable man do as he did shall be left to be determined by the jury; and in determining that question the jury shall take into account everything both done and said according to the effect which, in their opinion, it would have on a reasonable man.
> Homicide Act 1957, s.3.

It is clear from the above that the cumulative effect of periodic violence and stress over many months, as suffered by Sara and many other battered women, could amount to provocation according to the Homicide Act. The problem in her case and many others arises from judicial insistence that their own interpretation of the law is superior to statute law. Thus at Sara's first Appeal hearing Lord Justice Beldam dismisses her Appeal because 'ever since Lord Devlin's summing-up in *R. v. Duffy* (1949) the words "sudden and temporary loss of self-control" had been regarded as appropriate to convey to a jury the legal concept of provocation'.

By imposing a judicial interpretation made in 1949 on an Act of Parliament of 1957, Lord Justice Beldam not only placed judges above Parliament but distorted Sara's case by placing the main focus on the few moments when she went into the kitchen to fetch a knife. A distortion as blatant as analysing Hamlet's trauma in terms of the final sword stroke. The epithet 'sudden and temporary' makes sense in terms of instant male retaliation, but not long-term female reluctance to strike back. Sara's case is pivotal in English law because it exposed both gender bias in judicial interpretation and the failure of Parliament to make sure that its laws are fully enforced.

Lord Gifford QC told the Appeal Court that current interpretation of the law on provocation 'was apt to describe the sudden rage of a male' but not 'the slow burning emotion suffered by a woman driven to the end of her tether'.

Sara spoke to me shortly after losing her Appeal. We were both distressed. I told her of a similar murder case, also involving an alcoholic partner, where the defendant had just been given a suspended prison sentence. Joseph McGrail, from Birmingham, had 'killed his bullying and alcoholic wife'.

Shocked by this evidence of the law's double standards Sara broke down and sobbed. We discussed various options. She decided to go on a hunger strike for justice. She was moved to Holloway Prison, London, where medical facilities were supposedly better.

Media interest in her case and hunger strike was intense. Letters of support poured in. After three weeks her daughter Luise flew in from California and urged Sara to end her strike. She did so.

Sara decided to request a royal pardon. Edward Fitzgerald, her barrister, presented this to the Home Secretary. The royal pardon dates from the Middle Ages, when the king or queen had the power to bestow mercy on someone suffering a miscarriage of justice. In modern times this power resides in the Home Secretary, a political appointee who seldom has the wisdom and courage to rise above mundane pressures. After several months, Sara's request was refused.

By late 1991 the fierce energy which had sparked our love and fight for justice was thwarted by distance, loss of the precious moments of physical closeness possible in H-wing, and practical differences about the best course to take. Was our love dead or had it gone into hibernation? For some time we lost contact, but in September 1994, I visited Sara in Styal women's prison, near Manchester. For us both it was an emotional moment. As we sat facing each other across a small table Sara held out her hand to me. 'Look,' she said, 'it's shaking.' I held it as we talked. For me our love was more ocean than desert. Beneath surface storms there was still, as there had been in H-wing, an underlying strength.

We were next to meet in the offices of Penguin Books, in London, in September 1995. Sara had just been released on bail, pending her second Appeal. I had written to her, asking for a big hug when we met. 'Here it is,' she said as she walked in. We went over to a nearby pub later. As we talked, face to face, intense, smiling, it was as if the rest of the world did not exist. Just as if we were in the visitor's room of H-wing in Durham.

Now, though, nobody was watching us.

So what had become of that incandescent love on the wing? It flared brilliantly for more than a year, died down in 1992 and was later reborn as something calmer, adjusted to dramatically different experiences.

A bit dull, perhaps? Judged by the laughter and emotion of working together on this book, no. A new trust was demonstrated, and a different kind of love.

Afterword

by Sara Thornton

My departure for Bullwood Hall Prison in Essex forced a change in my relationship with George that neither of us could have foreseen.

Without the weekly visits and daily letters, I found myself making decisions and validating my newly acquired sense of inner authority. I still needed George's love and approval and he continued to be a source of inspiration and devotion. But the loss of my Appeal in 1991 and the ensuing hunger strike proved to be our swansong.

During the ten months I had spent in H-wing the goalposts of my quest for justice widened. I began to seek something far greater than earth-plane justice. I sought God/Goddess/All That Is.

A quest such as this is a unique and sometimes lonely experience that cannot be shared by another. Some of my experiences were so out of this world that I could not translate them into words of this world. I knew only that I had, by some miracle, accessed a Love that was total, healing and awesome. More importantly it was within me and is the true source of all life.

George and I parted amidst much pain and confusion. It took three years to understand and heal, and it wasn't until the summer of '94 that we met again.

This book is a testament to the power of forgiveness. We still argue, but we laugh too. George helped me to learn forgiveness and the power of human love. Without one, we cannot hope to find the other.

READ MORE IN PENGUIN

In every corner of the world, on every subject under the sun, Penguin represents quality and variety – the very best in publishing today.

For complete information about books available from Penguin – including Puffins, Penguin Classics and Arkana – and how to order them, write to us at the appropriate address below. Please note that for copyright reasons the selection of books varies from country to country.

In the United Kingdom: Please write to *Dept. EP, Penguin Books Ltd, Bath Road, Harmondsworth, West Drayton, Middlesex UB7 ODA*

In the United States: Please write to *Consumer Sales, Penguin USA, P.O. Box 999, Dept. 17109, Bergenfield, New Jersey 07621-0120*. VISA and MasterCard holders call 1-800-253-6476 to order Penguin titles

In Canada: Please write to *Penguin Books Canada Ltd, 10 Alcorn Avenue, Suite 300, Toronto, Ontario M4V 3B2*

In Australia: Please write to *Penguin Books Australia Ltd, P.O. Box 257, Ringwood, Victoria 3134*

In New Zealand: Please write to *Penguin Books (NZ) Ltd, Private Bag 102902, North Shore Mail Centre, Auckland 10*

In India: Please write to *Penguin Books India Pvt Ltd, 706 Eros Apartments, 56 Nehru Place, New Delhi 110 019*

In the Netherlands: Please write to *Penguin Books Netherlands bv, Postbus 3507, NL-1001 AH Amsterdam*

In Germany: Please write to *Penguin Books Deutschland GmbH, Metzlerstrasse 26, 60594 Frankfurt am Main*

In Spain: Please write to *Penguin Books S. A., Bravo Murillo 19, 1° B, 28015 Madrid*

In Italy: Please write to *Penguin Italia s.r.l., Via Felice Casati 20, I–20124 Milano*

In France: Please write to *Penguin France S. A., 17 rue Lejeune, F–31000 Toulouse*

In Japan: Please write to *Penguin Books Japan, Ishikiribashi Building, 2–5–4, Suido, Bunkyo-ku, Tokyo 112*

In Greece: Please write to *Penguin Hellas Ltd, Dimocritou 3, GR–106 71 Athens*

In South Africa: Please write to *Longman Penguin Southern Africa (Pty) Ltd, Private Bag X08, Bertsham 2013*

READ MORE IN PENGUIN

BIOGRAPHY AND AUTOBIOGRAPHY

Freedom from Fear Aung San Suu Kyi

This collection of writings gives a voice to Aung San Suu Kyi, human rights activist and leader of Burma's National League for Democracy, who was detained in 1989 by SLORC, the ruling military junta, and today remains under house arrest. In 1991, her courage and ideals were internationally recognized when she was awarded the Nobel Peace Prize.

Memories of a Catholic Girlhood Mary McCarthy

'Many a time in the course of doing these memoirs,' Mary McCarthy says, 'I have wished that I were writing fiction.' 'Superb ... so heartbreaking that in comparison Jane Eyre seems to have got off lightly' – *Spectator*

A Short Walk from Harrods Dirk Bogarde

In this volume of memoirs, Dirk Bogarde pays tribute to the corner of Provence that was his home for over two decades, and to Forwood, his manager and friend of fifty years, whose long and wretched illness brought an end to a paradise. 'A brave and moving book' – *Daily Telegraph*

When Shrimps Learn to Whistle Denis Healey

The Time of My Life was widely acclaimed as a masterpiece. Taking up the most powerful political themes that emerge from it Denis Healey now gives us this stimulating companion volume. 'Forty-three years of ruminations ... by the greatest foreign secretary we never had' – *New Statesman & Society*

Eating Children Jill Tweedie

Jill Tweedie's second memoir, *Frightening People*, incomplete due to her tragically early death in 1993, is published here for the first time. 'Magnificent ... with wit, without a shred of self-pity, she tells the story of an unhappy middle-class suburban child with a monstrously cruel father, and a hopeless mother' – *Guardian*